Contents

2011 Author's Preface

This is a book about what could be called radical nonduality, Zen, Advaita, or meditative exploration in the context of an actual life with all its messiness. This book isn't meant to provide final answers, but is rather an invitation to question some of our most basic assumptions, to look more closely, to explore and enjoy whatever is showing up Here / Now, and to discover what remains when all our words and ideas about this fall away.

The book was first published in 2003. Non-Duality Press acquired it in 2006 and has been publishing it ever since. Several prefaces and afterwords have come and gone, but the main text of the book has remained unchanged since it was first published in 2003.

The title of this book may be somewhat mystifying to readers outside the United States. The heartland refers to the center of this country, the Midwest as it is often called, a region of the United States that has the reputation of being ordinary, down-to-earth, plain-spoken, no-frills and no-nonsense. I was born in the heartland, in Chicago, and this book tells the story of my return there in middle age to be closer to my mother in her final years of life. The title refers not only to Chicago and the American Midwest, but it also plays on that sense of ordinariness, as well as on all the nuances and implications of the Heart.

When I subtitled this book "The Ecstasy of What Is," I wasn't pointing to ecstatic experiences. Experiences come and go. They are inherently impermanent. Liberation has nothing to do with feeling ecstasy all the time. The subtitle points instead to the ecstatic nature of life in its entirety: love affairs, hearts breaking, flowers blooming, people dying, babies being born, holocausts, earthquakes, tsunamis, thunderstorms, sunlight, clouds, spring breezes, airplanes flying into buildings, explosions in distant galaxies – the full catastrophe, as Zorba the Greek called it.

Please don't adopt anything in this book as a new belief system. I hope that this book will invite you to stop, look and listen – to explore for yourself. If you find any answers in this book, let them go.

Joan Tollifson
April, 2011

Give up the search for something to happen and fall in love,
fall intimately in love with the gift of presence in 'what is.'

TONY PARSONS, *As It Is*

Ram Tzu knows this...

You are perfect.

Your every defect
Is perfectly defined.

Your every blemish
Is perfectly placed.

Your every absurd action
Is perfectly timed.

Only God could make
Something this ridiculous

Work.

RAM TZU , *NO WAY for the Spiritually "Advanced"*

For Zen students a weed is a treasure.

SHUNRYU SUZUKI

If you truly want to see God, then take a look around.
Everything you see, touch, taste, think, hear, feel, know or
imagine is God!!

WAYNE LIQUORMAN

The Tao That Can Be Spoken

The first utterance about Truth
Is the first step
Down the path of deceit.

RAM TZU, *NO WAY*

A Sea of Jewels

One day at the post office in Oakland, I saw a little girl, who was maybe four or five years old, in line with her mother. The little girl was totally alive, looking at everything with amazement. She ran to the wastebasket in the corner and gazed down into it as if into a sea of jewels. She was ecstatic. The mother kept pulling the girl back, telling her to stop this and stop that. Every other word the mother said was "stop" or "don't."

Finally they are up at the window, and at the next window there is another mother who has a little baby in a basket sitting on the floor beside her. The first little girl stands beside the basket, and the baby and the girl gaze unabashedly into one another's eyes with total absorption. The mother of the little girl again pulls her back. As they leave, the little girl waves goodbye to the baby as if to her dearest friend.

It was such a clear display of the unobstructed love, wonder, and awareness that is *naturally* here, and the process of human socialization which trains us to pull back from this aliveness, to stop looking, to stop being ecstatic, to close down. We learn to shut down and to live more and more in a mental world of ideas, so that by the time we are adults we are uncomfortable looking for too long into a stranger's eyes. And it would *never* occur to us to run up to a wastebasket and actually *see* what's inside it as something we'd never seen before, with curiosity and interest. Because by the time we're adults, we think we *know* what's in there. We've got a word for it. It's garbage. We don't see it any more. And we don't see one another, or the love between us, because we're afraid of it. We've learned that a person who would look with wonder into a public wastebasket, or too long into a stranger's eyes, is a crazy person, a mad person. We're afraid to be in love, except in the allowable, relatively safe confines of romantic relationships, or perhaps in rare moments of communion with babies and very young children. For the most part, we're cool, detached, afraid of the natural ecstasy of being.

Our lives feel empty. We long for the spontaneity, joy, and wonder that we seem to have lost. We take workshops and consume mind-altering substances to regain it. We undertake rigorous meditation practices and throw ourselves at the feet of exotic gurus. We run up enormous visa bills, looking for what is simplest and most ordinary, for what is always already here.

When we finally "get it," we get nothing at all. We have not arrived at some fascinating foreign place. We're exactly where we always have been—right here. Here is all there is. But when we're looking for something else, we don't see how extraordinary here actually is. We're preoccupied.

Here and now is *alive*. It's the only thing that actually *is*. In the clear light of present awareness, *whatever* appears is vibrant, beautiful, sacred. The vibrancy, the beauty is in the awareness, in the presence, not in the object.

This Is It!

For one instant, abandon all labels, formulas, answers, beliefs, stories, explanations, expectations, and all efforts to understand or achieve a result of any kind. Give up everything you've ever been told, everything you've read, everything you've experienced, everything you know, every idea about what is or what might be. Let it all go. Completely give up. Hold on to nothing at all.

What remains?

If you are trying with your mind's eye to *see* what remains, give up that effort. Let it go completely. Simply be, without words, without knowing anything.

You are here. You don't need to look in the mirror to confirm it. You don't need any authority to tell you. You *know* you are here. *Ideas* about who or what you are (your name; the idea that you are a person; your body image; your life story; your beliefs; all your scientific, spiritual and psychological concepts), these are all added on later. They are an overlay. But *that* you are is undeniable. You *are* here. Here is *always* here. It's *always* now. Now is what *is*. Just as the eye cannot see itself, this is-ness cannot be seen. Presence cannot be known in the way we know objects and information, as something outside of ourselves. In that sense, it is utterly unknowable. But at the same time, we *do* know it, without any doubt at all. It is the one thing of which we are absolutely certain.

Call it emptiness, presence, awareness, the Tao, the Self, God, groundlessness, the Absolute, Consciousness, or refuse to speak about it at all. It eludes all attempts to capture it. It is truly nothing. And yet, here it is. Here *you* are. Presence. Awareness. *This*.

What *is* this?

What *are* you?

Are you the character in the story, or the aware space in which the story appears and disappears? Is the character even real, or is it an image—a creation of thought, memory and sensation; a product of neurochemical blips and firings in the brain; a mirage?

If the character is no more real than a dream, what is it that is dreaming?

This is no-*thing* "you" will ever find. Any *thing* you find is part of the dream. But who is the dreamer? Who are you? What *is* the dream itself? What are all the dream objects actually made of?

Any answer is a dream.

Returning to the Heartland: A Story

Death is not extinguishing the light; it is putting out the lamp because dawn has come.

RABINDRANATH TAGORE

In the Fall of 2000, I moved from California to Chicago to be closer to my then ninety-one year old mother in the remaining years of her life, however many that turned out to be. She was in good health, still active and living independently, getting around town on the bus, full of zest, but she was also getting frailer. It seemed like time to be closer, to enjoy her while she was still here and ultimately to walk with her to the door of death and say goodbye from up close rather than from far away.

Mom talks openly about dying. "If I go up in a puff of smoke, don't feel bad," she says, "because that's what I'm praying for. Just call the Cremation Society. The card is on the refrigerator." I asked her once if she was afraid of dying. "Oh no," she said. "It's only the body that's falling off."

My mother is a passionate woman who loves life. She loves animals, plants, and people. She sees the divine in everyone. She is fearless. She has friends of all ages, races, sexual orientations, and political affiliations, from all walks of life. She knows no boundaries. On her birthday every year she throws a party. Close to a hundred people cram into her apartment to celebrate with her. My father, whom my mother loved dearly, died over twenty years ago. He was a hermit, a loner, a solitary. I inherited a little of each of them.

My father was an atheist and an inventor who read books about the fourth dimension and believed in determinism. He told me that the sun would eventually explode, that the light from the stars was billions of years old, that there is no free will, that everything is one unbroken whole, that nothing can be other than it is, that everything causes (and is caused) by everything else. All of this instantly made total sense to me. When I encountered Advaita, the Hindu philosophy of non-duality, several decades later, it was like coming home to Dad.

My mother, on the other hand, believes in love and the power of positive thinking. Fear and worry have been banished from her vocabulary. She believes you can do anything if you put your mind to it. She is a woman of boundless, unflagging optimism and good cheer.

I was born in Chicago on the fourth of July, three years after the atomic bombs were dropped on Japan. A little firecracker, they called me. It was the era of Joe McCarthy and the execution of the Rosenbergs. I still recall a terrifying nightmare in which my parents were locked up and electrocuted. Growing up in suburban America in the Fifties was like that film *Blue Velvet*: the surface was idyllic, but an inferno was boiling up underneath.

I fled the Midwest as soon as I finished high school in 1966, heading first to New York and then to San Francisco. Coming back to Chicago in 2000, I rented a sunny, one-bedroom, fourth floor apartment. My two rooms each have large southern windows that look out on two big locust trees. It feels like I am living in the heart of these trees, in a cozy tree house with heat and carpeting. Mourning doves roost frequently in the branches. I hear traffic, screeching brakes and minor fender benders, wailing sirens from ambulances going to the hospital up the street, the train passing through. I see flights of birds, and planes going to and from O'Hare. At night, in the winter when the trees are bare, in the far distance, I can see the Sears Tower. I bought a very comfortable armchair and placed it across the room facing the windows, so I can sit and look out. I call it my bliss chair.

My neighborhood is a mix of Hispanic, Indian, Pakistani, African-American, Asian, Arab, Orthodox Jewish and assorted white folks, including a lot of immigrants from Eastern Europe. On nearby Clark Street, all the signs are in Spanish. On nearby Devon, it's all Indian and Pakistani. On the other side of Western, it's Orthodox Jewish. In the parks, at the train station, in the streets, you see Indian women in colorful saris, men in turbans, bearded orthodox Jews in black suits and black hats, Mexican and Filipino families, old Polish ladies, Arab and Jewish women in head scarves. You hear a multitude of languages. It's a residential neighborhood with lots of trees and big yards and no tall buildings.

People are very into the American flag in Chicago. Long before 9/11 they were prominently displayed on houses, on poles in people's yards, even on their cars. It was the presidential election year when I arrived, and most of the posters I saw in my neighborhood were for Gore/Lieberman, and one for Ralph Nader in the window of the nearby Heartland Café.

Around the corner are the house where my mother lived as a child, and the elementary school she attended almost a century ago. The streets of Chicago are as familiar to me as my own body. I've been on them since I was born and even before that. I have come home. To my surprise, I am growing to like Chicago.

Chicago is a meat and potatoes kind of place, home of steel mills and stockyards. Transportation hub of the nation, major financial and cultural center, Chicago is a diverse, cosmopolitan city, but the dominant tone is one of Midwestern ordinariness. This place is raw and solid and accepts no bullshit. It has no frills. Tough and streetwise, it was the home of Al Capone and the mob. But mostly, I find it to be a place of kindness and hospitality, the metropolis of the heartland.

The Bay Area, where I have lived for most of the last thirty years, is an airy place of transcendence and breathtaking beauty; the edge of the map and beyond; home to radicals, queers, sages, artists and outcasts; meeting point of East and West. Like many others who jumped or fell out of the American Dream in the Sixties, I landed there. At it's best, California births the new and defies all boundaries and limits; at its worst, it is a smorgasbord of insubstantial fluff.

Chicago is about earth, ground, heart, and roots. It has winds so strong they blow people off the sidewalk, winters so cold that people freeze to death, summers so hot that people die of the heat. The air quality is bad. The traffic is thick. At it's worst, it is everything I fled in 1966: traditional, conventional, straight, flat. At it's best, it is the perfect place to wake up.

And that's really why I'm here. My mother is a kind of excuse, or more accurately, part of the dance. I have always avoided commitment. I like to keep my options open. I've never owned a house or had an enduring committed relationship, a family or a career that tied me down. Coming here is the biggest commitment I've ever made. I'm here for as long as my mother lives. That might be a month; it might be six years; it might be twenty years. I've finally given up all my options to flee, to seek something better.

And to my surprise, here I am in this big, noisy, polluted, Midwestern city—the last place I ever imagined myself settling or discovering the truth. Oddly enough, it turns out to be a perfect metaphor. Because that's exactly where we do find the truth: right here, in the most ordinary place, amidst what we thought were weeds and distractions.

Being here is about dying in many ways: It's winter, I'm middle-aged and going through menopause, my hair is turning gray, I've left behind aging friends in California, and of course, the spiritual life is always fundamentally about dying, as Krishnamurti put it, "dying to the known." Death is at the heart of life, and is actually the secret of liberation, but when we *think* about it, it often seems to terrify the human mind, this disappearing of everything that has seemed so real.

The Urn

Mom calls to tell me that a former neighbor who lived down the street all through my childhood, Milly Whipple, has died. We will attend the memorial service on Saturday and perhaps the dinner afterward. I feel dread. Milly's son, Ted, was a hotshot psychiatrist who "cured" homosexuals. We will likely see many former neighbors, all of them rabid Republicans, like the one who served in Eisenhower's cabinet and was a friend of Dick Nixon and Don Rumsfeld. I imagine myself back in my old home town—the exclusive, affluent, and once all-white suburb of Chicago where I grew up—at a gathering of anti-gay, pro-Bush Republicans, on the eve of Bush's inauguration, trying not to explode or commit psychological suicide. I tell myself it is a wonderful spiritual opportunity. But inside, I feel dread.

Saturday arrives. We pull into the church parking lot, we're quite early, and immediately there is a procession coming straight toward us—Episcopal priests, family—and I see Ted, the psychiatrist-son, and he's carrying an urn, which I realize holds his mother's ashes. This is a situation

Emily Post never covered, what to say or do when you see someone you haven't seen in over thirty years coming toward you carrying his dead mother in an urn. There is no time for reflection. I roll down the car window and say, "Hi Ted," and he–holding the urn–leans in slightly and says, "Joanie..." and then the procession moves on.

And then the service. There in that church, in the presence of age and death, all the things that divide us, or seem to–our differing ideologies and lifestyles–all seemed very superficial and meaningless in the face of that which is so much deeper and so much more real– the momentary nature of the play, the beauty of it in its entirety, and the love that sometimes manages to shine through in spite of all the odds against it. Ted's wife kisses me on the cheek with genuine affection. Effie, the sister of the deceased, a woman Mom's age whom I've known all my life, holds my hand.

Three of the four officiating priests were women, one was African-American. Something has changed, even here.

We never did go to the dinner. Mom decided she didn't want to. And now today I know no more than I did before about the Republicans, except that they, too, end up in urns.

Giving Up Hope

What is complete attention without a single idea?

TONI PACKER

It is a dark afternoon, and windy. The birds are being blown every which way across the sky. Black clouds break open, and sunlight comes pouring through. For one glorious moment the bare tree branches shine with light. And then the black clouds close shut, the light is gone, and the all the birds are singing again, the songs they sing before storms.

It so happens that today is the first day of Lent, the season of repentance in the Christian liturgy. I read once in a book by Thomas Keating that the word *repent* means "to change the direction in which you are looking for happiness."

Where is it that we are looking for happiness?

So often, we are looking in all the wrong places. We scramble around after more money, more fame, more adulation, more power, another piece of chocolate cake, another café latte, another romance, another vacation, another drink, another snort, another cigarette, another piece of knowledge, another consoling theory, another sexual ecstasy, another guru, another spiritual experience, and finally, what we imagine to be the ultimate experience—enlightenment.

No matter how many substances, experiences, answers, and relationships we acquire, it's never quite enough. We realize we might lose it all tomorrow. Someone else always seems to have more. There is a persistent unease, a restlessness, a craving, a sense that something is missing, that this moment—as it is—is unbearable, not enough.

Is it unbearable?

Is it possible to stop all of our outward searching and be still and find out?

Is it possible to be right here, right now, with open eyes, open ears, open mind, and open heart—completely present, without judgement or resistance, without any effort to achieve something better?

Do we really *need* more money, more fame, more adulation, more intoxicants, more experiences, or the biggest possible experience? Do we actually even *want* any of these things?

I'm not saying that *any* of these things are bad, or that we should renounce them (a common spiritual mistake). But do they really give us happiness? Are we satisfied? Are we at peace? Or are we suffering, living lives of quiet (or not so quiet) desperation?

True happiness is found only in one place. It is here now. It is unconditional presence, empty of all knowing, empty of all limits, empty of all sense of separation and encapsulation, empty of you (as you think of yourself).

You may, and you undoubtedly will enjoy a variety of experiences and substances, and that's no problem. But if you imagine that any substance or any experience or any possession or any relationship will give you lasting happiness, you will be disappointed. When you are disappointed enough, you will be ripe for giving up hope—giving up the search for something better in the future, and turning your attention to what is. This is the beginning and the end of the spiritual life, true repentance, enlightenment.

Is this Advaita, Psychology, Memoir, Zen, Post-Spiritual Inquiry, or What?

The Tao that can be spoken is not the true Tao.

LAO TZU

I am never lost because I don't know where I'm going.

IKKYU ZENJI

What if we drop all the labels, categories and frames that we use to contain our experience? What if we're just here? Right now. What *is* this?

That's what this book is about.

It's not about finding an answer. It's about that aliveness that can't be objectified or grasped.

The mind is always looking for something else. It wants a winning strategy, future results, transformation, improvement. This book is not about that. It won't get you anywhere other than where you are now. *This* is the miracle beyond belief.

I don't just mean the *content* of this moment (the sensations, thoughts, experiences, and events that are endlessly appearing and disappearing), but more essentially that which is at the very *heart* of all these varied appearances: the simple fact of *being* itself. The hereness of here, the nowness of now. The eternal present. Presence. No-thing-ness.

Like all of us, I've assimilated a host of theories and explanations. I've been witness to an amazing proliferation of stories and narratives, movies within movies appearing and disappearing in dream-like fashion: the story of my life, the story of the world, the story of the universe, the story of your life according to you, the story of your life according to me, the Hindu story, the Buddhist story, the Judeo-Christian story, the multitude of scientific stories, the American story, the anti-American story, the modern story, the postmodernist stories.

A story is a way of seeing, a way of understanding, and for a moment, the fabrication appears solid and believable. Our story changes as the perspective changes. We look at life through a Freudian lens, a feminist lens, a Marxist lens, a Zen lens. With each new lens, the story gets re-framed, re-interpreted, re-visioned, re-invented and re-organized, and means something slightly or entirely different than it did before.

Even the way the so-called "bare facts" are reified from an infinite sea of utterly undivided, ever-pulsating, sensation and vibration, in other words, the way some *thing* is made up out of no-thing at all, is already a huge spin. Consider what I have told you so far about my life. The brain selects and sorts unfathomable chaos into seemingly meaningful categories and creates an apparently coherent narrative that is further modified by the distortions of memory and changed every time it passes from one person to the next. It is no longer any secret that what we think of as the factual and true story of our life, or the factual and true history of the world, is nothing but a very partial abstraction of something that never really happened at all. On some level, every twenty-first century person knows this. It's there in the new physics, in postmodern literature, in the cultural mirrors all around us. And yet, on a gut level, the deep-seated belief in the reality of the illusion persists. It is, after all, a very convincing illusion. Even the notion that there is any such thing as "twenty-first century people" who "have" this illusion is all part of the illusion! The whole thing is made up out of thin air. You, me, the world, the twenty-first century, the whole story I've created so far about Joan and Chicago and California: look closely, and you'll find no-thing at all.

Stories, mythologies, novels, plays, operas, movies, television programs, dreams, daydreams and fantasies are all an expression of the mysterious emptiness from which they spring and into which they disappear. Beautiful, horrific, fabulous, astonishing, breath-taking creations, they serve a function every bit as vital to the dream of human life as the spider's web is to the spider. They are totally real in a sense, and yet, they are phantasms, protean apparitions forever revising and erasing themselves. Like Rorschach inkblots, they become anything and everything. Like colored shapes in a kaleidoscope, they tumble endlessly into something new. Like the mirage in the desert, they vanish if you approach and try to catch them.

Stories make apparent sense out of what would otherwise be incomprehensible. They give meaning and importance to the fiction of myself and all that I identify with: my family, my civilization, my ethnic group, my political leanings, my sexual orientation, my subculture, my gender, my generation. Stories are entertaining. God apparently enjoys drama, play, hide and seek, lost and found.

Sometimes a story helps to expose and dissolve limitations; sometimes it creates and reinforces them. Stories can lull us to sleep or wake us up, reveal truth or conceal it. The same story can serve different functions at different moments. It's a great art to discern when a story is breaking open the heart and waking us up, and when it is lulling us to sleep, perpetuating illusion and generating suffering. Likewise, it is a great art to discern the difference between actuality and concept. The conceptual filters through which we think about everything are so ubiquitous and so seemingly real that it's easy to mistake them for actuality. No separate, independent, solid thing really exists, except apparently, in the story.

When I look for what I know to be true beyond any doubt, what I come to is presence itself, the simple fact of being here. Everything else is made up. This bare awareness is the only *real* truth, the only absolute certainty. We use words to point to it, but the words have a way of deadening and obscuring what they describe, for they turn the inconceivable and limitless into something conceivable and limited. Listen to the words in this book with your heart. Their intent is to dissolve structures, not to create new ones. They are meant to leave you with the open wonder of not knowing, rather than with a new set of deadening answers.

In recent years, I have grown ever more interested in awareness itself, simply what is: the sound of traffic, the sensation of a toothache, the song of a bird, the television images of devastation, the vague sense of dis-ease felt upon awakening in the morning, the sound of a lawn mower or a jet plane. I find that these are the moments of deepest truth, when there is simply *this*, as it is—when the urge to explain or get something out of it, to get rid of or improve it, or to have some ultimate transcendent experience above and beyond it—when all of that is gone.

That interest in what is, that willingness to be present, to not know anything, to simply be alive, to let the imaginary barriers dissolve—that willingness develops slowly. It goes against all our conditioning. It goes against the force of habit. It goes against the social grain. It goes against the prevailing mythology that I am a person adrift in a story on my way to a destination.

Spiritual life is very simple. Utterly simple, utterly obvious, utterly immediate, absolutely ever present and completely inescapable. It has been turned into something enormously complex and apparently hard to get. Intricate cosmologies have been invented; elaborate conceptual grids have been imposed on the indescribable. A whole class of highly trained religious professionals and spiritual experts have sprung up. There are special buildings, special clothes, special cushions, special beads, contorted body positions that are supposed to bring you closer to the truth, wafting incense, inspirational music, all kinds of complicated rituals and practices, maps of the journey, and glorious promises of salvation, *something* that may happen *to you* someday in the future, something much grander than what is. We hear about transcendental experiences, Kundalini explosions, ultimate attainments and final breakthroughs, and we long to have what we have heard described. We get lost in the complexity, the promises, the search. I'm not opposed to *any* of those things if you enjoy them. But they aren't any more spiritual than a seat on the city bus at rush hour. What I'm talking about is fully present right now, right here in Chicago, or wherever you happen to be at this very moment. It is what you *are*, not what you might someday become. This book is about the truth. And the truth is simple.

Joan, the apparent author of this book, is a character more or less like you. She has ups and downs, good days and bad ones, strengths and weaknesses. She's nobody special except in the sense that everyone is somebody special. We humans have a strong desire to put spiritual teachers up on pedestals and imagine that they are beyond neurosis, beyond confusion, beyond doubt, beyond anger, beyond petty personal concerns, beyond flattery and insult, and basically beyond being ordinary human beings. We love to believe in the Mythology of Perfect People. It's comforting and inspiring to the ego. But this book isn't about personal growth and self-improvement for the character you think you are.

This book is about stepping into the unknown. As far as I'm concerned, real spirituality is about having no answers at all. It is about living without formulas, without conclusions, without beliefs, without comforting ideas, without saviors. It has nothing to do with being a perfect person or having everything neatly resolved. It isn't about arriving anywhere, other than exactly where you are now.

In this Age of Information, we've all heard so much. We've read about "the power of now" and the "wonder of presence," how "Consciousness is all there is" and "You are That." We've been told to "be here now." We've longed for a life without problems, without uncertainty, without darkness. We've looked for something extraordinary, some tremendous result, some final understanding. And life as it is keeps disappointing us. In the face of that disappointment, what do we do? This is a crucial question, perhaps the most crucial question.

Do we brush our doubts aside and convince ourselves to believe in a lie or a fantasy? Do we fall under the spell of some collective hypnosis driven by magical and wishful thinking? Do we go back to getting drunk and smoking dope? Do we plunge into non-stop busyness and distraction? Or perhaps, are we willing to hang out more and more in a place of actual simplicity: not knowing, not seeking, not *doing* some theme park version of "just being," but actually just being present, without answers, without some grand assurance that all is well. Just *this*. That's what this book is about. It points to this, and it shares my own story, my own journey through spiritual obsession and wishful thinking to bare truth. Perhaps this particular story will help to de-mystify spiritual awakening, and encourage us all to be less afraid of what actually is, even when it *looks* chaotic, unresolved, messy, and disagreeable.

The story in this book is essentially a so-called "true story." In some instances, circumstances have been changed or condensed and composite characters created—all in the interest of protecting the privacy of the people I write about and making the narrative less cumbersome. Many events and people of real importance to me have been omitted for one reason or another-this is not intended to be a complete history of my life. I have changed the names of everyone except my teachers; public figures; Toni Packer's husband and son; and my friend Jarvis Jay Masters, a writer who is living on death row in San Quentin prison, whose real name I used with his permission in the hopes that it might bring some interest and attention to his case. This book is not intended as an objective account of any of the teachers I write about, nor should it be mistaken for an official version of their teaching. This is Joan's story; I speak for no one else.

When I started this book seven years ago, I believed many things that I no longer believe. Much has fallen away. Writing has been a way of exploring. The material is not always sequentially arranged, since time has a way of apparently flowing in all directions at once.

The Only True Teacher

In the Beginning: A Story

Life as it is, the only teacher.

JOKO BECK

Life always gives us exactly the teacher we need at every moment. This includes every mosquito, every misfortune, every red light, every traffic jam, every obnoxious supervisor (or employee), every illness, every loss, every moment of joy or depression, every addiction, every piece of garbage, every breath. Every moment is the Guru.

My right hand and the lower part of my right forearm were amputated by a fiber in the uterus during my mother's pregnancy. My mother tells me that when I was a baby, I used to reach for objects with my non-existent right hand and then look really surprised. Maybe I experienced a phantom limb. I like to think that this reaching for objects with a hand that turned out to be imaginary might have been my first visceral glimpse into the illusory nature of so-called material reality.

Having one hand has been a wonderful teacher. The funny thing is, I would never choose such a teacher, but now that I have it, I am truly grateful for it. I knew from early on that the body is impermanent, that there is a deeper reality than form, that true perfection must embrace imperfection.

Addiction has been another wonderful teacher for me. It taught me everything there is to know about the etiology of suffering and the question of free will. It took me to places I would never otherwise have gone. Again, I would never have chosen this teacher. But having gotten it, I'm infinitely grateful for it. Addiction is a superb and relentless teacher.

Growing up in an affluent community was another great teacher. I learned that money cannot buy happiness, that worldly success can be hollow and unsatisfying, that surfaces can be deceptive.

Whatever appears in your life is the perfect teacher for you. No two lives are the same. Don't get lost in comparing your experiences to anybody else's experiences. Each life is beautifully unique, and each reflects the whole.

In college on the East Coast in the Sixties, I encountered alcohol, psychedelic drugs, Eastern religion, existentialism, sexual freedom, and the collapse of the entire cultural construction of my childhood. After college, in 1970, I migrated to San Francisco where I led a wild life and nearly died from alcohol and drug intake. After that, I went through several forms of therapy, tried saving the world with radical politics, and eventually found my way to something that could be called Zen or Advaita, but is best not called anything at all.

In the 1980s, I practiced at the San Francisco Zen Center and its affiliates, lived briefly at Berkeley Zen Center, and eventually studied with Joko Beck, a radical and innovative teacher from San Diego who approaches Zen practice through the koan of everyday life.

By the early spring of 1996, I was living in rural Springwater, New York at a retreat center founded by a woman named Toni Packer. I was forty-eight years old. I was on staff at Springwater for the second time and had been there for about five years altogether. I had just proofed the galleys of my first book, *Bare-Bones Meditation: Waking Up from the Story of My Life*, which was due to be released in the fall.

Springwater had started out as a Zen center, but gradually the traditional, dogmatic, ritualistic, hierarchical aspects of formal Zen had dropped away. Toni Packer is a housewife and grandmother who grew up half-Jewish in Nazi Germany, married an American conscientious objector after the war, and eventually became a Zen teacher in north-western New York. Toni resonated deeply with Krishnamurti and left the Zen Center where she was teaching to work in a new way. Springwater is in the middle of nowhere. The yellow road sign at the turn off onto the gravel road that leads to the Center's driveway says, "Dead End." Toni is fond of its message.

Toni is someone who has consistently had the courage to stand alone, to put all the books, authorities and traditions aside, and to be here now in all simplicity without formulas or answers. In the spring of 1996, I had been with Toni for almost a decade, and I also continued to work by phone with Joko Beck.

Another one of my teachers was a woman from Idaho named Martha. Of course, I didn't think of her as my teacher. She was a fellow worker on the Springwater staff, and she drove me crazy, or so I thought, until I realized it was my own thinking that was driving me crazy. For a whole year after Martha joined staff, I hated her. It was a nightmare to live and work with her. We pushed each other's buttons endlessly. I felt she was mocking me, laughing at me, not respecting me. She felt similarly. I could never get away from her. She was there brushing her teeth at the next sink every morning and every night, she was there at every meal, she was there on every retreat. The sound of her loud footsteps in the hallway that we shared would make my skin crawl.

And then it broke open, I don't even know how, and she seemed lovely to me, and the same sound—her footsteps—evoked a deep tenderness and affection. I grew to love her.

The teacher shows up in many disguises.

꙳

Sometime in the early 1990's, I became interested in Advaita Vedanta, the Hindu teachings of non-duality, through seeing a European teacher named Jean Klein and attending several retreats with him in California before I came back to Springwater the second time. Jean was quite old and frail at the time.

"What do you do?" he asked when I met privately with him on a retreat in the desert at Joshua Tree.

"I'm writing a book about meditation," I replied.

His eyes lit up. " Wonderful!" he said.

"Well maybe not," I replied. "Maybe it would be better if I was silent..."

"*You're* not writing this book!" he said emphatically.

Suddenly there was a strong earthquake. The room began to shake and roll. Jean and I were both laughing.

He was right. Everything came out of nowhere: the impulse to write, the writing itself, the words. It was not personal. Nothing was.

❧

I discovered the Indian guru Sri Nisargadatta Maharaj, one of the clearest Advaita sages. He was already dead by then, but there were several wonderful books of his dialogs with people. I felt an immediate resonance and was irresistibly drawn to these teachings.

A friend gave me a video tape of a woman named Gangaji, an American Advaita teacher who was offering satsangs, gatherings where she sat at the front of the room radiating love and deconstructing people's stories with amazing deftness. I watched the tape over and over, compelled by what I saw and wondering if it was for real.

Before long, I had ordered more tapes. People wrote devotional love letters and sang songs to Gangaji. She threw flower petals at them. In the past, I had looked upon Americans who got involved with gurus and devotional relationships as people who were caught up in some kind of silly, immature projection. Secretly, I had also been somewhat fascinated.

Soon I was corresponding with Gangaji. Before that, if I found myself singing in the shower, or in the car while I was driving, I would often stop myself because I had this idea that it was better to be silently "aware." Now I *belted* the songs out! My heart was bursting open with love.

I was no longer in Kansas. I had tumbled down a magical rabbit hole into the wonderland of Oz, a world awash in flower petals, gaudy colors, ecstatic songs and love-drunk gopis swooning in erotic-spiritual bliss. Not that all of that was going on around Gangaji, because it wasn't, but it was in the air somehow—the aroma of Hinduism and India. On top of Gangaji's scene being Hindu, it was also very American. The packaging seemed so slick. There was more missionary zeal, entrepreneurism and promotional thrust than I was used to. I didn't completely trust it. Gangaji seemed like a movie star, and maybe I was a lovesick fan going rapidly off the deep end. But I couldn't resist or deny the truth in it either.

There was something utterly delightful, liberating and heart-opening about this neo-Advaita world, something refreshingly different from the sober, Quaker-like atmosphere of American Buddhism and Springwater. It was breaking my attachment to plain and simple, dissolving my righteous Puritanical streak, confronting all the disowned shadows of my personality (money, fashion, beauty, devotion), allowing the intoxicated bhakti fool in my heart to emerge. For me, it was akin to the leap from modernism to postmodernism.

The whole spiritual adventure became playful. It had a sense of humor. It was juicy and amusing. It was about *being* and not *watching.* It was a mystery beyond the grasp of the rational mind. It became at times a parody of itself, so over the edge that it jumped out of the frame and illuminated the set behind the movie, exposing the transparency of spiritual authority. It was theater. The whole thing lost its deadly seriousness. Rules broke down; multiple realities co-existed. It was utterly genuine and totally fake, off the mark and right on target, all at the same time. The rational mind couldn't contain it then, and it can't now. It was exactly what it was. If I had to pick one word to sum it all up, I'd say love.

Gangaji has a keen intelligence, a sharp eye, and an exquisite ability to cut through the mind and its stories. She also has a beautiful heart. It was with her that I first realized that truth is ever-present and cannot be lost or found. I saw how I clung to the old stories of "not awake yet" and "something missing." I saw that I was actually *afraid* of ecstasy and unrestrained love, afraid to be enlightened. It seemed dangerous somehow. It was safer to be a neurotic seeker, "just little old me," perpetually not quite here yet. That was familiar. That was the habit. And Gangaji was challenging that habit.

Suddenly I was headed to Asheville, North Carolina, where Gangaji was giving a weekend satsang series.

"Oh, you came!" she said when she saw me the first night. There was incredible energy between us from the beginning.

I was intoxicated, swimming in bliss, bursting with kundalini. Gangaji seemed delightfully free. There was so much laughter and love. Unlike the modest, austere, bare-bones style of Zen to which I was accustomed, satsang with Gangaji is a theatrical event with hundreds of people, videotape, spotlights, huge photos of Gangaji's guru and his guru, flowers, candles. Gangaji sails in wearing her exquisite clothes and sits on a sofa at the front of the room. I hear through the grapevine that she gets $100 hairdos and always flies first class. I hear other things through the grapevine, too. She doesn't socialize with her students, she demands royal treatment, she can be ferocious and cold.

I heard many disturbing stories about Gangaji's guru, Papaji. He spends days on end telling sexist jokes, he tells women they need to get fucked. Devotees gather at his feet for darshan while he watches television. He yells at people, calls them stupid pigs. He does not sound very much like his guru, the great sage Ramana Maharshi, whose lineage Gangaji claims to represent. But people love Papaji. They say he's a wild rascal, a crazy wisdom teacher, and I want to believe this. I do love the way he tells people to "call off the search." Like Gangaji, he's wonderful at waking me up to the truth that I'm already awake.

Lots of people around me had their opinions about Gangaji and her whole scene. And I had my opinions, which changed from one day to the next. It was shattering all the ideas I had about spirituality.

Toni questioned me: Is Gangaji coming from listening, or is she operating from a subtle system, like someone who gets the hang of koan work and knows how to pass them, but isn't really awake?

I don't know.

I told Springwater I would be leaving in the winter. Formal meditation had begun to feel unnecessary and contrived, and my heart was increasingly with Gangaji. Furthermore, I wanted to begin talking with people about awareness and waking up. I wanted to share and explore and go deeper into what I loved most. I wanted to teach. I felt in my heart that this was my true calling. I knew I needed to be on my own to let it happen. I needed complete freedom for it to unfold in whatever way it might. I considered moving to Colorado where Gangaji was living, but in the end decided to go home to California.

In November, we went on retreat, my last retreat at Springwater before I would leave. I went deep into the silence. It was a week of snow and ice storms and cold, and the deer hunters shooting in the woods. I went off caffeine. For me, that means days of headaches, body aches, exhaustion, and meeting up with all the mind-states and emotions I try to evade. It is painful, and yet, there is always something I love about withdrawal. It is the stopping. You finally stop running, and you sink in. You meet what you've been running from. You don't move. And it feels like a huge relief. Like some enormous noise has finally stopped. And you're just here.

One night after the retreat, driving Toni home on a foggy, slick, icy road in the dark, I was talking to her about my plans to give meetings and workshops when I got back to California, and I said to her, "I hope you would at least tell me if you thought this was a bad idea." I heard myself wanting Toni's blessing, some unmistakable imperative and sanctioning.

"I don't think it's a bad idea," Toni replied.

I had hoped for something a little bit more exuberant, although why I would expect that when I was throwing myself at Gangaji's feet was surely irrational at best.

"You're good with words," Toni said after a long pause, "but are you really here, really seeing? *That's* the question!"

For a moment I felt defensive, like she was telling me I was all talk and no substance, but afterwards I realized it was a question to live with.

I cried profusely at my going away party. I don't cry easily or often, and I hadn't expected that to happen. But the tears just poured out of me and wouldn't stop. Toni and I went for a walk before the party began. She talked to me about working with people. Listening is everything, she said. Not knowing. Not having any system at all.

꙳

So at the end of 1996, I left Springwater and returned to my home in California. I moved in with Adele, an old friend in Oakland, a psychotherapist and body awareness teacher who spent hours rolling on the floor or sitting quietly. We lived together easily and playfully.

It was a wonderful relief to live with someone who was also a contemplative, someone who liked a quiet lifestyle. Our society loves extroverts. If you enjoy solitude or quiet, you are often considered neurotic and maladjusted. There is tremendous pressure to stay perpetually busy and have a full social calendar. It was a great relief to live with someone who never turned on the TV, who enjoyed staying home more than going out, who liked to sit quietly in an easy chair staring out the window, who spent hours rolling on the floor.

Gangaji and her husband moved to California at exactly the same time I did. So, unexpectedly, there she was. I became a volunteer, helping to put on her satsangs. I was a serious devotee, and Gangaji was encouraging me in my desire to teach. I'd come home from her satsangs in speechless, ecstatic states, my heart bursting with love, and Adele would look at me like I was on drugs.

Adele found my interest in Gangaji unsettling. Adele has a naturally reserved personality, tending toward understatement, minimalism and frugality. Like many of my friends at the time, she recoiled from the devotional and upscale scene around Gangaji. She also wondered why I needed to pursue yet another teacher.

I wondered about that, too. This book went back and forth as I went back and forth. I was struck by how I would revise and rewrite the scenes, making them guru-positive or guru-negative, depending on where I was at. It was a great lesson in how unreliable all history is. Without changing the facts, I could slant the same exact scene in different ways, so that it would have a completely different meaning. I was fascinated by this process.

There were other questions that unfolded in my life and my writing. Was I awake? Was this it? Or was there some kind of even bigger awakening that I hadn't had yet, a total and irrevocable shift like some teachers seemed to be describing, an event that turned you inside out forever, after which all identification with the bodymind, all sense of personal doership, and all belief in the illusory me were completely and permanently erased, never to return? I was still seduced and mesmerized by the promise that maybe there was more to be had, a bigger Big Bang *for me*. I discovered that it's never too late to climb back onto the treadmill of samsara and go for another ride. I went for many rides.

And speaking of treadmills, was there any way to stop biting my fingers? I'd been gnawing on them for years, unable to stop. I'd bite for hours sometimes, making bloody wounds. I'd recovered from alcohol and drug addiction, and had given up cigarette smoking. But this I could not seem to stop. I'd worked on this compulsion with two therapists and every one of my spiritual teachers, and it had gotten better, but it still hadn't stopped completely. Why not? How do addictive patterns end? Is there anything to do, any choice, any practice, any way to make change happen, to encourage it? Or was everything utterly beyond our control?

What was this whole spiritual trip *really* all about? Was it the opium of the masses after all, another narcotic delusion, one more false dream? What were we all doing? What exactly *was* it that I wanted to talk or write about? Before I fell down the rabbit hole into Advaita, I thought I knew. Now I knew nothing.

Somewhere along the line, I remarked to a friend that I couldn't finish this book yet because the issues involved were still unresolved. My friend questioned why they needed to be resolved. Perhaps what I was writing was not supposed to be "the final answer," but rather, the questioning itself. Perhaps there actually was no answer!

I wanted so much to write a pure book, a book that spoke only the highest truth. But I keep discovering that what people seem to appreciate most in me is my honesty. Being a fucked up mess was beginning to seem like my vocation. Not exactly the one I had been picturing! I had hoped to be an awakened guru. But then, awakening is truly nothing more or less than recognizing God right here in the middle of this actual mess.

You Are the Present Moment

We are conscious of only a tiny fraction of the information pouring into our senses every moment. Moreover, there is a half-second time delay in transmission, so that all perception is actually of the past. We *are* the present moment, but we can never perceive it. We can only *be* it.

The present moment is presence itself. It is inconceivable.

This is not just another intellectual tidbit to file away. This is mind-shattering, world-dissolving: *everything, without exception, that you perceive, think and experience is the past. It has no reality.* Contemplate this deeply. Let it sink in. It destroys *everything*. It leaves *nothing*. This is horrifying news if you imagine that "you" are located "inside" the bodymind, looking out at an independent "real world." To suddenly realize that *everything* you see and think is nothing but an unreliable and partial printout from the past leaves you with no way out.

Your whole life has been about finding a way out. You've tried therapy, coaching, meditation, bodywork, creative visualization, positive thinking, network marketing, blue-green algae, *everything* you can possibly try to save you. And suddenly you realize there is *no way out*.

There is a complete stop. You are simply here. There's no escape. Right *here* is the possibility to discover that you are not trapped inside the bodymind at all. *You* are a dream. The bodymind is a dream. The world is a dream. Spirituality is a dream. *Everything* is a dream. Only *this* is real.

What is *this?*

No words can capture it. Bare presence is tremendously alive. It is pure energy. Fall into it, and you fall into nothing. Nothing is inconceivable. The mind finds this frightening. The mind is uncomfortable with anything that seems unpredictable, unknowable and out of control. There is no "me" in bare awareness, no story, no drama, no future, no hope, no meaning, no purpose, no body. To the mind, "nothing" is a terrifying idea: a barren, desolate vacuum, a nihilistic vacancy. It sounds dreadful, like death, like being buried alive. What could be worse?

And so, we pull back from bare presence. We keep very busy. We avoid this terrifying nothingness that lurks just under the surface of everything. We avoid silence. We avoid gaps in the conversation. We turn on the radio or the TV. We read books. We have "meaningful" careers. We raise families. We go on vacations. We chase gurus. We drink. We smoke. We consume. We talk. *Anything* to avoid this dreadful nothing.

But if you allow yourself to stop running away, and you let yourself fall into nothing, and *be* nothing, what do you actually find? Is it the desolate vacuum that you have been imagining and running away from? You may be very surprised!

The only way to find out is to do the experiment. No one else's results will mean anything to you. You have to take the leap for yourself. And the paradox is that there is no "you" to do that, and no distance to be covered. The "leap" is the dissolution of that entire mirage.

Can You Find A Boundary?

Right now, close your eyes and simply be aware of all the sounds and sensations that are here, listening openly to the whole thing. What happens if you try to sense where "you" begin and end? Can you actually find a boundary?

You can *think* about some boundary, like "the skin," but in simple open awareness, can you actually *find it?* Does it have any real substance? Or is your actual *experience* the undividedness of everything?

Are the sounds you hear right now inside or outside you? Again, you can *think* that they are "outside," but in your actual direct experience, if you listen openly, is there a boundary? Can you find the place where "inside" becomes "outside" and visa versa? Is anything outside or separate from awareness? Is there a "you" apart from, or other than awareness itself?

Who Am I?

The universe is uncaused, like a net of jewels in which each is only the reflection of all the others in a fantastic interrelated harmony without end.

RAMESH S. BALSEKAR

Certainly there is *some* reality to the idea of separation, you may say. I can lift my arm, but not your arm. Likewise, I can feel the headache in my head, but not the one in your head. There must be *some* real separation between us and *some* kind of independent, individual intelligence contained inside each of us. Certainly "the world" was here long before "I" was born into it, and will persist long after "I" have died. Surely, it is "out there," separate from "me."

It's a very convincing picture. But *where* is all of this actually happening? Notice that right now, absolutely *everything* perceivable or conceivable is *inside of you*, inside of awareness. You can *think* about "somewhere else," you can imagine and conceptualize it, but that thought is always happening here, in present awareness.

The only "you" that "I" know about is made up of sensations, perceptions, conceptualizations and memories appearing in present awareness here and now—visual images, sounds, smells, touch—organized conceptually into the *idea* of "you," supposedly "out there" in space, separate from "me." It all happens here. That is true of every apparent "I" and every apparent "you." We are sensations and memories inside one another, so which is which? How real is the separation?

There is certainly *apparent* diversity, differentiation and uniqueness, but is that the same thing as *actual* separation and independence? I can't live for more than a few minutes without oxygen, and not for more than a few days without water, or a few months without food. I am utterly dependent upon the environment that seems to contain me. In fact, there is no real separation between me and the environment, between mind and body, between me and you. The mind draws imaginary lines and uses different words, but in actuality, it is one undivided whole.

We say, "I can lift my arm." In this one simple, common, and seemingly innocent sentence, language creates the illusion of subject and object, the illusion of agency, the illusion of time, the illusion of cause and effect, the illusion of separation. It's all done with smoke and mirrors, better known as words. Something utterly inconceivable happens, and the words we use to describe it shape our perception of what it is.

"I can lift my arm." Where is the I? This is a wonderful question to explore. Take a moment to lift your arm several times. How exactly does it happen? We say "I" do it. But look closely at the actual experience as it happens. How exactly do "you" do this action? How do "you" initiate it? Where does the first impulse come from? In this case, you read a suggestion in this book to lift your arm. Where did this book come from? How did it come into your life? And then you "decided" to do what the book suggested. How did that "decision" get made? Can you actually find this elusive "I" that claims to be in charge of all this? The more you look for this "I," the deeper into nothingness you plunge. And the more closely you look at any simple action (lifting your arm, visualizing a flower, making a decision, writing a letter), the more mysterious it is.

We believe that thinking is something that "I" am initiating, but again, when we observe carefully, thinking also seems to come out of nowhere. We could say it comes out of conditioning, or out of the brain, but where do they come from? Can "you" control what your next thought will be? Or is any semblance of control, and of "you," merely another thought?

From the moment we are apparently born, we are told our name, our gender, our place in society. We learn to control "our" body. We are alternately praised and scolded for what "we" do, and told that we are responsible for "our" lives. It's like being gradually hypnotized into a kind of trance. By the time we have reached adulthood, we fully believe that "I" am truly independent and in control of "my" life. "I" *could* screw the whole thing up. We become obsessed with trying to control the uncontrollable. It never occurs to us that this entire manifestation (movie after movie), along with the main character, along with the entire spiritual search, might all be nothing more substantial than a dream, a play of Consciousness.

By paying attention to our direct experience, we can begin to distinguish the actual subjective *experience* of "I," which is nothing more or less than unbounded awareness, from the *story* of "me," an ever-shifting series of fictional narratives about a made-up character in a virtual reality, like a television program.

When the story of separation is believed, solidity and reality are given to limitations and divisions that don't actually exist. Feelings of guilt, blame, self-doubt and self-hatred arise from the story. When we live out of the story, we are lost in daydreams. We miss the miracle of life as it actually is, because we are forever seeking something else. We can't relate to other people in a truly free and intimate way because we see only our ideas of them, our projections. We keep tripping over imaginary obstacles. On the global scale, we drop bombs on people we have never met, imagining that they are our enemy. God has incredible powers of imagination and visualization.

"We" don't do any of this. That's all part of the story. None of this is personal because the apparent "persons" are only imaginary disguises hiding the One Reality, the Absolute. When that truth is seen clearly (by no one), suffering ends. There may still be pain and what we would think of as terrible circumstances. But there will no longer be suffering. Suffering happens only *in* the story. Suffering is created by the mind.

Whatever *appears* is only the One Reality. It looks like chairs and tables and bodies and airplanes. Those are all thought-forms, concepts, ideas, ways that perception organizes itself in order to function. And that very functioning that sorts and labels and struggles to survive is itself an activity of that same reality. "I" am not separate from or in control of this activity, anymore than "I" created my own brain. "I" is a thought-form, a sensation.

⁓❧

Is the One Reality also a thought-form?

Yes, obviously as soon as we label and conceptualize it, it is. It points to the open space of not knowing, the undividedness of being. But in the blink of an eye, the mind turns no-thing-ness into a *thing*: a Giant Expanded Ego, an objectified Blankness, an upgraded version of God the Father, some Primal Substance, an assurance that all is well, that we are in good hands despite frequent appearances to the contrary. This book isn't about believing in some idea that feels comforting. It is an invitation to let every belief go, even the belief in oneness.

Is the World Real?

Row, Row, Row your boat, gently down the stream
Merrily, Merrily, Merrily, Merrily, life is but a dream

Children's song

Thus shall ye think of all this fleeting world:
A star at dawn, a bauble in a stream;
A flash of lightning in a summer cloud,
A flickering lamp, a phantom, and a dream.

BUDDHA

The real position of an awakened person in relation to existence is that of a person in the process of reading a book—I am the reader and I never forget that....But my fundamental non-implication in the hero's turns of fortune in no way affects the reader's pleasure, nor even an identification with the hero!

STEPHEN JOURDAIN

To see the illusory nature of the universe is primarily to see the illusory nature of oneself.

RAMESH S. BALSEKAR

The World is Illusory;
God alone is real;
God is the world...

When your standpoint becomes that of wisdom,
you will find the world to be God.

RAMANA MAHARSHI

Distressed and outraged by the idea that the world is nothing more than an insubstantial and fleeting appearance, someone once asked an Advaita teacher if the starving Africans are real. The teacher replied, "They're as real as you are."

How real is that? That's a great question to live with.

Seeing through the illusion of a movie or a novel or our life doesn't mean we can't enjoy the play. In fact, I would say that we can't *fully* enjoy it *until* we understand that it is an illusion. And is a movie or a novel "just" an illusion? Calling "you" and "the world" an illusion doesn't mean there is nothing here. There is, but it's not what we think it is.

A dog, an ant, and a human all looking in the same direction do not see the same thing. Two humans don't even see the same thing. Countless studies have shown that people often see what they expect to see, even when it is not actually there. Memory is notoriously capricious and creative. And as we've already noted, *all* perception is actually the past. So, does anything actually exist outside present experiencing? Is there such a thing as objective reality, or are there just infinite, momentary, subjective apparitions? And how would we know one way or the other?

⚜

Human beings, with our ability to think abstractly and use language, have labeled and classified the universe that we perceive. These labels and classifications are useful for our survival and our day-to-day functioning. We can call this make-believe world created by perception, memory, thought and language the relative world. It is a world apparently divided up into many separate, independent objects. It is a world of opposites. *It is a world that exists only in the mind.*

When attention is absorbed in this virtual reality, it seems like there is "you" and "me" and "dogs" and "cats" and "events" and "problems" and "happenings" and "dilemmas" and "decisions" and "duality" and "non-duality" and "awareness" and "enlightenment" and all kinds of things going on. It's like turning on the TV and getting absorbed in one program after another. It *seems* real. But how real is it?

This is a question to live with and to explore, not philosophically or abstractly, but through direct inquiry and attention, moment to moment. How real is yesterday? How real is my life story? How real is this problem I seem to have? How real is this room I seem to be in? How real is my body? Where is all this occurring? What *is* it? What am I?

Our language and abstract thinking have divided "the arm" from "the leg," they have divided "New York" from "New Jersey," they have divided "you" from "me." They have divided "up" from "down," "good" from "evil," and "the relative" from "the absolute." But in actuality, no such divisions really exist. The arm is not really separate from the leg, anymore than New York is really separate from New Jersey, anymore than up is really separate from down, anymore than I am really separate from you, or good is really separate from evil.

The absolute is the whole thing, which is no thing. The whole is container-less, boundless, limitless. The relative is all about containers, limits, boundaries, and the resulting objects and dualities. The absolute isn't separate from the relative. It includes it, but it isn't confined or divided by the imaginary boundaries and limits that language and thinking create.

The absolute is never not here. Our attention can be preoccupied with the relative, with the map, with the words and the world they create, with our beliefs and concepts to such a degree that it *seems* like the absolute has been lost. But has it? Where could it go?

Actually, the absolute is the only "thing" that really *is* here, but it is not a thing, so it defies all attempts to capture it mentally.

Every *thing* that you can see, name, think about, describe, experience, or understand depends on awareness to be. It is an impermanent appearance, a momentary pattern, an image in the brain or in Consciousness.

It has no independent reality. But we don't usually *feel* that way about ourselves and the world we perceive. Despite everything we know intellectually about the unreliable nature of perception and memory, we nonetheless tend to regard our own perceptions and memories as reliable, factual and true. We tend to regard ourselves and the movie we're appearing in as solid fact. It's a very convincing illusion.

What gives every-thing its apparent reality is the presence in which it all appears. Presence is invisible. When you look to find it, you find nothing. Anything you find is not it. And yet, paradoxically, presence is the only "thing" of which you are entirely certain, without the slightest doubt. It is the one "thing" that cannot be denied.

⤴

The absolute is not the opposite of the relative. The absolute is outside the frame of duality. All duality is in it. The absolute includes everything. You don't have to burn the menu to enjoy the meal. And you don't have to deny the world in all its magnificent diversity and texture to recognize that it has no independent existence.

The mind can get itself all tangled up in knots trying to work this stuff out mentally. It won't be worked out. The answer isn't in the mind. It's right here as soon as the mind relaxes its grip and gives up the search.

The Divine Dance

Giving up or doing nothing is not something the mind can "do," anymore than falling asleep at night is something the mind can do. In both cases, it is a kind of relaxing or surrendering—doing nothing, as opposed to doing something. It might begin with simply *noticing* the tension of seeking and efforting, without trying to change it or make it go away.

Hearing is happening. Seeing is happening. We don't have to *try* to hear the traffic or the birds. Awareness happens on its own. Awareness is not a strategy. The me who wants to "do" awareness is a thought, the imagined subject of a thought like, "Am I doing it right?" This thought appears *in* awareness. This thought pretends that it refers to something real, that this something ("me") possesses awareness. Actually, it is the other way around.

As the whole, as awareness, we have no problems, no goals, no purpose. Only the illusory me has problems and destinations, and once we imagine that we are this illusory me, there is no end to apparent problems, no end to imaginary destinations.

We lose track of the fact that thought is thought. We don't realize that thought is *creating* the world we apparently live in; we think that thought is merely *describing* an objective reality. We think and imagine and believe that we are somebody, that something is lacking, that we have to get somewhere, that we have time to get from here to somewhere else. We imagine that the future is really out there. This all *seems* very real.

But is it?

There is an old Hindu metaphor of a rope that is mistaken for a snake. When it looks like a snake, we experience fear and the sense of danger. The danger seems real. But actually, the danger is only imaginary. The rope is *always* only a rope, even when it *looks* like a snake.

Are you ever *really* lost, or do you only pretend to be? Perhaps if you observe carefully, you will find that you actually enjoy getting lost, just as you enjoy going to the movies. But sooner or later, it is time to be found, time to come home. How to do that? Very simple. You *are* home. You can't *be* anyplace else. The rope only *looks* like a snake. The problem doesn't really exist.

Selling Water: A Story

I started offering two weekly meetings in the Bay Area. I held private sessions with people. Readers of my book wrote me letters and emails, and I wrote back. I talked to some of them on the phone. The New York

Open Center flew me to New York City to give a weekend workshop on meditation. I made more money that one weekend than I usually made in a whole month. I gave talks at several Buddhist centers and a university, and got paid for some of them. Sounds True recorded my book. Maybe my dream of making a living doing what I truly love was actually materializing!

A German publisher bought the German rights and I got a nice advance on that, and then there was a Dutch translation. In addition, I took a job at Peet's Coffee in Oakland, and after that, did part-time office work for a chiropractor. Along with my book royalties, other writing projects, income from my meetings and workshops, the last remaining bits of an inheritance I had gotten twenty years earlier, and some generous gifts from my mother, I was surviving quite nicely. But the end seemed always to be in sight. I've never felt very good at making money. That's one of the stories I tell myself, and I often believe it.

I dreamed once that Toni Packer was giving dharma transmission to Martha, my arch-enemy at the time, instead of to me. In the dream I screamed at Toni, "Toni, I *get* the Absolute. It's the relative I don't understand."

We have a strong value on independence in our culture, a notion that we must each individually pull ourselves up by our own bootstraps, stand on our own two feet, carry our own weight, and be self-supporting. There is certainly something to be said for being able to take care of yourself. But in our society, a view that takes the truth of things into account seems largely absent. We feel personally responsible and in charge. In fact, the universe *is* supporting each one of us to do precisely what it wants us to be doing, like the lilies of the field that Jesus spoke of. How could it be otherwise? But the mind doesn't always believe it. The mind tells me that Joan has to pull herself up by her own bootstraps, and she damn well better hurry up and do it before she shrivels up and dies, having ruined her whole life. The mind wants Joan's destiny to be spectacular and painless, not ordinary and terminal. In truth, each lily in the field is utterly spectacular, but only in the most ordinary and momentary way. And each lily is *completely* dependent upon the ground, the air, and the light. No lily worries about pulling itself up by its own bootstraps.

I went through all kinds of agitation about whether it was okay to charge money for my meetings. There were so many ideas floating around about spirituality and money. Vipassana teachers worked only for donation. Monks were supposed to possess nothing and traditionally begged for their food. Likewise, many Indian gurus never touched money, but their society supported them. All these people depended on those who *did* touch money!

Ramana actually *stole* the money that took him to Arunachala, his beloved mountain. Once there, he sat down in samadhi, allowing the insects to chew up his legs while grateful devotees put food into his desireless mouth to keep him alive. He never charged money and wasn't concerned in the least with marketing, financial success, or even the survival of the body. I wasn't about to do anything that radical. Money was therefore a necessity. And *maybe* there was nothing inherently more spiritual about a life of material renunciation.

The old Zen masters saw the humor in what they were doing and happily noted that they were selling water by the banks of the river. But they took it lightly, as a joke. I took it all very seriously, fearing that "I" might do the wrong thing.

When I think about it, it seems obvious enough that in our culture, money is the medium of exchange. The person who provides a spiritual service has to eat and pay rent just like everybody else. If that person has to do other work to earn the money they need to survive, then they will have less or no time and energy for the spiritual work they want to offer. In India, that was understood. If you sat down in bliss at the foot of a mountain to contemplate God, people fed you. They took care of you. It was a deeply respected occupation, doing nothing. In our society, we pay our car mechanic, our hairdresser, our therapist, our entertainers, our baseball players, our consultants. Why not spiritual teachers? When it comes right down to it, isn't *everyone* selling water at the banks of the river?

Was money inherently evil, corrupting, and unspiritual? Or was it just another funny shape that the divine was taking in its cosmic play?

I loved doing the weekly meetings. It was clearly a living process, and while I was shaping it in a certain sense, it had a life of its own and was being created through all of us by something beyond us. I had no idea what would come out of my mouth next or what it all might look like next time. I learned a lot from people's questions and my responses. It was easy to see, in the others, the absurdity of the stories, the flimsiness of the imaginary webs that seem to bind us. Whereas when it was my own story, its apparent reality had a greater hold. So everyone was a mirror in which I could see the emptiness of all beliefs, and the absolute undeniable radiance that is always here.

There was also a certain sadness that came after the very first meeting I held. I'd been *thinking* about doing this for so long. It had been such a big deal in my mind. And suddenly it was actually happening, and I could see that in a sense it was totally ordinary. I was not being transformed like Cinderella into a totally new and perfect Joan. In fact, here I was, still biting my fingers, still making mistakes. The mess remained. This obviously wasn't going to save me either; another dream of salvation bites the dust. I could see my Zen teacher Joko Beck smiling. She always thought disappointment was wonderful.

As the weeks went by, offering meetings made me appreciate more than ever the way that Toni works: spacious, not knowing, not imposing an answer. As I gave talks, I was listening to the talk myself, not knowing what would come out next. I never planned them. I let them emerge from silence, from the listening stillness. I loved being present without a plan. I loved the people who were showing up.

Meditation: The Joy of Nothing at All

That there is nothing which can be attained is not idle talk; it is the truth. You have always been one with the Buddha.

HUANG PO

The spiritual life (true meditation or satsang) is not something we do occasionally at a special time and place. It is rather our whole life, or put another way, it is this moment right now. It is not a method or a technique. It requires no special posture, location, or surroundings. It can happen anywhere, under any and all circumstances. Every moment, just as it is, is meditation. Actually, there is only one timeless moment. *This* is meditation.

There is truly nothing to attain. And yet, whenever that is not seen to be so, there will be suffering. It isn't "you" doing it. It's an impersonal appearance, like the weather. It, too, is the One Reality. But it will hurt.

In the absolute sense, there is truly nothing to do about it, *other than what you do*. You will do whatever you do. You won't be able to do anything else, except what you do. Whatever you actually do is perfect. It is exactly what is needed. Getting dead drunk for several years was an important and indispensable part of my own path. You never know what is needed; you can only see what is apparently happening. The mind will have lots of better ideas for what you could or should do instead. It will provide elaborate criticisms and justifications. It will strategize, take vows, and make plans. And still, you will do whatever you do. The "you" is a mirage, an optical illusion. Actions happen, including thoughts, but there is no individual entity at the controls. Whatever you do is your practice: meditating, watching TV, getting drunk, mowing the lawn, biting your fingers, listening to the traffic.

The notion that something is a mistake, or that something needs to be other than it is, is simply that, a notion. Any intentional "practice" runs the risk of perpetuating the illusion that your true nature is not fully present now, that "you" could ever be separated from it, that "it" is something to be achieved or acquired.

At the same time, just about anything *else* you do is also likely to reinforce that illusion, and at least meditation is *aimed* at seeing through it, which most other activities are not. Doing nothing is sometimes misunderstood as "you *should not* do anything," as in, you should not meditate or engage in any form of intentional activity. *This* "not meditating" is just as much a doing as deliberately "meditating," and is equally rooted in the idea that something is needed (in this case, "doing nothing") in order to somehow improve. If you cling to "doing nothing" as if it was something to do, you have missed the point, which is also perfectly okay, and not "your" doing! Doing happens by itself. "Doing nothing" points to the recognition that there is nothing that "you" need to do, or *can* do other than exactly what happens. That might be meditating, and it might be swigging scotch.

If you get stuck on one side or the other of any apparent duality, you have missed the whole truth. The problems are imaginary, and yet the suffering hurts. As my first Zen teacher Mel Weitsman put it, "You are perfect just as you are, but that doesn't mean there is no room for improvement." The mystery is too subtle for any position to take root. The truth is in groundlessness.

Meditation is about groundlessness. Formal meditation is an artificially simplified space where you can pay attention to what is. What we call "artificial" is actually as natural as anything else. It all comes from the same nowhere. Meditation is about resting in the absolute, which just means the sound of the traffic, the sensations of breathing, the tightness in the shoulder, whatever is.

What is takes no effort to achieve, and in fact, cannot be achieved. It *is*. Any effort to achieve it is rooted in the assumption that this isn't quite it. And the falling away of that effort cannot be achieved through effort. In fact, that falling away does not even need to happen. The very notion that it needs to happen is the same illusion. If effort appears, then effort appears. There is no problem with that, unless you have the idea that this effort "shouldn't" be here, that it has to be eliminated. In fact, nothing needs to be eliminated. If the efforting hurts, simply relax. It really is that simple. If you don't relax, then be tense. No problem. Meditation allows everything to be as it is.

We could say that true practice is wherever life takes you. It might involve getting dead drunk for a few years. It might involve a rigorous formal Zen practice. It might be art making. Or therapy. Or body awareness work. Or an intimate relationship. Or getting a job. Or quitting your job. It might be spending time in prison. There is no single right way because there is no way at all.

If you want a practice, I'd say listen to the traffic, the birdsong, the barking dogs, the leaf blowers, the cicadas, the wind, whatever is appearing. Feel the body: the sensations, the energy, the breathing. When thoughts arise, notice that they are thoughts. The habit is to automatically believe them, take them seriously, get involved in them, and become absorbed in the dramas they create. Instead, begin to see thoughts as nothing more than meaningless mental noise. Question the reality of what the thoughts tell you. Notice that the personal stories and dramas you think about are no more serious or real than television soap operas. Let go of every belief, every idea, every aspiration that can be let go. What remains? Give up every answer that arises. Just listen to the traffic, the birds, the wind. Feel the body. Allow everything to come and go. Hold onto nothing. Simply be.

If this sounds depressing or disappointing, I would suggest it's because you are listening to the mind, and not to the traffic, the birdsong, the barking dogs, or the leaf blowers. When you really listen to these ordinary sounds, you hear God. And I don't mean you hear anything *other* than what you are hearing right now.

Enjoy the miraculous sound of running water, the miraculous sound of traffic. Instead of tuning in to your thoughts, tune in to what is. That can happen in any moment of an ordinary day. Enjoy drinking a cup of tea without doing anything else. Just enjoy the tea. Smell it, see it, taste it. Be completely devoted to it. Don't get too precious about it, turning it into a practice and trying to "do" it perfectly, or trying to "do" it all the time.

Experiment with sitting in a waiting room, or on the bus, or on an airplane without your Walkman or your cell phone or your laptop, without reading a magazine, without knitting, without doing anything. Just *be*. Feel the aliveness of presence itself. There's nothing unspiritual about reading a magazine, gulping your tea, or imagining your next holiday while you are washing the dishes. Letting all this go now and then is just something to play with. It won't get you anywhere. It's just pointing you home to where you *are*.

Take walks in silence. Leave your cell phone and your Walkman behind. Go alone. Feel the wind. Smell the flowers. Or the fumes. Enjoy every leaf, every building, every piece of trash. Walking is wonderful and costs nothing.

Have you ever taken time to simply look deeply at something that is utterly commonplace? The bark of a tree, the twisted shape of the branches, a leaf, a cloud. The back of your own hand, a fork, a spoon, a telephone, a lamp. Can you look at something ordinary and familiar without knowing it, in the same way you might look at an abstract painting, enjoying the shapes and colors and gestures of it, the dance it is doing? If you look deeply enough, what is it? What you thought was familiar and ordinary turns out to be utterly new, ever changing, boundless, and extraordinary. The shift is not in the object; it's in the quality of the seeing. Again, I'm not suggesting you rush around "doing" this in a self-conscious way. But perhaps it will invite you more and more, the simple wonder of everything.

I speak of listening or seeing, but what I'm talking about doesn't depend on the senses. Someone who is blind and deaf can listen and see in the way that I mean it. I'm talking about alert presence, awareness, open attention. The senses, and the entire body, are a vehicle for that listening, but the essence, the source, is prior to the senses, prior to the body, prior even to consciousness. What I'm speaking about is effortless; it is already happening. Simply notice that this is so. Tune in to the silence, the spaciousness, the emptiness that is everywhere. In this listening presence, "you" dissolve. All separation dissolves. Only pure being remains, only listening.

Our society is becoming ever more frantic and frenetic. Any moment of silence or idleness is instantly filled with sound and busyness. We flip restlessly through magazines, we channel surf, we surf the net, we have radios and TVs and stereos going every minute, we do as many things at once as we can. There is a kind of dread of emptiness or silence, and a compulsion to fill it up. Nature is too slow. We come to crave the over-stimulation of constant speed, noise and activity.

When we slow down and quiet down, we begin to tune into subtler realms of reality. We notice subtle shifts that wouldn't be perceptible at high speed or full volume. We become more sensitive. It doesn't mean you should never read a magazine or turn on the TV or go fast. But perhaps, if you're interested, you can experiment with seeing what happens if you do nothing at all except be fully present where you actually are.

There are many moments in an ordinary busy day when nothing needs to be done, maybe just for a minute or half a minute. Instead of rushing to fill that space with something (some activity, some noise, some stimulation, some thought, some busy-ness), simply be still. Just breathe. Just listen. Just be.

Listen to the rain. Listen to the traffic. Not as a practice to get you somewhere, but simply to enjoy what is. Is it possible to be here now without trying for any result, without seeking any improvement? Can we put all our techniques and methods aside and simply be alive?

That doesn't mean you are in a state of ecstasy all the time. There will always be a variety of passing experiences, sometimes including boredom and flatness. There will be hours spent doing your income tax and balancing your checkbook. There will be upset and confusion and irritation and pain. There will be fantasies. That's the nature of life. But when we stop *looking* for round-the-clock ecstasy, or for some ideal "empty mind," there is the possibility to be alive to *this* moment, exactly as it actually is.

Nothing fancy needs to happen. Nothing needs to disappear. Nothing needs to be attained. Slowly and instantaneously we grow more and more willing to simply be alive.

※

Sitting quietly, doing nothing is a lovely way to be, as often as it invites you. It is a refreshing and clarifying way to start and end the day. It doesn't matter whether you sit on the floor or in an armchair, what posture you take, whether your eyes are open or closed. Experiment; try different possibilities. Enjoy the view out the window. Watch the birds and the clouds. Just be present. Instead of reading a book, or turning on the TV, or phoning up a friend, experiment with doing nothing at all.

See what reveals itself. Again, this doesn't mean that watching the clouds is spiritual and watching TV is not. It's just a possibility.

Instead of trying to *make* something happen, be fully present to what actually *is* happening. Let everything be just as it is. Without trying in any way to manipulate or control your experience, simply hear the sounds of traffic, the hum of the refrigerator, the cheeping of birds, the laughter of children, the barking dog, the lawn mower, the snow blower, whatever is appearing right now. Feel the sensations in the body. Let go of any effort to do it right, to improve, or to have any particular kind of experience.

If anxiety, restlessness, or boredom should arise, let it arise without trying to control it or make it go away. Instead of telling stories about it, simply *feel* it in the body as pure sensation. Notice how, when you pay careful attention, sensations move and shift, dissolve and reappear. At the very core of these sensations, what do you find?

Observe how thought tries to formulate and understand, how it strategizes and looks for answers and solutions, how it tells stories and passes judgment, how it tries to work everything out mentally. Notice that thoughts are only thoughts. You don't need to make them go away. Just see them for what they are. They *seem* believable, a reliable source of information. But *are* they?

Notice the thoughts coming and going. Feel the body. Hear the traffic. Nothing more, nothing less. If thought pops up and says, "There has to be more to life than this," just notice that this is a thought.

You don't have to "do" all of this perfectly or correctly. You don't have to achieve anything or turn into a better person. Just allow everything to be as it is. Just listen. I don't mean to suggest that you have to "be aware" all the time, as in a mindfulness practice that never lapses. That is a fantasy. There is no you to do any such thing. Rather, notice that awareness, *by its very nature*, includes and allows everything. This total acceptance is always, already the case. True meditation, true prayer, true devotion, true satsang is simply what is, as it is.

The mind endlessly says, "Yes, but," and "So what?" and "What's next?" and "What if?" The mind can't find anything of substance in this that is being pointed to. It's just nothing! But if you're reading this book, chances are you've come to suspect that "nothing" is worth exploring.

When we are listening deeply, stillness arises naturally on its own, and for awhile, we may be completely motionless. Stillness allows for a subtlety and depth of attention. If you watch animals, you'll see that they spend a great deal of time in absolute stillness. They're alert. They don't move at all.

There is something rich about physical stillness, not moving away from discomfort and upset. Typically, when we are upset or afraid, we squirm. We get restless. We try to escape. Stillness is about not escaping. It is about turning to face what we are running from and experiencing it fully. It's especially interesting to sit quietly if you feel agitated, restless, irritated, depressed, or upset. Experiment; see what happens.

Many formal meditation practices have you sitting absolutely motionless for timed periods of fixed duration, often hour after hour, day after day. I did this kind of sitting for many years, and there was something powerful that I learned from it. I don't regret having done it. But it was even more liberating when I finally dropped it.

I no longer recommend this kind of rigorous, forced practice, although if you are drawn to it, by all means do it. What you learn in sitting through these uncomfortable, restless, painful places translates into an ability to find peace at the center of the storm in daily life. But in my book you don't need a timer or a schedule, and you don't need to deliberately subject yourself to excruciating pain. Life will provide you with ample opportunities to face pain without creating them artificially. The body is not designed to sit absolutely immobile for hours and days on end. Stillness will arise naturally if you allow it into your life and make time for it. Maybe at times it does help to have some structure. If structure is needed, it will appear. But you don't need to wear a hair shirt or sleep on a bed of nails in order to wake up. You're not going anywhere. You're here!

Be gentle with yourself. Allow this exploration to be pleasurable, not grueling. Not that life will always be pleasurable. It won't. Unpleasant things will arise, and when they do, it's an especially rich opportunity for stillness and attention. It's eye opening to discover how much of the suffering in life is mind-generated, how much of it comes from resistance, how much of it is optional when the mechanism is clearly seen.

～❧

You might find it interesting and enjoyable to take a day or two, or even a week to be in complete silence. Turn off the phone, pretend you're out of town, leave your computer off, don't read or write or listen to music or watch TV. Do absolutely nothing. Just be alive. See what happens. If you can't do this in your own home because of family or housemates, there are many retreat centers now where you can go and do your own self-retreat. It's also possible that your family or housemates might be willing to let you do this in their midst, and they might even be interested in joining you.

Allow yourself to be completely unscheduled, to discover the organic rhythm of every hour, every day and every moment. Don't impose anything. In doing this, we are not retreating *from* life; rather, it is an intensive exploration of what we ordinarily ignore.

You may find that it is an enormous relief to let all the noise and busyness go. Most likely, you will also encounter some difficult moments. You will be faced with the empty hole that we try desperately to fill with activities and substances. Instead of running away, this is an invitation to dive right into the center of this apparent hole. You may discover that the hole and the diver are both a mirage.

If you are finding yourself getting attached to peace and quiet, and beginning to regard everything else as a distraction, let that be a little wake-up bell. Nothing is actually a distraction. It is what it is. But if we have the idea that what is should be different than it is, we call it a distraction. Dividing the sacred from the mundane is missing the point. Everything is sacred. There are no distractions, no mistakes, no obstacles. If we *feel* like something is a distraction or a mistake or an obstacle, we are believing our thoughts, and resisting what is.

Years ago, when I was leaving a Zen sesshin (a week long silent intensive), the teacher said, "Now the real sesshin begins." Real satsang can happen anywhere—in a traffic jam, at the office, in the supermarket. It can sometimes *seem* easier to realize the truth in a quiet natural setting, but if we imagine that we *need* any particular setting, or that there is *more* truth in one place than another, we are limiting the truth and missing the essence.

~&

Sometimes we think that spirituality is about being calm and blissful, and losing our temper is something else. But actually, life gets *most* interesting and *most* juicy at precisely those moments when things seem to be getting the most difficult. These are also little wake-up bells. They tell us we're holding on tightly in some way to the illusion. They are doorways into truth. They are sacred moments.

The next time you're upset, or you find yourself being critical of someone else, perhaps it's possible to be interested in what is happening, to observe it. This is the last thing we want to do. We want to be right. We want to wallow and gossip and chew on old bones. But slowly we begin to realize, or at least get a glimmer of the unreality of these dramas and the suffering they create. We begin to wonder if there's another way. We develop a willingness to question our story. And we discover that when the story ends, there is love. Our lives change.

So the next time you're upset, instead of getting lost in the drama, see if it's possible to tune into the bodily sensations. Feel the tightness in the chest, the shoulders, the jaw, the throat, the stomach. Experience it with infinite curiosity and patience. Let it unfold. If the storyline starts running, notice it as a story. Notice how compelling it may be, how we want to keep going on with it. Is this story really true? What happens to me, to my relationships, to the world when I tell this story? What would life be like without this story? Do I really need this story? Do I really believe it?

Notice how mechanical the whole upset is. Something "pushes our buttons" and the story begins to run automatically. Thoughts trigger emotions; emotions trigger more thoughts. It's a self-perpetuating cycle. There's nothing personal about it. It's a pattern. The awareness that sees it is not mechanical. Awareness is free. If the buttons get pushed, and the anger explodes, awareness is unharmed.

The force of habit wants desperately to go outward, toward past and future, toward objects, stories, and results. If we try to force that to change, or sink into self-hatred and despair when it doesn't, that's all just more of the same. This isn't about self-control and becoming a perfect person. To simply be aware of the movement of conditioned habit and reactivity, to see it, to learn about it, to do nothing about it, to let it be as it is, *that* is a whole new way of being. That's already outside the habitual loop.

Awareness beholds everything in the same way a mirror reflects images, without judgement or preferences. Awareness has no limits, no boundaries, no gender, no age, no point of view, no agenda, no qualities of its own. It does not belong to any body. It includes everything and sticks to nothing. It is unconditional love.

⁓❧

I've offered a number of suggestions in this chapter: sitting quietly, taking time to be in silence away from your usual busyness, paying attention to upset. I want to emphasize again that these are not intended as a recipe for enlightenment or as guidelines for a spiritually correct life. These suggestions are merely pointers to what is. You won't achieve anything by following them. There is nothing to achieve.

If you have been meditating for many years, I encourage you to recognize what never comes and goes, and to stop pursuing it in any specific or exclusive experience. If you enjoy meditating, by all means meditate. But if you are separating meditation from the rest of life, recognize that every moment is meditation. Give up the whole concept of "meditation." Give up attaching importance to *any* particular state of consciousness, however "enlightened" or "unenlightened" it seems.

Stolen Car

My housemate Adele is out of town, and I walk out of the house in the morning on my way somewhere, and my car is gone. There's just an empty space on the street where it was. I can't quite believe it. I walk back in the house and come out again. I look up and down the street. No car. It's definitely gone. I see some broken glass in the street where they must have smashed a window to get in. I'm not experiencing any of the emotional upset I might have expected, no anger or grief. Instead there is simply action happening. I call the police. I call my insurance company. I wait for the police to arrive. I talk to the officer who comes. I eat some lunch. I take a bus into Berkeley and get a rental car.

It strikes me that this is all happening in a field of total acceptance and calm that would not have been the same if Adele had been home, not because of any fault in her, but because of the way we humans typically set each other off and work ourselves up in relationship through sheer habit. Had Adele been home, I can imagine I would have rushed back into the house and announced in a dramatic tone that my car had been stolen. Adele would have responded with shock and astonishment, and together we would have rushed outside to look, feeding one another's outrage and upset, telling each other the story that something terrible had happened. I would have been appropriately upset. Maybe it wouldn't have been like that at all, obviously it's all speculation. But I have a sense that if I had not been alone, it would have set into motion a whole drama that simply did not happen.

Later that night, my neighbor called, having heard the news, and she was prepared to console and sympathize and be upset with me, but instead, in a matter of seconds we ended up laughing hysterically over the whole incident.

It showed me how human beings habitually create drama and suffering, especially when we're feeding off each other, and how it's entirely possible to meet something that would normally be upsetting without there being any upset at all. But it didn't happen the way it did because I was *trying* to respond that way; it happened on its own. *Trying* not to get upset is a losing strategy. Either you get upset anyway, and then feel terrible about yourself, or else you get cancer or hives or migraines or *something* from the internalized pressure of holding yourself in. This wasn't like that. This was effortless. It happened on its own.

~❧

Coming home on the freeway one night in the rental car, in the dark—heavy traffic, everyone going seventy m.p.h.—suddenly a car to my left goes totally out of control and comes straight at me across four lanes of traffic, narrowly misses me, hits the wall, bounces, spins, goes back across four lanes of traffic (all this is now happening in my rear view mirror) as cars everywhere swerve and collide. And I am untouched. Wow. Wakes you right up. No tomorrow.

A few days later, the police found my car. Blessedly, it had not been trashed.

The Nature of Experience

We search for the perfect experience. We hope that someday, in the future, we will attain it: the perfect car, the perfect relationship, the perfect job, the perfect house, the perfect spiritual teacher, the perfect enlightenment experience. But the nature of all experience is the same: what begins must end; every up includes a down. They go together. They are inseparable. They create each other.

We imagine that someday the teeter-totter of polarity will stabilize in the up position. We will finally arrive. But it never works that way. The teeter-totter always goes up and down. For as long as we are alive, no matter how many times we take out the garbage, more accumulates.

The desperate search for permanent pleasure (or final enlightenment) is suffering. Pain is inescapable; it comes with organic life. Suffering is imaginary; it comes from the story. Liberation accepts everything and seeks nothing. This is not an ability that "you" will someday acquire; "you" *are* the resistance and the seeking. The promise of "someday" is the fuel that sustains the mirage. Liberation is your absence. It has no future. It is just what is.

Disappointment

Years ago, on the first sesshin I did with Joko Beck, she began by saying something like this: "In a little while, you're all going to be really disappointed, and that's a wonderful thing." Why did she say that?

We work so hard to win, and we keep being disappointed, and this disappointment is wonderful, Joko says. Because we *can't* win, and when we finally stop *trying* to win, we're here. *Here* is the jewel.

Who Is Pulling The Strings?

Do We Have A Choice?
Who Is Pulling the Strings?

No one can will anything but what the Totality causes him to will!

RAMESH S. BALSEKAR

Your suffering is your own activity. It is something that you are doing moment to moment. It is a completely voluntary activity....You will continue to pursue every kind of means until you realize that all you are doing is pinching yourself. When you realize that, you just take your hand away. There is nothing complicated at all about it. But previous to that, it is an immensely complicated problem.

ADI DA SAMRAJ (A.K.A. DA FREE JOHN)

Paradoxically, although we are 100% responsible for our lives, I sense that we have, nonetheless, absolutely zero control over anything. In fact, we cannot even control our belief (or disbelief) about this whole issue of control. However, although we don't actually have a so-called "free will," it still seems to be very important to PRETEND that we do. But, as they say "Que sera, sera."

CHUCK HILLIG

Events happen, deeds are done, but there is no individual doer thereof.

THE BUDDHA

Choice implies consciousness—a high degree of consciousness. Without it, you have no choice. Choice begins the moment you disidentify from the mind and its conditioned patterns, the moment you become present.....Nobody chooses dysfunction, conflict, pain. Nobody chooses insanity. They happen because there is not enough presence in you to dissolve the past, not enough light to dispel the darkness. You are not fully here. You have not quite woken up yet. In the meantime, the conditioned mind is running your life.

ECKHART TOLLE

The sense that things should be other than they are, is suffering.

WAYNE LIQUORMAN

Whatever action happens, whether you eat icecream or meditate, at that moment you could not have done otherwise.

RAMESH S. BALSEKAR

What makes it unbearable is your mistaken belief that it can be cured.

JOKO BECK

To any conceptual problem there cannot be any valid answer except to see the problem in perspective as an empty thought. There is no such thing as a "problem" which is other than merely conceptual.

RAMESH S. BALSEKAR

To see something you must look at it. To do this you must first separate yourself. This is the illusion.

H.W.L. POONJA

Find out who it is who has free will or predestination and abide in that state. Then both are transcended. That is the only purpose in discussing these questions. To whom do such questions present themselves? Discover that and be at peace.

RAMANA MAHARSHI

Controlled or not controlled?
The same dice shows two faces.
Not controlled or controlled,
Both are a grievous error.

Mumon's Comment,
"Hyakujo's Fox," The Gateless Gate

I've spent much of my life investigating the age-old question of free will, along with the koan of addiction, which I define very broadly. For me, these are not abstract philosophical issues. How change happens has been the central question of my life. How do habits end? Can we wake up from entrancement on the personal and global levels? Is there a choice? Is it possible to stop biting my fingers? If so, how? Does it even *matter* that I bite them, or that nations are at war? What do I say when someone calls me up and tells me that they are drinking themselves to death, they want to stop, they've been in and out of treatment programs, they always go back to drinking, they've lost their job, nothing seems to work, and they ask me, what should they do? How do I respond?

Do I act *as if* they have a choice? *Do* they have a choice? Do *I* have a choice?

One thing I've learned from investigating these questions is that they defy answers. That's often a tip-off that the question itself is in some way flawed. It's easy with questions like this to get into a war of conflicting dogmas and doctrines, arguing with others who have different beliefs and defending our own as if our very survival depended on it. Often we're at war because we're using the same words in different ways, and if we really checked it out, we'd discover we're both saying the same thing. And even if we *aren't* saying the same thing, we might *both* be right. Or we might both be wrong. The question itself might be absurd because the very elements to which it refers turn out to be imaginary. So, right now, in investigating this question, is it possible to stay completely open to not knowing, to being surprised?

Looking anew right now, is there free choice?

It *seems* like "we" make choices all day long. We apparently choose whether to have corn flakes or oatmeal, whether to wear blue or green, whether to marry Joe or Ed, whether to take the job offer or not, whether to live in this or that town. It also seems that "we" have control over certain "voluntary" actions: I can raise my arm, sing, or twirl around.

We also have the experience of sometimes having no control. Certainly, we didn't have much control over being born or growing our body. Every day cancer cells, car accidents, earthquakes, tornadoes, floods, wars, and psychopaths routinely and capriciously wipe people like us out. Whenever one of these events touches close to home, we are reminded viscerally of how little control we have. Sooner or later, this body and everything it loves will die. It could happen in the next second. *Anything* could happen in the next second.

Addiction is an interesting phenomenon because it seems to embody both control and the absence of control. Putting my fingers in my mouth and taking them out again is usually thought of as a voluntary action. Yet when I compulsively bite my fingers, it *seems* that I cannot control it. Anyone who has struggled with an addiction or a compulsion has experienced this phenomenon. Probably, to some degree, everyone has experienced it. We vow or intend to do (or not do) something, and we fail.

Performing, or not performing, a given action (whether it's smoking, finger-biting, gunning down innocent people in a shopping mall, dropping bombs, or polluting the earth) has to do with more than just the neuromuscular capacity to perform the task. Conditioning (chemistry, genetics, habit, nature and nurture, thought and belief) and awareness (clouded over or shining clearly) determine what happens and what doesn't within the range of what is physically possible.

Can "I" *choose* to be present and aware, free of conditioned habit?

Rather than looking to what various authorities have said about such questions, perhaps we can begin to look directly at our own experience. Actually begin to observe, in your own life, the making of choices. It can be the big ones, like whether to move across country or get married or quit your job. Or it can be the very little ones, like whether to stand up after you've been sitting down for awhile. Watch very carefully to see how it happens. You're considering whether or not to take the job, going back and forth in your mind, and suddenly you act decisively one way or the other. The decision has been made. Can you actually find the decisive moment? Were "you" in control of it? Likewise with getting up from your chair: how did that decision actually happen? Begin to observe this for yourself. This takes a subtle and careful attention, not just a quick look with the conclusion already in mind.

Scientific evidence indicates that the decisive thought ("Stand up") is actually an after-thought. The body is already involved in initiating the movement when that thought occurs. So if "you" didn't set yourself in motion, what did?

Are we, in fact, free to stop addictive habits? Do they have to continue? Who or what is pulling the strings? Who is pinching who? And who exactly is stepping back to take a look?

Addiction

I'll define addiction very broadly as the habitual, compulsive, often destructive, apparently uncontrollable and irresistible movement away from something unwanted, often some fundamental sense of unease or lack, toward something desired—some kind of soothing gratification, heightened pleasure, numbness, distraction, change of state, or enhanced functioning—something associated with happiness or pain-relief. I'm not using the word *addiction* pejoratively, but simply as a description of what is. In a sense, anything that we feel we *have* to have or do, aside from basic biological necessities, is an addiction in the way that I am using it. This can include anything from heroin and alcohol to a particular train of thought or even a compulsive meditation practice. It can be a substance, an object, or an activity. The basic mechanism is the same, although of course certain addictions are quite benign and may even be beneficial in some ways, like mine to green tea, while others are fatal attractions that wreck considerable apparent havoc in our lives and in the lives of those around us. All serious addiction is a kind of ritualized dramatization of the fundamental gesture of dilemma and resistance that we call egoic life or human suffering. In that respect, it's a great window into the entire mechanism of illusion and suffering: "I" create a problem, suffer from it, try desperately to solve it, and all the while "I" am biting myself. And I am doing this for a reason. It's a distraction, an avoidance, a kind of pleasure. That which this movement of addiction seeks to avoid *feels* like it will kill us. And in a certain sense, it will.

Is it possible to not move away?

～❧

The prevailing views on addiction are that you are a weak-willed, good-for-nothing wastrel, a blight on society; or you are the victim of an inherited illness or a chemical imbalance, and you should either join a twelve-step program or take psychiatric drugs to correct it; or you have total responsibility and should "just say no." Which is it?

Thirty years ago, I was a gutter drunk, using every drug there was, smoking three packs of Camels a day, having sex with strangers. I woke up in jail, I woke up in the hospital, I woke up in strange cities and foreign countries, but fortunately I always woke up. Then it ended. I sobered up. What happened? What made me a drunk, and what made me sober up? At what moment, and how did the switch actually occur in my life from alcoholism to sobriety?

I tried at least half a dozen times to stop smoking. I'd stop for a day, or a week, or maybe even a few months. Then I'd start again. Then one time, it never came back. What changed?

I've been compulsively biting my fingers since I was a child. I bite the flesh, not the nails, and I make bloody wounds, and sometimes I am unable to stop for hours at a time. This still happens. Sometimes this habit disappears for a day, or a week, or even for several months. But then, so far, it comes back. My fingers are bandaged as I write this. Why isn't it finished, like drinking and smoking?

～❧

Addiction *feels* out of control, yet paradoxically it is a mechanical pattern, a controlled way of being out of control in order to get control.

We can always stop an addictive behavior if we *want* to stop. But the problem is, we want to indulge, sometimes more strongly than we want to stop. "Wanting to stop" becomes a future plan. Indulging is the instant gratification, the pleasure that we want now. Stopping is our future hope. Someday we will be saved; life will be better; we will stop. But meanwhile, we'll have just one more.

Can we choose what we want? Don't answer from belief, look and see.

⌒&

The addictive habit is an old and familiar pattern that we have learned. It happens automatically. Some feeling or thought arises, and suddenly we want a drink, a cigarette, a sexual encounter, or our favorite train of thought (maybe dreaming about what we will someday become, or thinking compulsively about all the ways we've been mistreated and victimized).

And this isn't just a vague take-it-or-leave-it kind of desire. It feels like an irresistible, compelling force. It seems like something we *must* have or do, like our very survival is at stake. And in some cases, as the addiction progresses, we will do amazing things to satisfy it. We will drive for miles in the middle of the night to buy cigarettes, and we will keep smoking even though we are dying of emphysema. We *have* to do it. Or so we think and feel.

If it becomes obvious that this habit is also painful, we experience the desire to stop. Now we have two conflicting impulses: one that urges us to indulge and one that urges us to stop. At different moments, each of these impulses seems to be "the real me." One is the Good Girl, and one is the Bad Girl. When I was in therapy sobering up, my therapist had me do "gestalts" where I would move between two chairs, alternately taking the voice that said "indulge" and then the voice that said "stop." It was illuminating to hear what they each had to say. I recommend this exercise.

"You should quit smoking because you're going to get lung cancer, and it's costing you a small fortune, and you'd feel a lot better if you stopped."

"Oh come on, stop trying to be such a good girl. You should smoke because you love it; it feels good. Who cares if you get lung cancer? You're having fun, and you're going to die anyway. It's sexy to smoke, and besides, you won't be able to write if you don't smoke. What the hell, lighten up and light up."

Each voice seems to have some real validity and value to us. The one who wants to stop is the caring, intelligent, rational, healthy, mature, adult. The addict is the irrational, reckless, daring, spontaneous child. In myself, I called them the sober nun and the drunken lover. They each represented a vital part of my life. If society manages to suppress the wild and reckless part, then it may be that it can only come out through addictive behavior. The challenge is to find less painful and more creative ways of allowing all aspects of ourselves to come into being. As I sobered up, that was indeed the process I went through. I had to discover that I could dance, say what I felt like saying, write books, take risks, be spontaneous, and make love without being drunk.

~❧~

"I have to smoke a cigarette," is a thought. "I can't stop," is a thought. "I should stop," is a thought. "I will stop," is a thought. Where do these thoughts come from? Are "we" in control of them? And what determines whether we act on them? Are we in control of that?

Again, watch it in action as it happens in your own life. Notice how compelling certain thoughts are, for example if you're angry at someone, or worried about something, or lost in some pleasurable fantasy.

The more any habit is repeated, the stronger the compulsion gets.

Likewise, the more presence and awareness there is, the more presence and awareness there is. Putting it into words that way makes it seem like presence is something that comes and goes, something that can get bigger or smaller. Perhaps a more accurate way to say it would be, the more awareness is aware of itself, the more the content is seen for the transient, insubstantial, dream-like appearance that it is.

Before we truly "sober up" once and for all, there are many moments when the addiction is over, when we actually don't *want* to drink or smoke or bite or whatever it is. But then it comes back and seemingly "overwhelms us." How does that happen? How does it shift?

The same thing happens with so-called awakening. There are moments of clear seeing, and then the old view comes back and seems to overwhelm us again. Empty, spacious awareness appears to contract back down to the tight little reactive capsule of "me," the character in the story. How does that happen? How does it shift? Is there any choice involved?

This is a question to live with. Watch and see, moment to moment, how these shifts occur, between clarity and mind smog, between freedom and compulsion. Taking the smog personally, or viewing it as an obstacle, is just more smog. Simply be curious about the whole movement—the flip back and forth—see it, observe and investigate it. Don't settle for anyone else's answers. Look for yourself.

To whom do these apparent flips occur? Is there some individual who *owns* these experiences, who *has* them? Or is that merely an idea, a mental image, a sensation?

~❧~

When we say "I" have changed, what do we mean? Where is the "I"?

"I" was a drunk, and now "I" am sober, we say. Who is the I?

When we observed carefully those activities that seemed to be voluntary and in my control (like lifting my arm or making a decision), we discovered that we couldn't really pinpoint the decisive moment, or how it actually happened. When we look for the doer of these actions, we find empty space.

At the same time, it would be absurd to say that I cannot talk, or lift my arm, or direct my attention. There is something *right here* that can act. And yet, when we look for the source of that, we can't find anything.

There is simply activity: biting, thinking, drinking, not drinking. *"Woman sitting in chair biting."* Even the nouns are actually verbs. The so-called *chair* is a disintegrating sub-atomic dance of particles and waves, with no real boundary, utterly inseparable from the so-called *woman* who is a disintegrating process of cells and organs and particles and waves and electrical firings. It is a process, an activity. The apparent solidity and differentiation are composed of nothing but thought-forms.

Perhaps there is no "you" here who "has" this experience of addiction and who needs to be saved from it. Perhaps there is just activity and sensation (some of it pleasant, some of it unpleasant), and thoughts *about* that activity (interpreting it, judging it, giving it meaning, strategizing about how to keep or get rid of it), all an impersonal process, like the weather, or like the flu.

Control is an idea, a way of thinking. It doesn't exist or make any sense without the central reference point ("me"), because there has to be something separate to be in or out of control, fated or free. Words emerge, the arm lifts, the body moves. Joan isn't in control, because Joan is a mirage.

And yet, *right here,* there is the capacity to act. Action happens. *You* can act. Not "you" as Joan, the mythological character in the story, but *you,* the One Being. When life happens out of undivided aware presence, rather than out of the trance of separation and mis-identification as "me," there is a sense of total freedom. The mind is not producing imaginary obstructions and doubts. Action flows freely, responsive to the whole situation, unhindered. This is not the freedom to do whatever "I" want, as if "I" was a separate piece who could go my own way. It is rather the freedom that wants only what is. The separation, which was only a mirage, has vanished.

What Is Choice?

What exactly do we mean by this word "choice"?

It seems to mean that thought can imagine two or more possible alternatives in the projected future. Thought evaluates them and finally appears to select one. It is a process that functions by artificially dividing the world into parts, most basically by dividing subject from object: the chooser and the chosen.

An apparent fork in the road appears, and there is the *thought:* "*I* am at a fork in the road. I could go down Road A or Road B." Then further thoughts: "If I go this way, this might happen. If I go that way, that might happen."

Then, *Going-Down-Road-A* happens. And then the thought, "*I* am going down Road A. I *chose* Road A. I *could* have gone down Road B."

But the "I" separate from Road A is imaginary. It is a creation of thought. Actually, "I" and "Road A" are one event. "Me going down Road B" exists only as an imaginary idea, a thought, occurring now, as part of *Going-Down-Road-A.* There is no such actuality outside that thought.

Going down Road A is one whole event, undivided from the fork in the road, and the road before that, indivisible from *everything.* There was never a choice, only the *appearance* of one. There was no one separate from *what is* to choose one direction or the other. The decision, the choice is only a way of conceptualizing and *thinking about* what has occurred. Nothing could actually be any different from how it is. Past and future are in the mind. Time itself is in the mind; it is a way of thinking; it has no actual reality. Only *this* is.

But because we *think* it could be different, and because we think "we" have a choice, there is suffering. We think: "I should have taken Road B; that would have been better." We imagine that this possibility actually exists, that "I" could be separated out from "here," and that what is could be other than it is. We imagine time and space, past and future, "me" steering my ship. This picture is so deeply conditioned and reinforced that it seems entirely believable and factual.

Acting out of this picture, we think more thoughts. We look at our spouse, our child, our parent, our employer, our employee, our friend, or our favorite enemy, and we think: "That idiot went down Road B! I told him to take Road A. *I* took Road A. Why the hell did he go down Road B? He's really screwing up. He should be punished."

When you "decide" to do or say something, what has actually occurred? An impulse arose. From where did it come? Did you choose it? If "you" like it and follow it, did "you" choose that response?

Choice is always about the future. Whether that future is a second away or ten years away, it is always about the future. It is therefore always hypothetical, imaginary, and unreal. If you (apparently) decide that "I am going to cook dinner now," that action (cooking dinner) is in the projected future. It is not happening at *this* moment. When that thought ("I'm going to cook dinner now") is followed by cooking dinner, you feel that you have made a decision and carried it out. The illusion of choice and free will is reinforced every time this happens. But the actualizing of that so-called decision is entirely dependent on a host of variables over which "you" have no control whatsoever. For example, if your apartment bursts into flames as you are walking into your kitchen, the desire to survive will undoubtedly override the decision to cook dinner. Likewise, the decision to quit smoking can arise, and it *may* happen that you never smoke again. But if something in your circumstances, your neurochemistry or your circuitry overrides that decision, then you'll smoke.

Where does the impulse to do something come from in the first place? Why does one person get the urge to write books and not someone else? Why is one person tempted to become a heroin addict and another feels no such temptation? What forces turn one person into Mother Teresa and another into Jack the Ripper? And are they *really* two separate people, or are they aspects of One Being?

If you take up the life of meditation, if you inquire deeply into your own direct experience from moment to moment, you will soon discover that something very vast is living you, doing you. There is no one outside of it (or inside of it) to be in or out of control, or to go off in some direction other than what is. All separation is notional. You *are* the whole thing. Consciousness is doing or imagining *all* of it. You have no choice at all, *and* you are choosing absolutely everything. There is actually nothing to choose because every apparent "thing" is *really* all the very same no-thing: the One Being, Consciousness itself.

The sense of having a choice is actually mental confusion. In the moment, it is always obvious what to do. Only when the mind gets lost in projecting the imaginary future does it get confusing. In the next moment, our direction may shift 180 degrees, but in each moment there is a kind of choiceless clarity that *knows*. Action happens.

When life moves only from presence and clarity, without endlessly looking back, without second guessing, without doubt or hesitation, then it *feels* like the seamless flow that it actually always *is*. It feels effortless. There is no strain, no resistance. There is a sense of total freedom. We could call this enlightened activity, unobstructed by mental confusion. This kind of activity is responsive, not reactive. It comes from love, which is another word for awareness, intelligence, acceptance of what is. Such activity is non-harmful.

But very often, at that moment of knowing what to do, the thinking mind comes in and muddies it up. It throws up doubts and fearful specters ("How will you survive if you do that?" "What will happen to you?"), or else it holds out alluring promises ("Oh, it will feel so good! Go ahead!"). It churns out elaborate rationalizations. It says, "Yes, but" and "What if?" It paralyzes us in indecision. We agonize, imagining all possible outcomes. We hesitate. We worry. And then, driven by desire or fear, confused by mental smog and upsetting emotions, we do things we "know" are off the mark in some way. We are out of sync. We stumble and fall. It feels constricted and unpleasant. The seamless flow is still here, but we no longer feel it. We could call this deluded activity. It is often harmful from our human perspective, meaning that it creates suffering.

In reality, there is no such thing as enlightened activity and deluded activity. The distinction is purely notional, and from the perspective of the universe, there is no mistake and no tragedy either way. The disorder is all part of a larger order. If one passageway is blocked up, the river of energy finds another channel. But from our human perspective, *because we take it personally,* we want to be the "open channel," the enlightened one. The stones in the river that block the flow of water have no such ideas about themselves; therefore, they don't suffer from their situation. Neither does the universe. Only the human mind suffers, and as always, the suffering is rooted in the mistaken belief that we *are* this one little stone, and that what happens is personal, within our control, and should be different than it is.

Spirituality is not about "you" as a person becoming a perfect channel. Nor is it about you always *feeling* a sense of seamless flow, or having a sustained *experience* of oneness. It is rather about realizing that you *are* the whole, all the blockages and all the openings, all of it a dream-like appearance that vanishes in an instant. The bodymind is a conditioned organism that undulates endlessly between open and closed (inhaling and exhaling, heart beating, eating, eliminating, pulsating, vibrating, being born, dying, opening and closing). In fact, the bodymind is a thought-form, and all thought undulates between the polar opposites. The body, the emotions, the thoughts, the behavior ("you" as a person) will never be permanently open. It is impossible.

Is there an openness that is always open, that includes *everything*, all openings and all closings, an openness that has no opposite, no beginning and no end?

Prescriptions and Descriptions

All descriptions of reality are inevitably incomplete and cannot capture actuality. The mind turns these inevitably inadequate descriptions into *beliefs*, and then into *prescriptions* for how to live a spiritually correct life. So, if we hear there is no choice, the mind turns it into "I should not choose." Deep down, we still think there is a "me" here to choose or not choose, so we find ourselves "trying not to choose," as if we had a choice! We try to use "choicelessness" or "non-doership" as a prescription or a strategy to get us somewhere.

Or you hear there is no choice, so you think, "Okay, I have no control, so I'll keep on smoking; everything is just happening to me." The mind is using the description as a rationalization for behavior; the description has become a belief in the service of habit. Yes, even that simply happens, like the weather. But again, that is a description, not a prescription.

Right now, if you make a fist and then open your hand, and if you observe carefully as you do this, you will not be able to find any doer. But at the same time, the action can be done. If you decided that you could not open your hand anymore because there is no separate, individual doer, that would be absurd. Or if you had a stroke or some other kind of brain injury, and temporarily lost the ability to open your hand, it would be absurd to refuse physical therapy or whatever was required to re-learn that skill on the grounds that you are not the doer and there is nothing to do. And yet this is precisely the kind of confused muddle that the mind can get itself into when it *thinks* about all of this without fully understanding it.

Just as there is an ability to open your hand, there is also an ability to open your mind, to direct your attention from one place to another, and to tune in to the silent stillness of pure awareness that is here before and after all objects. It isn't "you" as an independent entity who is doing or initiating *any* of this, and yet, to say it cannot be done is untrue. It cannot be done if the force of habit and conditioning is too strong, if the neurochemistry or the mental smog is too thick, or if the force of the universe is going the other way, and "you" are not in control of *any* of that because "you" are only an idea, a mental image. The *origin* of any action is not "you" as a separate little entity, because all such separation is only a way of thinking and perceiving. The real source of any apparent action is Consciousness or Life Itself. *This* is what acts. And *this* is what you are.

The impulse or thought to open your hand (or your mind) comes from beyond the person, as does the neuromuscular apparatus and functioning that carries it out. You as Jane Doe cannot "choose" something that is not already arising in consciousness. You as Jane Doe cannot "choose" to go off in a direction contrary to and independent from the totality, because you are not a separate piece. That separation is an illusion. But the totality functions through every Jane Doe. Our apparent capacity for discernment, our apparent ability to move our body, to direct our attention, and to apparently "choose" or "intend" this or that is all part of that functioning. The illusion is that we think that "we" as an independent entity are the source of it.

If we hear there *is* choice, and we don't realize the true source of it, then it will reinforce the idea of a separate little me who is, or should be, in control. When our efforts at choosing or intending something don't always work (because sometimes the force of habit will be too strong, or the movement of the universe will be going in a different direction from our mental ideas—which is all the apparent person really is), we will feel like we have failed. This leads to guilt and blame, holding ourselves and everyone else responsible for everything that we all do. And likewise, if we succeed at something, we will imagine that "we" did it, and we will take personal credit for the work of the infinite.

The notion of choicelessness is deeply upsetting to most people. It suggests that I'm nothing but a kind of robot. But when all sense of separation becomes transparent, there is nobody left to be a robot, or to *care* about being a robot. There is simply what is. Action can happen freely, without being bogged down in *any* kind of conceptual mirage.

Truth can't be put into words. Concepts can never catch the paradoxical aliveness of the mystery. They can only point.

⁓❧

Language and concept not only *describe* what is perceived and believed, but they also *create* what is perceived and believed. Words create perceptions. The baby does not look at this room and see "chairs," "tables," "rugs," and "people." Those are ideas. Thought draws boundary lines and we *learn* to see "a chair" and "a rug." To the infant, it may well be one undivided flowing whole, or it may be divided on a completely different basis, by color instead of function, or whatever. Nations are thought-forms with no inherent reality, and yet we take them so seriously that we fight wars over them.

If we believe this is a hostile universe, that's what it is. If we believe it is a loving universe, that's what it is. If we believe we are powerless, then we are powerless. To an amazing extent, thought creates the reality we *appear* to live in. What we pay attention to, and what we think and believe, is what we get. We attract what we focus on and expect to find. In a very real sense, that's what actually creates whatever appears. I'm not suggesting that disease, disability, poverty, addiction, and everything else in this world are caused only by thoughts, or certainly not by anyone's individual thoughts in the way that some New Age teaching has put forward. I'm only pointing to the power of thought and attention to create reality. Outside thought, what is there? This is a wonderful question to live with and to consider. It has been said that the same glass can be seen as half empty or half full. Believe one view, and you are disappointed. Believe the other, and you are happy. Believe nothing at all, and where are you?

What Causes Addiction?
What Causes Sobriety?

People tell me fingerbiting is a compulsive disorder, a malfunctioning in the neurochemistry linked to anxiety and depression. I could cure it by taking anti-depressants. Others tell me it's self-injuring, a psychological problem often associated with early trauma, whereby people, usually women, inflict non-lethal harm on their own bodies in a ritualistic way. Still others tell me it's a manifestation of kundalini. I've called it an addiction. Theories abound about all of these categories. Is it physiological or psychological in its etiology, voluntary or involuntary in its expression? Is it rooted in the body or in the mind; is it an addiction or a compulsion, or maybe even a spiritual experience? Where do we draw the lines between all these things—between body and mind, between addiction and compulsion, between spiritual and non-spiritual, between voluntary and involuntary? We make up explanations, but do they really explain anything?

I can say I became a drunk because I suffered intrauterine trauma, or because I had only one hand, or because my parents were uncomfortable with the expression of certain emotions, or because I was queer in 1966, or because it was a time of tumultuous social upheaval, or because there was a lot of drinking going on at my college, or because I had a genetic predisposition, if such a thing even exists. But there were certainly many other people who had all or many of those same conditions who never drank, or never to excess.

So what caused it? The only conclusion I can come to is that *everything* in the whole universe caused it. An unfathomable mix of genetics, neurochemistry, hormones, nature and nurture, weather, circumstances of all kinds, explosions in distant galaxies. In short, everything. Or nothing. There is no single cause. No easy explanation.

And my sobriety? Some say I had great courage or strong will, but I know how cowardly and weak-willed I can be. Some say it was my wonderful therapist, but others who went to that same therapist kept right on drinking. So what did it?

At the moment when I met my therapist—which happened "accidentally," I wasn't looking for a therapist—at that moment, I *knew* I was going to sober up. I had no doubts. It was totally clear to me. I've tried since then to reproduce or manufacture this kind of doubtless certainty, and it can't be manufactured. It emerged out of life itself. It was simply *there*. In fact, it almost seems like *in that moment*, my sobering up had already happened. Would I have stayed sober without my therapist? No way to know. But I can't really explain why I stopped. Or why the person sitting next to me in the bar never did.

Is wanting to know also an addiction?

❧

When I sobered up, my therapist used the model of choice. I had made an unconscious decision to kill myself, to drink, and I could now become conscious of that, and make a conscious decision to be sober. My therapist asked me to make a contract with her that I wouldn't drink without talking to her first. She did not think there was any such thing as an alcoholic. She didn't buy the disease model or the twelve-step ideology. My therapist was influenced by Transactional Analysis (*Games People Play, Scripts People Live, Games Alcoholics Play*), by Gestalt therapy, and by feminist and radical therapy. She believed a former alcoholic drinker could even drink again eventually without getting drunk. This proved to be true, although I rarely ever drink.

When we worked on my addiction to smoking, my therapist would have me change *can't* to *won't*. Instead of saying, "I *can't* stop," I was to say, "I *won't* stop." Changing the word was a way to help me see that I was *choosing* to smoke; I was getting something out of it; I was pinching myself. It was my own voluntary activity.

This approach, emphasizing choice and freedom, breaks the trance of powerlessness, victimization, helplessness. Addiction *seems* out of control, it *feels* that way, but actually this is just thought and belief. Really I'm pinching myself, and if I truly want to stop, the solution is obvious and easy enough. All I have to do is stop!

Right? Then why doesn't it always work?

Toni Packer pointed to choicelessness. Everything is one whole undivided, inseparable happening. There is no "me" to choose one thing over another. This approach breaks the trance of agency, and the whole deeply conditioned picture of me separate from the totality, me who is—or should be—in control. Believing this myth of individual control leads to blame, guilt, self-hatred, shame, vengeance. Every day we are confronted with mistakes, our own and other people's. We believe that if someone was unkind or cruel to me, it's because they chose to be. If they committed murder, they chose to. They could have made a different choice. They could have done better. This is the mentality that institutes the death penalty, externally and internally.

When there is powerful chemistry and no insight and thought is believed, this organism will light up, or commit murder, or whatever thought says must happen. It's like a hypnotic trance. And the "me" who tries desperately to stop is part of the trance. If the spell isn't broken, the action will happen. And how is the spell broken?

I don't know. That's the truth.

Both my therapist and Toni *listened* to me, and they listened without judgement, with full acceptance, which is love. In the presence of each of them in turn, I started listening with that same openness to myself—to the thoughts and beliefs that were running this life. I became more able to rest in actuality, to simply experience sensations and emotions in the body. As that aware space opened up, and as those beliefs came into awareness, this life changed. Was there a causal relationship? I don't know. My therapist said it was a choice. Toni said it was choiceless. We could call it either one, or we could call it grace.

Awareness & Thought

We make choices all day long, but on what basis do we make them? Zen practice looks into that question.

PARAPHRASE OF JOKO BECK

Thought is always in duality, divided. Awareness is non-dual, whole.

Thought can't see what is. It can only think *about* it. Awareness *sees*.

Awareness is open to anything. It doesn't "know" anything from the past; it is totally alive now—empty of preconceptions. Awareness sees no other. It says "yes" to what is. It includes everything and holds onto nothing. It is the aliveness, the energy, the core of everything. It is unconditioned, formless. (All perception is conditioned, but not awareness itself).

Thought thinks in opposites. It divides and classifies, resists and excludes. It knows what everything is, based on memory and projection. There are limited possibilities and many self-fulfilling prophesies. Thought is forever trying to get somewhere or accomplish something. It is mechanical, conditioned, habitual, patterned.

Thought depends on awareness; awareness does not depend on thought. Awareness is upstream from thought; it contains thought and makes thought possible.

The action of awareness is unconditional love, infinite intelligence. Awareness has complete response-ability. It is spontaneous, free, open. The action of thought is reaction based on memory, projection, habit and survival. It is divisive, manipulative and strategic.

The danger in talking about all this is that the mind (which is a bunch of thoughts) is likely to conclude that awareness is "good" and thought is "bad," and soon we are desperately trying to "be aware" and "stop thinking," as if both are something "we" possess or do. We decide that enlightenment equals non-stop awareness, interpreted as mindfulness that never lapses, and no more unnecessary thinking ever. This is suffering. This is delusion. This is thinking.

Awareness *is* non-stop. It cannot be attained or practiced. Thought comes and goes in it. No "me" owns either experience. The "me" is simply a thought-sense that arises in awareness, an appearance with no actual reality.

All this can begin to feel philosophical and abstract to me if I *think* about it. But if I watch, moment to moment, and observe the making of any simple choice, like whether to stand up or stay seated, then it's my own direct exploration, my own direct discovery. To actually watch the whole process of fingerbiting, this is a very rich unfolding. This is entirely different from metaphysical speculation. Then it becomes a living inquiry, a meditation. It comes alive.

Is There Anything You Can Do to Stop an Addiction?

As far as I know, there is no magic bullet, no infallible solution, no golden key to stopping an addiction. And yet, perhaps there is something that can be said that may or may not be helpful. It's a delicate job putting it into words. The mind wants to *use* awareness to achieve the desired *results*, and this very movement is the exact opposite of what needs to happen because it is a falsehood, an illusion. Awareness is not about results. It is only here now. It is total, unconditional acceptance of what is. It isn't going anywhere else. This is it. It never gets any better or any holier than this. Right now.

The suggestions that follow are all about tuning in to awareness and presence. They are about developing the ability to recognize thoughts without believing them, and the ability to rest in the bodily experiencing of uncomfortable, anxious, or scary feelings. These suggestions are about being totally intimate with the *actuality* of what is. The you that I am addressing is *that* which can open or close the hand, *that* which can shift the attention, *that* which you truly are. *That* is bigger than the mind, bigger than your ideas and agendas for what you *think* ought to happen. These suggestions are not about will power and control. Awareness is totally non-judgmental. It includes everything. Awareness meets addiction not as your enemy, but as the Beloved.

Be interested in this addiction. Not the *idea* of it, but the actual texture of it. Be curious about it. Pay attention to it. Be gentle with it. When I talk about exploring the texture or the actuality of an addiction, I'm not talking about thinking about it, analyzing it, theorizing about it, or telling and re-telling yourself the story of its long history. I'm talking about *feeling* sensations, *listening* to sounds, *hearing* thoughts without believing them. No words can describe actuality, or the direct experience of what is. It's not a mental process. It's about awareness and presence.

Let's use the addiction to cigarette smoking as an example. Let's say that you want to stop smoking, but you can't seem to do it. Before you light up, pause for at least a few minutes and completely *experience* the desire, the urge itself, the urgency, as *pure bodily sensation*. This is what we're running away from. This sensation is exactly what we think we can't stand. This is what we imagine will kill us or drive us crazy. Can we risk finding out?

Just to let yourself experience these sensations all the way through for a few minutes is wonderful. You don't have to start off with the expectation that you'll never smoke again. Just stop for two minutes. Now is what matters, not "forever."

What are these sensations actually like if I just let them be here?

We may discover to our surprise that we can live through the feelings we thought would kill us. We may also find our lives transforming. Maybe if we stop smoking, we'll find we can't really tolerate our job or our living situation anymore. We'll have to open ourselves to the unknown. Fear tells us this is dangerous, it might not work, we might starve to death. And it's true. We might. It's a risk. But chances are, life will open up in new and unexpected ways. What do we really want? A cigarette? Is that what we really, deeply want?

If smoking happens and *seems* uncontrollable, let that be okay. Start where you are. Experience smoking as pure meaningless sensation. Be completely aware of how it feels to hold the cigarette, how it feels on the lips and between the fingers, how it feels to inhale and exhale the smoke. Notice what is pleasurable about it. Feel the sensations in your entire body. Listen to the sounds in the room: the traffic, the birds, the hum of the refrigerator, whatever is there. Don't be reading or watching TV, but give your complete attention to the act of smoking. Have no ambition to change. Just experience smoking, without any judgement or resistance.

What happens if you exaggerate the movements? What happens if you change your posture? What if you switched hands? What is your breathing like between puffs? Is it deep or shallow? What if you change it? You don't need to analyze this data mentally or try to draw any conclusions from it. The body itself will process it. Giving the habit complete attention, observing it with curiosity and interest, is a whole different movement than trying to impose change through will power.

Begin to hear all the conflicting, crisscrossing thoughts: "I want a cigarette," "I want to stop," "I should stop," "I can't stop," "I'll just have one more," "I'll die if I don't have it," "I can't control this," "I will control this," "This is hopeless," "I'm a terrible person." Can you begin to see how thought actually *creates* reality, while giving the appearance that it is merely *describing* it?

"I have to have a cigarette or I'll go crazy," is a thought. It's a very compelling thought. But is it really true? What is the result of this thought when we believe it? What would happen if we didn't believe it? Do we *really* believe it?

"I don't know how to stop." Is it true?

Habit is deeply conditioned, and the force of it is very strong. Anyone who has struggled with an addiction knows this. But the amazing thing is that this whole momentum can completely dissolve in awareness. Not forever, not once-and-for-all, but right now. It can completely vanish.

Notice that in some way, we don't want it to dissolve. It may be killing us, but we enjoy this habit! There is something immensely pleasurable about it, something we're getting out of it. We don't always want to wake up.

In fact, we often associate the waking state, or sobriety, with suffering, tension, and the onslaught of endless problems. In many ways, we'd rather pull the covers over our head and relax back into the carefree bliss of being nobody, doing nothing. We'd rather get dead drunk, in other words, than be sober. Addiction is a kind of imitation of true liberation. It *looks like* surrender, it *looks like* letting go, it *looks like* freedom. But it's not the real thing, and ultimately it is painful and not liberating at all. So is it possible to discover the relaxation and the peace of deep sleep, the bliss of being nobody, while in the waking state, without getting drunk or taking drugs or lighting up in order to make it happen? Is it possible that this bliss is actually omni-present, right in front of you, closer than your nose, never absent?

You Are Awareness, Not An Addict

Please understand that there is only one thing to be understood, and that is that you are the formless, timeless unborn.

NISARGADATTA

Our personal agenda is simply a bunch of thoughts. It may or may not tally with what life at a deeper level is up to. The thought may arise that it's time to stop smoking, because that sounds nicer for you, but what the universe is up to is ultimately beyond your ability to comprehend. Conditioned habit patterns will run their course until they stop, regardless of what you think should happen.

What if this addiction *never* stopped? What if this tension *never* went away? Is awareness itself ever contracted or addicted?

Awareness is always whole. Awareness is undefiled. The fire in the movie never burns up the screen. Be aware of awareness itself, not as an object, because it isn't one, but as the space, the aliveness, the listening presence, the stillness, the light that is unharmed by anything, this that *is* before any name or concept, without which the movie could not exist or be seen.

Is There Really a Problem?

Enlightenment is to Awaken from the seriousness of experience.

ADI DA

You can't not be in grace. Everything about you is totally absolutely perfectly appropriate. All the things you think are wrong with you are absolutely right.

TONY PARSONS

I don't give a damn about society, the five billion inhabitants of the earth, the starving Chinese, not to mention my internal organs.

STEPHEN JOURDAIN, *Radical Awakening*

To know that pain and pleasure are one is peace.

NISARGADATTA

Nisargadatta, one of my two favorite Indian gurus, smoked. He sold cigarettes for a living. He ran a tobacco shop. He died of throat cancer. His Guru, Siddharameshwar Maharaj, also smoked, and is often pictured holding a cigarette. Nisargadatta's disciple Jean Dunn died of emphysema, still smoking. She had no problem with it. I call it the Cigarette Lineage.

Jean Dunn lived in a trailer in Vacaville, smoked Merit cigarettes, watched soap operas on TV, and died of emphysema. I've heard that when Jean needed money, she would go to Las Vegas and play the slots.

Chogyam Trungpa Rinpoche, the renowned teacher who brought Tibetan Buddhism to the West, apparently used to fall off his cushion while giving dharma talks because he was so drunk. He was in the mishap lineage. Trungpa reportedly said that enlightenment is the great and final disappointment, the dissolution of all our egoic fantasies and grand hopes.

Ultimately, if we're banking on form, we're banking on an illusion. Perhaps all of the horrors and catastrophes that life offers so abundantly are ways of showing us this truth and inviting us to discover what is big enough to contain it all.

What we're looking for is here. It can't ever be anyplace else. We're not on the way anywhere. Here is all there is. Right here, there is no problem to solve. The search for a solution and for a way out is all part of the dream. You are beyond the dream. No thing in the dream will last. Not even your neurosis. Not even "you."

Helplessness Is Freedom

Usually, when people decide to stop an addiction, and it stops, they think that they did it. If they used a twelve-step program, they think twelve-step works. If they used a therapist, they think therapy works. They are convinced that anyone can do what they did. All you have to do is decide to quit and stick with it.

If alcohol, drugs, and cigarettes had been my only addictions, I would have come to that same conclusion. But my long struggle with finger-biting has impressed upon me, beyond the slightest doubt, our utter helplessness.

Does this mean I'll be biting forever? No. I might never bite again. Or I might be doing it, off and on, until the day I die. Does this mean I won't decide anymore to stop? No, it means I'll do exactly what I do, whatever that is.

There is no single cause, no infallible cure. If there was, don't you think we all would have found it by now and done it? As one Advaita teacher, Wayne Liquorman, is fond of saying, If you were really in control of your life, wouldn't you be doing a much better job of it? When you finally admit your absolute helplessness (which, of course, is not something "you" can do!), when you finally give up, you discover tremendous peace and freedom right here where you would least have expected it. You realize there is no one who needs help. There is actually no problem.

The mind will of course insist that there *is* a problem, and it will lay out all the convincing evidence. But how real is it? If you're reading this book, you have at least an inkling that the whole thing is make believe. The invitation is to investigate it for yourself. Really look and see. How real and how serious is it? Even if it is life threatening, how serious is that?

With my own addiction to fingerbiting, I tried every cure imaginable. I took vows and then felt despair when the biting came back in spite of my best efforts. After I moved to Chicago, an enormous patience arose in me, an ability to be with the slow, back and forth process that might take years, perhaps an entire lifetime, and might never be complete. More and more, the devotion was to the process rather than the result. Slowly, the habit was dissolving. Biting happened less frequently, and less severely when it did, and either way, in every moment there was just whatever was arising at that moment.

After awhile, all intention to stop fell away. The whole problem lost its importance. Biting came and went, and when it came, there was complete acceptance, just letting it take its course, bandaging up the wounds, allowing it all to be. It no longer mattered. I stopped trying to solve the problem, in fact, it was utterly clear that there was no problem to solve.

Intention

But isn't it helpful to have the intention to stop?

It can be very useful, but like everything else, it is ultimately beyond your control. There is obviously tremendous power in the mind, and there's no reason not to use it, if you can! I saw the power of intention when I studied martial arts. We had to break boards by punching them. If you visualized your punch going through the board, it did. Amazing! And then, if you imagined hurting your hand, sure enough, the board didn't break and you hurt your hand. Intention can be helpful! But, here's the catch: despite my best efforts to visualize my hand going through the board, sometimes I visualized the opposite. It wasn't in my control! It *seemed* like it was when my intention matched what happened. But the truth is that intention, like everything else, comes out of nowhere. But that said, the only way to play the game is to play the game. In a sense, we have no choice except to pretend that we're making choices. And in that play of apparent choosing, intention is extremely useful.

Suzuki Roshi often cautioned against being idealistic and having "gaining ideas." And yet at the same time he also said, "In some sense we should be idealistic; at least we should be interested in making bread which tastes and looks good!" Of course! We naturally want to produce good bread, metaphorically speaking. Doing your best, working to improve, training hard, visualizing success, utilizing intention, and taking care of business are in no way antithetical to deep realization. There seems to be a natural aspiration in us that wants to heal, clarify, repair, correct, and improve. That aspiration is part of the functioning of life. There's nothing wrong with it. When we know that nothing matters, we also know that *everything* matters totally, but not in the way we first thought it did.

The secret is to realize that "I" don't really know how healing should look, or how long it should take, or even what constitutes health, sickness, success or failure in the larger scheme of things. *True healing always begins with the ability to embrace what is.*

So, if you are punching boards, by all means *do* visualize your hand going through the board, *if you can*. If you're trying to stop an addiction, by all means *do* visualize success. But if the addictive activity recurs, which it may, don't get caught up in stories about how "you" failed, what a terrible person "you" are, how hopeless "it" all is. That kind of thinking is all part of the addiction. Just recognize (if you can!) that whatever happens could not be otherwise. The battle is all in your head. Relax. Enjoy the show.

The End of Fingerbiting?

What is to stop anyone from quitting the use of a substance?
Whatever appears as the answer to this question is the sound
of the Addictive Voice.

JACK TRIMPEY, *Rational Recovery*

During my second year in Chicago, a friend mentioned to me in passing
that her brother was using a book called *Rational Recovery: A New Cure*
for Substance Addiction by Jack Trimpey to sober up. I recalled having
seen it in a bookstore a year earlier. I had picked it up back then and
browsed through it, momentarily excited because it seemed close to the
approach of the therapist with whom I had sobered up. But Trimpey's
book was different in some ways, plus he had a big axe to grind and
opinions on several subjects that I found disagreeable, so I didn't buy the
book until my friend mentioned it.

The author still had his axe to grind and some opinions I disagreed
with, but this time around, something in the book really grabbed me.
Recovery, Trimpey said, is not a process; it is a decision. You either decide
to stop forever and it's finished, or else you keep up the addictive behavior.

Trimpey's cure centered around recognizing what he called "the
Addictive Voice," and realizing that this voice is not you, that *you* have
the power to recognize and reject it, to refuse its suggestions and
commands. The Addictive Voice is *any* voice, from inside or outside you,
that tells you that you must, should, could, or will indulge, that you are
helpless and out of control. Like my therapist, Trimpey did not buy the
twelve-step or disease model, instead stressing the ability to discern truth
from illusion and choose truth.

Here's the part that really excited me. When people came to Trimpey
for help, he would begin by asking them, "Are you going to drink anymore?" Or, "What is your plan concerning the future use of alcohol?"
The person would hedge and make conditional statements, expressing an
intention to try to stop but always with the caveat that it was out of their
control. Trimpey would point out how they were leaving open the option
to drink again. They would insist that this was because they couldn't

always control themselves around alcohol and might drink again despite their best intentions. Trimpey would show them that *this* was the Addictive Voice talking, and that by believing it, they were setting themselves up to relapse.

This was eye opening to me. I saw something I hadn't seen before. I saw how I had been believing and giving credence to a particular thread of the Addictive Voice which I had mistaken for objective truth. It is the voice that says, "You've always failed before, you'll probably fail this time." But even more importantly, I began to wonder if it was also the voice that says, "You're helpless, you have no choice, choice is an illusion." However true that statement appeared to be, perhaps in the very act of conceptualizing and *asserting* it, it became dangerously false. Because once you tried to formulate it, the expression was limited, and the whole truth or the subtlety of the truth was lost. By asserting that there was no choice, perhaps that assertion became the Addictive Voice, setting you up to relapse. Was that possible? I began to re-examine everything.

Once again, I had real hope that I could finally put an end to fingerbiting! In fact, it wasn't hope; it was certainty. I was pinching myself; all I had to do was stop. This *seemed* so true; it had to be true. And yet, I couldn't completely reconcile it with my own undeniable *experience* of helplessness and failure, and with the understanding, through careful observation and investigation, that there is actually no choice at all, until there apparently is.

Could *both* somehow be true? Perhaps the truth was like those magic eye drawings or autostereograms that contain two different pictures in a single image, or those optical illusions that can be created where cubes flip this way and that as you gaze at them. Perhaps recovery was *both* a process *and* a decision, *both* choiceless *and* intentional, depending on how you looked at it. Perhaps the truth was impossible to formulate. If you say there *is* a choice, it is false; if you say there is *no* choice, it is equally false. The truth is what is left over after *all* the objective positions have been negated.

My therapist had considered addictive behavior a choice. In her view, the original choice, the one that first started the addiction, was unconscious. The addiction *seemed* out of control only because we did not fully see and understand the mechanism. Once we saw it, we could then make the conscious choice to stop. The power rested with the person (or we could say, with awareness), not with the substance. Once sober, we would be faced with the original pain that had driven us to seek escape in the first place. If we learned how to be with that in a new way, we could remain free of the addiction.

Using this model, I had stopped drinking and smoking. I'd been sober for thirty years now, and I hadn't had a cigarette in twenty-five years. But fingerbiting had persisted. I had certainly tried to apply this understanding to fingerbiting, but it hadn't worked, at least not consistently. For the last twenty years, I had pursued a spiritual path that emphasized choicelessness.

And then suddenly this book about rational recovery comes to my attention. Did I choose to find this book? No. It appeared out of nowhere, "accidentally," the same way my therapist appeared thirty years earlier.

After reading Trimpey's book, I made the irrevocable decision never to bite my fingers again. It was crystal clear: I don't have to bite. Nothing real is binding me. The chains are all entirely imaginary; they have no real power. The mechanism had been rendered powerless. Fingerbiting was over.

For a few days, the Addictive Voice kept arising, but each time it was instantly seen through. It had no power. Within a week it stopped arising at all. My fingers healed. The compulsion left me. It was totally, completely gone. Months went by.

Was this a decision, a choice? In some sense, yes. It was predicated *entirely* on the notion of choice. And yet, despite all my best efforts, somehow this choice was not available until the moment when it actually was. In the deepest sense, it happened by itself.

The person who appears to be choosing this or that is a disguise, a costume, a mask behind and through which Consciousness operates. When "you" believe in the reality of the disguise and lose sight of who is pinching who, then "you" enjoy the Divine Drama: the struggle, the horror, the hope, the advances and the setbacks, the whole apparent adventure, including the whole fascinating quandary of whether or not "you" are free to choose. When it is seen (by no one) that there is no one behind the mask, then the pincher and the pinched dissolve together. The hand moves away effortlessly. The dilemma evaporates.

Or maybe the pinch continues. After all, not every flower blooms, and only in the mirage of personal identity does this appear tragic. Consciousness (or God) has an interest, it seems, in experiencing absolutely *everything*: even failure, even addiction, even the holocaust. Unconditional love embraces it all, just as it is.

As it turned out, biting came and went many more times. Trimpey's approach was a piece in the puzzle, not the ultimate cure-all. What was being slowly worn down in all of this was the tenacious illusion that there was a self here who could take control and win. Again and again, this illusion was shot down. The amazing thing was how many times it could pop back up. But gradually, the mind was being forced into a corner, and it was being seen that liberation had nothing to do with improvement. That dream of getting control at last and finally triumphing is the Last Big Hope, the final disappointment. We no longer believe that a million dollars or an academy award will bring us lasting peace and happiness, but we still imagine that our ersatz version of enlightenment will. We're still taking the phenomenal dream and the "me" character to be real. We've switched from a worldly movie to a spiritual one, but we're still in the frame of duality and personal identity, trying to get somewhere in the movie. Even trying to get out of the movie is only another movie, featuring the same illusory main character. True enlightenment is not final victory; it is final defeat. It's outside the frame.

Identifying as Joan and seeking improvement is agitation. Peace allows everything. But it's not that peace is good and agitation is bad. Agitation can be fun. The story of being bound and trying to get free is a very entertaining story. Hollywood has made billions on it. The movie arises and disappears. The agitation comes and goes. Awareness accepts it all. There is never really a problem. The rope only looks like a snake. Look deeply into agitation, and you find only peace.

There is no choice because there is no thing at all. That word (enlightenment) truly points only to this that never arrives and never leaves. The mind just can't quite believe it. It's too simple. Too transparent. Too all-inclusive. It is literally beyond belief. Right here, right now. Just as it is.

Awareness Has No Agenda

When all efforts to improve and get somewhere fall away, what remains is the traffic, the birds, the breathing, the listening presence, the empty space in which it is all happening, awareness itself: the simplicity and wonder of what is.

If you hear yourself thinking, "I've tried awareness over and over, and it doesn't work, I'm still smoking," that's thinking, thinking about awareness. It's thinking about "you" (a thought) using something called "awareness" (an idea) to achieve an imagined result (another idea)! That's not awareness; it's wishful thinking, followed by frustration and despair. Awareness isn't looking for results or feeling depressed by past failures. That's all thought activity. Awareness sees without commentary or judgement. It has no agenda. It accepts everything as it is.

Suffering is the illusion that something needs to be different. Awareness is all-inclusive. Nothing is left out. Paradoxically, it is this very quality of total acceptance that has the power to dissolve all suffering. It's a great joke, a great mystery that the key to transformation is the complete acceptance of what is.

Addiction is not an obstacle standing between you and enlightenment. Blame and guilt come from the divided mind. Ultimately, even the divided mind is God. All division is imaginary.

In the end, it isn't about whether you smoke or not. I remember a story about Gurdjieff telling a prospective student who was a heavy smoker that he wouldn't work with him unless the student quit smoking. So the student quit and a year later went back to see the great teacher. Gurdjieff welcomed him, invited him to sit down and then proceeded to offer him a really fine Turkish cigarette so they could smoke together. First Gurdjieff broke the student's attachment to smoking, then he broke his attachment to being a non-smoker. He was pointing the student to a deeper liberation, free of both smoking and not smoking. A dangerous tactic perhaps, not for the faint-hearted, but true to the deeper truth.

The root addiction is the illusion of separation and control, the sense of there being somebody at the helm, the sense that what happens is personal, the urge to escape, the search for something better—whether that something is a cigarette, final enlightenment, or a new and improved "me." Sobriety and awakening are about the falling away of a hypnotic trance. Sobriety is the falling away of the belief in the Addictive Voice. Awakening is the falling away of everything.

The mind hears "the falling away of everything" and immediately pictures *something* (a huge event, a radical change in vision), and it chases what it pictures: some *thing*. Enlightenment is the falling away of the picture and the chase. It is the falling away of the one who feels separate and incomplete. It is the end of imagining that there is anything *other* than the Holy Reality. It is the end of the search, the end of escape. It is the discovery of grace.

Everything Is Grace

The Night I Couldn't Breathe

During my first winter in Chicago, when the windows were iced over and closed, and the apartment was heated, and the air was stale, I got sick with terrible head and chest congestion and a bad cough. It was the sickest I had been in years. The nights were the worst. I couldn't sleep. It was dark, and I was all alone. It felt claustrophobic and frightening, especially when I began to feel like I couldn't breathe, like I was suffocating. It triggered a deep, primal fear in me, one that felt psychological as well as physical. I'd get out of bed, turn on the lights for comfort and sit in my armchair terrified and alone. Then I'd get up and pace the apartment, and sit back down, and get up, and sit back down. It was nightmarish. It felt like death was closing in on me.

Finally it dawned on me that I was desperately resisting what was happening, trying to get away from it. I began to hear the stories I was telling myself: "I'm all alone in a strange city dying in the middle of the night." Instantly, in seeing this, I relaxed. I sat down in my chair and stopped resisting. I opened up completely to the situation, even to death itself if it should come. I surrendered to actuality. Next thing I knew, I was sound asleep.

Enjoying the Dentist

I'd always been afraid of dental work. I was always tensed, expecting some unbearable pain that I had only imagined. Try as I might, I simply could not seem to relax. Finally, I inadvertently scheduled my first crown on the day after one of Toni's silent retreats in California. I was deeply relaxed and present, not anticipating what the dental work might be like, willing to experience anything. To my great surprise, as the drilling got underway, I found that I was not tensing up and resisting the imaginary pain that might occur or any actual discomfort that did occur. Instead, I was open and relaxed. I actually enjoyed lying back on the dental chair, watching the birds and clouds out the window during the procedure. Ever since, my relationship to dental work has been different.

Many months after that experience, I was home alone in Oakland on a Friday night, and developed a severe toothache. It became excruciating. I took aspirin. Nothing changed. An hour went by. The pain got worse. It felt unbearable. I found myself desperately pacing around the house, frightened, trying to get away from the pain. Suddenly I became aware of what I was doing. I immediately stopped, sat down, relaxed, and completely opened to the actual sensations. Right away, the pain was bearable, and next thing I knew, it was actually interesting. I sat there experiencing and exploring the sensations. The exploration was enjoyable, although the sensations themselves were still unpleasant. It was a deep meditation. I was even a little bit sorry when it was finally over. "I" didn't *do* this; it happened.

When the Darkness Visits

Everything is grace. When we say yes to what is, we say yes to grace.

FRANCIS LUCILLE

Our natural reaction when we feel pain or threat is to contract. Instead, as I discover again and again, the way out is through the very center, allowing rather than resisting, opening rather than closing, relaxing rather than tensing. When disturbance and upset come, whether the pain is physical or emotional, the secret is to go right into it, to fully experience it as it is, without resisting in any way. Particularly with emotional pain, it often takes a long time to understand exactly what that really means.

What we usually call "feeling depressed" is in fact a way of remaining entranced in the mental overlay (stories, beliefs, explanations, analysis, past and future scenarios remembered or imagined) and *not* fully feeling the sensations. We may *think* we are feeling them, because after all we "feel terrible," so therefore we must be feeling the depression. But completely feeling it is a kind of deep meditation, in which we stop running away, and we completely meet whatever this thing is, with no resistance at all. With my terror the night I couldn't breathe, for example, I wasn't fully experiencing it until I stopped running from it, until I gave up and was willing to die. Likewise with my fear of the dentist or the excruciating pain of my toothache, it was when I stopped resisting and met it with complete openness that the whole thing dissolved.

It often takes a very long time (years!) to come to that willingness to stop running away. It happens when it happens. You cannot force it to happen, and if you are trying to make this relaxation and surrender happen *so that the pain or the depression will go away*, that is already a kind of subtle resistance. True surrender has no agenda. It isn't looking for an outcome. It is totally present to what is. It accepts and allows everything, even resistance and contraction. It doesn't oppose anything. Once that surrender actually happens, depression is over. It may not be over forever, although maybe at some point it does stop coming back, or maybe it never stops coming back—it doesn't really matter.

For some people, old habits may dissolve quickly and permanently. For others, they may come back again and again. It only sustains them to take them personally and get caught up in comparing ourselves to others, wishing the darkness would go away forever, despairing over its persistence. No matter how many times it happens, the only time that matters, the only time that really exists, is right now.

If the habits are persistent, it is an opportunity to fully experience the force and strength of habit. If you get to experience that yourself, you will better understand why there is so much suffering in the world. You will have more compassion, more wisdom, more humility.

Since my book came out, many people have contacted me. I was amazed to discover how many different people identified with my story, people whose lives on the surface seemed very different from mine. I discovered I was not alone. I met and heard from many seemingly successful, high-functioning people who revealed to me that they were dealing with self-injuring, serious depression, addiction, anxiety, troubled children, massive debt, and a host of other apparent problems. If you met these people, you'd never guess that they were cutting themselves with razor blades late at night, or that they hadn't slept with their spouse in seventeen years. On the surface, they looked happy, together and successful. Some of them were therapists and spiritual teachers.

Maybe you're one of the lucky ones who has enjoyed a happy childhood, a healthy body, a healthy mind, and a relatively unblemished life. I've met people like that, too. But I've discovered that even those people have felt pain and disillusionment. Nobody escapes this life unscathed. We are not alone in our human suffering. How much or how little is not important. Nothing is personal. It simply is, as it is.

❧

The world itself seems to be in acute distress these days as resources dwindle, the environment is increasingly damaged, land is consumed, population explodes, famine and epidemic rage, and old hatreds fester—armed with increasingly destructive weapons. If you read the daily paper, it can look pretty bleak, especially if you take the world drama seriously and consider the death of the earth a tragedy. At the same time, who knows what technological breakthroughs, transformations in consciousness, or stray asteroids smashing into the earth and obliterating an entire continent may suddenly change the whole picture in completely new and unexpected ways. Up and down, scary and promising, hopeful and hopeless, the drama goes on. And when death itself is finally faced, is it actually tragic or scary?

❧

As I look back over my life, I see how many different parts I've played and how totally convinced I've been at different times of completely opposite ideologies. I was a Young Republican who supported Barry Goldwater, adored Ayn Rand, and wanted to nuke Vietnam. I was an ultraleftist radical who idolized Malcolm X and Ho Chi Minh and wanted to smash US imperialism. I was a Christian, a Buddhist, a Hindu, an agnostic. I was an unpublished nobody collecting rejection letters. I was a published author with a government grant. I was a janitor, and I was a college professor. The blessing of a life like mine is that you get to see very clearly how illusory it all is. But any life will show you that if you're willing and able to look.

❧

We tend to think that we must always be happy, energized, successful, clear, healthy, productive, and on top of the world. We don't allow any space for periods of lying fallow, periods of confusion, periods of exhaustion, periods of upset, periods of inactivity. We forget that the phenomenal manifestation has its cycles and that there cannot be pleasure without pain, or up without down. We don't allow any space for so-called failures and mistakes. And yet these are all part of life. Even the horrific is part of life. It's here. Learning to welcome and give space to whatever actually is, is part of the art of living.

❧

Frida Kahlo is an artist whose life and work has always fascinated me. Frida had lifelong health problems: polio, a bus accident that shattered her spine and left her in chronic pain, multiple miscarriages, depression, kidney infection, repeated spinal surgeries, abscesses and infections, gangrene, amputation, pneumonia, chronic exhaustion. She was dead at fifty. We could imagine that without all these health problems, she would have had so much more time and energy for her art, and would have become even greater. Logically that seems to make sense. But with Frida, it's so obvious how false that reasoning is. Her suffering was the subject, the source, the essence and the heart of her art. It *was* her art in a very real sense. Her work was about transmuting suffering into beauty. Her passionate and vibrant paintings celebrate the ecstasy of what is, even in its most horrific and painful aspects. Hers was an unflinching, honest gaze into the face of death and darkness. Frida's greatness was totally inseparable from the chronic problems she had with her body. And this is actually how it is with all of us. Everything about us is exactly as it needs to be.

Abandonment

Lovers don't finally meet somewhere.
They're in each other all along.

RUMI

Bring only Love and Openness to me, for everything else that arises is of the mind and an illusion.

NGETON

What we're really talking about is the capacity to bear the bliss of being.

GANGAJI

My friend Elaine and I were hiking on Mt Tam. We were planning to attend a satsang that evening with Ngeton, an American teacher from Hawaii, a tantric Advaita guru, blues pianist, Tai Chi master, former drug and sex junky, and mother of five, who had been with Muktananda, Adi Da, a few Tibetan teachers, and finally with Jean Dunn, a disciple of Nisargadatta. Ngeton was rumored to be an eccentric character, a wild card. I didn't care if we got to this satsang or not. But we did get there.

Coming into the room, I saw women in dazzling fashions, gorgeous men, a middle-aged woman seated on the floor singing bhajans and playing the harmonium. Incense was burning; the room smelled sweet and exotic. Eventually the bhajans rose to a frenzied pitch, and as they did, this tiny radiant being came into the room dressed in diaphanous flowing robes and a richly colored scarf. Ngeton had a long braid of dark hair all the way down her back and looked to be maybe sixty years old.

She gazed around in total love and openness, smiling and laughing and greeting people. She was so relaxed, so utterly uninhibited and present, so totally alive. She was literally vibrating with unprotected, pure ecstasy. I loved her.

I went back the next night, and the next, and the next. And then I went on the weekend retreat.

Ngeton describes a moment on the beach when she completely woke up. She says she had several awakenings before that, but this thing on the beach was the real thing. Instantly that brought back my obsession with final awakening. I, too, wanted the "real thing." And once again, I imagined that this wasn't it, that it was somewhere else, in the future, just out of reach.

"Oh fuck, I have no idea what I'm talking about," Ngeton might say right in the middle of satsang, laughing hysterically. This was totally unlike the sober, restrained formality of Zen and Springwater. At Springwater during retreats you're supposed to sit absolutely still and be silent, and while it's not forbidden to laugh or cry, it almost never happens. You get the feeling it's not an entirely okay thing to do, and certainly not something you would indulge in often. Here, on the other hand, you could laugh uncontrollably and not stop. You could sway and shake and move your body with the waves of kundalini. You could shout; you could sing; you could say anything. It was very liberating. Ngeton transmits abandonment. It was even wilder and looser than Gangaji, and it was less formal and more down home. There were no video camera, no lights, no huge crowds.

We did movement/energy work to get us out of our heads and into our bodies. We did devotional singing to open the heart. We did eye gazing, where you sit face to face with a partner and gaze into their eyes without looking away; you can laugh or cry—anything is okay, as long as you don't look away. There was a lot of love, a lot of ecstasy, a lot of laughter on this retreat.

At one point, I was wearing a bindi on my forehead (one of those little dots) and ecstatically singing Hare Krishna. It used to be my worst fear that I'd end up in a group like this, wearing a bindi on my forehead, singing bhajans, sitting in ecstasy at the feet of some guru surrounded by a bunch of obsequious devotees. The very thought of such a scene would have made me shudder with revulsion. But oh, to be perfectly honest, I would also have been secretly fascinated, wishing in some dark and forbidden part of me that I could allow myself such a wild indulgence as this. And now, my worst fear had been realized, and I was so happy!

Finally, none of it makes sense. There's just sensation. Just what is. Just the absolutely beautiful, crazy, unknowable, ungraspable mystery that produces the giraffe, the camel, the zebra, the elephant, the orchid, the neon colored tropical fish, the dolphin, the shark, Toni Packer, Da Free John, Ngeton, Mother Teresa, Rajneesh, Gangaji, Billy Graham, Ramana Maharshi, Oral Roberts, Joko Beck, Papaji, and the Pope—all in the same Universe. One can only laugh. Sing bhajans. And be amazed.

⁓᪣

Gangaji was definitely not pleased when I told her that Ngeton was my new guru. With ferocious tenderness and love, she threw me out. I felt sorrow. And then I felt relief.

What on earth was I doing, chasing after these gurus? The mind went to work in its usual fashion, trying to make sense of it all.

I called Toni to discuss all this, and she went on and on about some movie she'd seen, and I felt a little bit irritated. I wanted to discuss this important dilemma, and she was talking about some stupid movie. Then in a postcard from Toni in Switzerland she tells me of hikes taken on beautiful mountain trails, and finally at the very end, "Thanks for your letter. Read it on the way to Toronto. Much ado.... Love, Toni." I was angry: Hey, this is *my life* she's talking about! This isn't nothing! Then I see the joke. It *is* a movie!

Toni said to me recently, it's amazing how much complication can go on around something that is inherently so very, very simple.

~❧

Light rain. The rush of the freeway. The night train wailing. The croaking of frogs and crickets coming from the creek that runs out behind the house. The sound reminds me of Springwater, but here in Oakland, the cricket song merges with the freeway song, and occasionally the police helicopter song. Rain batters the windows at dawn. All these sounds are an outpouring of love.

"I was ecstatic when I did this painting," my friend Elaine says. "The dragon is fucking me in every possible orifice, and I'm vomiting."

~❧

My own meetings blossomed in some way after the break with Gangaji. I was becoming friends with several people who came regularly. A sense of on-going community was beginning to emerge. I'd gotten more and more honest, dropping whatever pretense I started out with of being somebody special. I truly felt now that we were all in this together.

Vedanta / Mid-November

*Sitting here is without any purpose. Contemplate profoundly
what it means: being without purpose.*

JEAN KLEIN

I am out at the Vedanta retreat Center in Olema where I go occasionally to spend a few days or a week by myself in silence. Quail are gurgling in the wet grass awash with sunlight. White deer step through the trees. Water glistens everywhere. Cows moo passionately, echoing each other.

Calves, wet with rain, stand in the emerald green field, white deer amongst them. Frogs are croaking. Fog is lifting from the rippled face of Elephant Mountain.

A lizard runs across the carpet. Outside the deer sleep. A jet plane passes overhead. Rain batters the house for days. The language of rain is meaningless sounds and shapes. There is no need to understand. We can just *enjoy* these sounds. The language of rain is ecstasy. Can *everything* be enjoyed this way, as meaningless shapes and sounds?

A banana slug lies dead atop a large pink mushroom, a trail of green vomit issuing from its mouth, and a little heap of excrement at the other end. The rim of the mushroom is partly eaten. Deer watch me pass. Fog slides past the wrinkled face of the mountain. The song of blackbirds fills my heart with joy.

A fly now buzzes through my room.

"We are never at any moment in the dilemma we fear ourselves to be," Da Free John says. "Your suffering is always a *present activity*."

◦❧

Back home to Oakland at the end of the week. Zelda who comes to my Tuesday night meeting tells me of running through the trees in the moonlight kissing them, and she says the moon was surrounded in pink mist. She is a woman in her late sixties who used to be an opera singer. She has invited me to move the meetings to her home.

Homecoming

I am once again coordinating Toni Packer's New Year's retreat in California, as I have for many years. Everything got so quiet and simple on this retreat. I felt finished with chasing gurus.

Many times I've thought that I was done with Toni, only to re-discover her anew. It isn't her personality that brings me back, nor some intoxicating devotional love affair. It isn't the promise of final enlightenment. It's the clarity, the spaciousness, the simplicity of being here without hype or pretense of any kind, without needing anything other than what is.

Toni offers nothing except bare attention: simple listening, *this* moment, however unspectacular this moment may *seem* to be. That's all. No millennial vision, no grandiose or comforting ideas, no inflated image of Toni as Avatar, Divine Mother, World Teacher, or Savior. It's not very glamorous. But when we actually *listen* to this moment, this moment is a miracle. Infinitely subtle, infinitely miraculous, infinitely quiet. It lacks nothing.

Rain pours down. Hissing, trickling, gurgling sounds. A solitary orange plops down from the tree in the early morning rain, landing in the wet black earth and the glistening leaves. Rain comes and goes. Clouds blow past. I spend the next night, until 2:30 a.m., in the emergency room with a retreatant who might have had appendicitis but didn't, and that strange twilight world of triage, injuries and heart attacks is no different from the beautiful courtyard with the orange tree and the silence.

The whole obsession with final awakening fell away completely.

Toni asked me: "Is there fear of standing completely alone, unsheltered, this lively, changing, changeless moment?"

᭦

My weekly meetings have moved to Zelda's home. Seventeen people came to the first one there. One woman cries, talks of there being no solution. I see myself scrambling for the right thing to say to save her. And then I see, it's really to save myself. Because her pain opens my pain. Seeing that, I realize that there is no need to save her, or me. There is no need to solve or fix anything. It can all be here, exactly as it is. What a relief!

What is a Teacher?

Because you imagine differences, you go here and there in search of 'superior' people.

NISARGADATTA

Observe things as they are and don't pay attention to other people. There are some people just like mad dogs barking at everything that moves, even barking when the wind stirs among the grass and leaves.

HUANG PO

[The teacher] has nothing to give you, because there is nothing to give and nothing to get....There is an insistent need to create illusions when we are afraid to face bare facts.

TONI PACKER

I would say seek out a teacher who gives you nothing at all, no hope, no method, no personal offer to take you there, because of course there isn't anywhere to go. Look for someone who destroys all of your belief systems and who is always throwing you back onto "what is," right here.

TONY PARSONS

The real job of any teacher is to make themselves irrelevant.

NIRMALA

I personally have no interest in making a big deal about "enlightened" people. That's a notion that implies permanence and solidity....So many of us have suspended our discernment in the interest of thinking there was someone out there who could do no wrong....I feel badly that I've actually supported people in being outlandish because I thought there was something I just didn't see. So I've colluded by putting them outside my common sense.

ELIZABETH HAMILTON, DHARMA HEIR TO JOKO BECK

Teaching is a matter of creating the space where learning can occur.

PARAPHRASE OF MOSHE FELDENKRAIS

Sooner or later you are bound to discover that if you really want to find, you must dig at one place only—within.

NISARGADATTA

You are the teacher you've been waiting for.

BYRON KATIE

A true teacher gives you absolutely nothing, only empty space. They *are* empty space. They pull the rug out from under you whenever you think you've found a place to stand. They point you to here and now, to what is.

I spent a long time looking over my shoulder to see if my latest authority figure would approve of me, wondering if I was doing it "right," looking for the Big Bang enlightenment experience that somebody else described and claimed, measuring and comparing myself, awed by the wizard of Oz.

What I see now is that no one has any special authority to teach. It's made up. The Pope, the Zen roshi, the abbot, the rabbi, the guru, the wizard behind the curtain, the doctrines, the lineages, the cosmologies—it's all made up. Jesus and Buddha weren't sanctioned by anyone. They spoke from their own experience, from the heart. They weren't in anybody's lineage. I'm not opposed to religious systems for those who want and enjoy them. But they're make believe. And that's okay. Play is fun, if you know you're just playing.

What has most deeply interested and drawn me is the truth, the bare truth. And that's simply what is—presence itself—the aliveness here and now. Of course, many other desires have pulled on me as well (for comfort, security, answers, pleasure), but the deeper desire, the one that seems to be the bottom line, is this desire for truth. And truth is simple. Ever-present.

Nobody owns it.

When I meet with people, I find that all I really have to do is show up. Whenever I think I have to provide answers, solve problems, or fix people, I'm off the track. When I remember that I don't have to do anything, then the magic happens. Not my magic, but just magic. In writing, I've noticed that my work is most alive when I speak from my own heart, and most dead when I try to sound like somebody else who I think has got something I don't.

We humans have a deep desire for answers, for authority. I'm increasingly interested in what happens when there are no answers, no authority, no system. In truth, there is nothing to teach. And no one to teach it.

As a personality, any so-called teacher has quirks, warts, blemishes, and neurotic tendencies. They are blessedly imperfect. I say blessedly, because if they were perfect (as personalities), you might be tempted to put them up on a pedestal far above you and fall into permanent infantilism and idolatry. And, of course, there are many teachers who encourage you to do exactly that. But a true teacher is quite happy to appear imperfect and human.

When you come up against a teacher's shortcomings, or maybe just up against aspects of their personality that clash with your personality, it gets interesting. The romanticized, idealized myth crumbles before your eyes. You are disappointed, irritated, unhappy, upset. This is wonderful because it pushes you to focus on the truth and not on the personality, the message and not on the messenger. It shatters the idol your mind was trying to create, deflates the self-serving projections, disappoints your illusory hopes, and forces you back to the utter simplicity of what is.

If this deflation doesn't happen, it is all too easy to project a flawless, all knowing, enlightened Parent Figure who will take care of and save you, the ultimate authority who has all the answers. That illusory picture invariably leads to dishonesty, denial, confusion and dependency. When that supposedly perfect person displays abusive or confused behavior, it is all attributed to crazy wisdom. We are told that whatever they do is done with absolute selfless purity.

What *everyone* does is done with absolute selfless purity! That's all there is, selfless purity! But if we think only the guru is pure, we get into big trouble. In the extremes of such foolishness, the devotees line up to swallow the poisoned Kool-Aid. Some very intelligent, very insightful, very caring people have swallowed some amazing stuff. And that's perfectly okay, too!

There are many teaching paradigms, from spiritual companion to Messiah. Some of my teachers, like Toni and Joko, were sober and bare, careful and precise. Others, like Ngcton, were ecstatic, intoxicated, care-free, loose. I'm grateful for all of them. I've loved them and hated them; I've fallen in adoration at their feet and then argued with them; I've put them up on pedestals and torn them down again; I've compared them to each other; I've critiqued them; I've envied them; I've followed them around; I've left them behind. Many apparent dramas have transpired. I've left and returned, been kicked out and welcomed home. As Toni said: much ado, much complication. The truth is simple. No one can save you because there is no one to save. But that may have to be found out the hard way by apparently going down many false paths until the thought that "you" have time and a future is transparently false.

I've been momentarily seduced by glamorous facades and inflated claims, but it never lasts. Those teachers fall away. The ones that endure, the ones I find really trustworthy, are the ones who don't set themselves above everyone else, who meet their students as friends, who are willing to question everything anew, who are honest and open about their own human foibles. They don't tell you their enlightenment experiences ad nauseum, nor do they act as if they as individual people have totally and completely transcended the conditioned mind. They are unglamorous, and they don't promise miracles, other than the miracle of every moment, which doesn't depend on them. They talk out of their own direct experience, not out of theory and belief. They don't offer anything seductive or comforting. They challenge you. They look the most ordinary, but they are the rarest of jewels.

Pay attention to what happens when you are around a teacher, how you feel, what arises. Is there clarity and presence or more and more seeking? Is questioning encouraged? Is there a party line, and what are the consequences if you don't buy it? Do you find yourself becoming ever more dependent on this teacher, or increasingly independent of them? What about the other students, how do you feel about them?

Of course, the right teacher for you may be the wrong teacher for someone else, and the right teacher for you yesterday may be the wrong teacher for you today. Krishnamurti took me right into present awareness; others found themselves tangled up in analytical mind-spinning when they heard him. At one moment for me, Gangaji was a clear window into the deepest truth; at another moment she was a seductive dream. However you feel around a teacher at any given moment, don't blame it on them or on you. There is no "you" and no "them" in this or any other relationship; there is only the meeting itself. It is what it is. There are no mistakes.

❧

There are some teachers who seem very invested in being wise and special. There are any number of them around today claiming to be avatars, messiahs, and even God. These teachers tell you that they speak *only* the Truth, and that *they* can take you to where you want to go, apparently somewhere other than where you are now. In fact, they'll even tell you that you can't really make it there without them. These teachers appeal to that place inside of us that is frightened and uneasy, that wants certainty and answers. People gather at their feet, waiting to be zapped, waiting forever for the future to arrive.

Most of us, if we're honest, would probably, in some shadowy part of our psyches, love to be able to believe that someone somewhere really was God, and that by going to them, we could be enfolded once and for all in the love and protection of the Divine Parent, assured of getting the genuine goods, and maybe eventually becoming certified gods ourselves. But it's an illusion. *Caveat emptor.*

Once, when I was living in California, I went to see a teacher named Byron Katie, who does what she calls "The Work," a process of questioning our thoughts and beliefs. I went up on stage and did The Work with her (on the question of evil, and whether or not everything is really God), and at one point I said to her, "Yes, but, Katie, when you turn on the news and see something like a school shooting or a massacre, don't you feel sorrow?"

Katie looked me in the eye. "Don't ask me," she said. "Ask you."

Ask you and then investigate the answer that arises. See if it's really true. Keep asking and keep investigating. Then you arrive at real truth, not a borrowed truth.

We hunger for an authority with the right answers, a path with certainty. Again and again we turn ourselves over to someone or something we imagine to be wiser. We look to what the experts have to say. We try desperately to fit ourselves into some pre-existing template, to conform to some model of what we are *supposed* to think or feel or do. We try to replicate the experiences that others have described.

Or else we go to the opposite extreme of compulsive rebellion and false egalitarianism, and that's just the flip side of the same coin. When we get past *both* idolatry and rebellion, then it's possible to have a relationship of *mutual* respect and love. Then, as Nisargadatta once said, "What does it matter who is who?"

The whole context in which we meet somebody plays a huge role in how we experience them. Are they up on a stage or sitting with us in a circle? Have we been told in advance that they are the incarnation of God or an awakened master? Do they arrive with great fanfare or in complete simplicity? Do we get to see them off stage in regular life? What we expect to find is very often what we do find. It's easy to begin fabricating experiences when you want them and have imagined them, based on what others have described. Does a particular teaching paradigm show you that there is nothing to seek, nothing needed, nothing lost? Or does it promote a kind of narcotic spiritual consumerism rooted in the sense that something is missing?

Wherever you find yourself, that's where you belong, not forever, but right now. How do I know that for sure? Because that's where you are! What looks like confusion, stagnation, or outright insanity may be the road to clarity. *You can only be where you actually are.*

For many years, I thought there was something wrong with me

because I went to many different teachers, and sometimes back and forth between them. I had this idea that you were supposed to settle in one place. You were supposed to find one teacher, one way of working, and stay there forever. For many people, this is what *does* happen. But in my case, it was not what happened. Finally I realized that in my case it was not *supposed* to be happening, that this was just an idea in my head. I realized that true settling is nothing more or less than "waking up moment to moment," as my first Zen teacher Mel Weitsman told me long ago.

So don't try to imitate someone else's path or swallow anyone else's apparently better idea about what's right for you. Ultimately, you can only be true to your own heart, the guru within, and you can only *be* where you actually *are*, not where you or anyone else *thinks* you maybe could or should be instead.

❧

Teachers, spiritual books, and spiritual company are wonderful, and then, at a certain point, these things *can* become an addiction, an escape. Often I reached for a teacher or a book or a tape exactly as I might reach for a drink or a cigarette or a new lover, to fill the hole of emptiness and fear, to get away from something that seems unbearable. There comes a time when the only way to arrive is to stop travelling. In the end, you're on your own.

It may take a long time for the search to fall away. The search, after all, is entertaining. It's comforting; it's familiar; it's habitual; it fills time, and it has "me" at the center of it. When the search ends, *everything* is the Guru. Every scrap of garbage is beautiful and holy. Everything is enlightened. The sound of the traffic says as much to you as the words of the teacher.

Devotion

Who is it we spend our entire life loving?

Kabir

I dreamed once that the Guru instructed me to bring sweets to the satsang dinner. Dessert was my assignment. Dessert is the useless course, the ecstatic course that nourishes the heart but not the body. It is like the extravagant feast in that wonderful Danish movie, *Babette's Feast.* Dessert is the course I spurn, like Babette's puritans, in my pursuit of holiness and perfection. It is the delicious course my mother delights in so completely, the favorite of children. It is the metaphoric antidote to my fixation of doing everything right: that which is *wanted,* but which one *should* not have. I was not happy when the Guru told me that my assignment was dessert. Every righteous fiber recoiled. I wanted to bring broccoli or salad. But beneath the recoil, there was some sweet desire to completely lose control, to be engulfed in dessert. One of my fears has always been that if I lost my grip, I'd turn into some mindless bhakti type swooning in devotion. Utterly useless, foolish, without shame. Fully in love, completely mad.

Is it possible to be a mindless swooning bhakti devoted to the rain, the traffic, the wind in the leaves, the utter simplicity of bare awareness?

The Egret

It is early February. I am at the Berkeley marina at sunset. It is a dark overcast afternoon; the setting sun is totally hidden behind a low ceiling of black clouds. Suddenly, a narrow slit breaks open at the horizon, instantly flooding land and sea with red light and revealing the fiery orange ball dissolving into the ocean. There is now a peculiar mixture of light and darkness happening at once.

On the slope of the glowing emerald green hillside only a few yards from where I am standing, a white egret floats down gracefully and lands in the exquisite red light. It waits, absolutely still, on its tall, thin legs, poised and intent, hunting for dinner. Swiftly it strikes the ground and comes up with a small animal in its beak, a mouse or a vole perhaps, squealing. The egret holds the tiny animal in its beak, then swallows it down live in one gulp. I see it pass down the long, rose-colored throat.

The egret stands tall, feathers rippling in the wind, the warm meal still alive inside the white belly of death. Such awesome beauty and grace, and the truth so clearly revealed. The body is food. In the end, it is somebody's meal. Quickly extinguished. Completely undone. The sun sinks; the glowing red light dies; the white egret rises from the ground and floats away.

Vedanta / February

Sheets of rain are blowing this way and that. Never in my life have I seen so much rain. It poured one night and all the next day without ever stopping.

A white egret is dancing with a black cow. Quails rush past. Who thought up all these amazing forms of being? Where did they come from? What *are* they?

It rained in torrents for hours and hours, day after day, night after night. Coming home, I saw mudslides, and the little stream by the roadside had swollen to a raging river with rapids.

Oakland

Pelicans fly across the water at the marina. A woman in a wheelchair rolls past. Chinese children frolic, running with delight after a dog. Back at home, ants file through the house in long columns and find their way into our clothing. A spider web glistens on a bush out front. Rain falls for days, pouring down. The backyard slides into the creek. Lightning flashes in the sky. I pass accidents on the highway.

Our neighbor Harvey was out at dawn yelling at the old woman from Asia who comes and picks through people's recycling bins on recycling day looking for bottles and cans she can get money for. Harvey told her to go back where she came from. Adele and I were horrified. The next morning Harvey was outside calling for Fluffy, his pet rabbit, who was lost. He went up and down the street for hours calling for Fluffy. He had tears in his eyes. Each of us is such an astonishing mix of light and dark.

⚜

Someone told me I was hiding my light under a bushel, focusing on all these gurus, chasing experiences when I was already awake, doubting and denying what I knew to be true, climbing back on the treadmill of samsara again and again. Perhaps it was nothing more than an old habit-pattern of this personality playing itself out: persistent self-doubt, a sense of lack and inadequacy, a tendency to think others had something I didn't.

I called Joko Beck. "*Everything* that's going on in my life right now seems to be about holding back," I told her. I felt anguished.

Joko said, "So? So hold back!"

If I'm holding back, I'm holding back. No problem. Just see it; experience it.

"You're doing fine," Joko says. She tells me there's no need to be perfect. What is, is. Out of just being here, the way emerges.

I had many questions about what I was doing offering meetings in the midst of all this apparent confusion. But, as Suzuki Roshi once said, the life of a Zen master is one continuous mistake. So I continued with my weekly meeting, and offered occasional one-day retreats. When these events were happening, I loved it. When I was *thinking* about it, I would sometimes have doubts. I felt a persistent pull to let everything go: my meetings with people, my writing, this whole obsession with spirituality. It was all beginning to make me sick. I just wanted to live an ordinary life, whatever that might be.

Joko told me to pay careful attention to the urge for a guru or a savior when it arises, feel it in the body. I told her, "I hope I don't go back into this guru trip again."

She replied, very matter-of-factly: "You might."

⁓☙

Over the next several years, I attended occasional satsangs and retreats with a number of other Advaita teachers, but I never again tried to make any of them into my savior-guru in the way I had with Gangaji and Ngeton. Something had played itself out and was finished. But the essential simplicity and freedom of Advaita continued to beckon. So did the mirage of final awakening, which appeared and disappeared on the horizon as the understanding came in and out of focus. I spent time with Francis Lucille, Isaac Shapiro, Wayne Liquorman, Tony Parsons, Adyashanti. I went several times to hear Byron Katie. I began a friendship and dialog with Steven Harrison, who considers himself post-spiritual.

And I found myself going more and more frequently to Chicago to see Mom.

What We See Is What We Get

Once at a satsang with Isaac Shapiro, in the back of the room where I was sitting, a beeping noise started up and didn't stop. Somebody's pager or cell phone was going off. In those days, I had an intense dislike for the ever-growing presence of cell phones and pagers in public places. They seemed perfectly symptomatic of everything I found pathological in our culture. It was no exaggeration to say that I *hated* cell phones and pagers. And now, somebody had one in their purse or backpack, and it was going off in the middle of satsang (outrageous!), making it hard to concentrate on what Isaac was saying, and I was furious. Furthermore, no one was doing anything about it! A few people were looking around, as I was, but no one was turning it off. The idiot who owned it was oblivious. I got angrier and angrier. Modern technology and human stupidity were ruining my chance for enlightenment! Suddenly, someone near me spotted the pager. It was a cricket. A cricket had somehow gotten into this room in the middle of the city.

Instantly, the whole movie changed. I love crickets. They're part of nature, which is dear to my heart, and they remind me of Springwater. I found it charming and miraculous that there was a cricket in the room attending satsang. I was suddenly so happy.

The sound itself was exactly the same as it had been before, only now I had a different conceptual picture, and a different set of stories and beliefs. Instead of a pager or a cell phone (representing everything in life I hated), now it was a cricket (representing everything in life I loved). Nature produced it, not evil human technology. And furthermore, "the idiot who owned it" didn't exist, and wasn't really oblivious to his non-existent pager after all. Now it was a pleasant sound, a miraculous sound. It no longer made it hard to concentrate on what Isaac was saying. In fact, it seemed to perfectly compliment his words.

Some years later, when I was teaching at a city college where people's cell phones were frequently ringing during class, I noticed that I no longer hated them. In fact, I found the ringing and the whole phenomenon rather charming.

Bondage & Freedom

If I'm sitting at my desk, and suddenly I have the thought "I've ruined my whole life," which I sometimes do, and if I take that thought seriously, if I believe it, if I buy it as an objective report on reality, what will be the result? Depression, anxiety, suffering. Pretty soon I'll be having a whole train of negative thoughts, and emotions, and more thoughts. But if, when that first thought comes, I see it for what it is, just a thought, then it actually amuses me. It's absurd! I begin to laugh! This is freedom.

Visit to Springwater

I arrived at the Oakland airport in the pre-dawn darkness. I was going to Springwater for a retreat and a visit, my first visit since I left staff. They had over booked the flight, and asked for volunteers to get off in exchange for a free ticket on a future flight. I considered it, but decided against it since I really wanted to get to Springwater as early as possible. The plane sat on the runway for several hours. We were told it had mechanical problems; they weren't sure if we'd be cleared for take off or not. Eventually we taxied back to the gate, and all of us ended up on the later flight alongside our fellow passengers who had gotten off earlier in exchange for a free ticket, the only difference being that we had not gotten the free ticket.

This next plane was delayed for several hours because of bad weather ahead. The sun had gone down, and it was dark by the time we made it to Chicago, my transfer point for the flight to Rochester. I had long since missed my connecting flight. Chicago was having the worst lightning storm in its history, accompanied by pouring rain and gale winds. Minutes after we landed, the airport was shut down, and all flights were cancelled. Hundreds of travelers were stranded, hundreds of flights canceled and delayed. By morning, the airport was a mob scene.

I spent the whole next day in the Chicago airport in a sea of stranded travelers, trying to get a flight to Rochester. Flight after flight was cancelled. Each one that did go had more potential passengers hoping to get on it than could fit into the plane.

Many people were quite angry. Some were yelling and screaming at the airline employees, giving themselves and everyone else a very bad time. These people had a horrible two days.

I had a very pleasant two days. There was complete acceptance of the situation (an acceptance I could not have engineered; it happened). I met a lovely man who invited me to the Red Carpet Club as his guest, so I spent the whole second day in luxury. I would rather have been at Springwater if I'd had a choice, but I didn't have a choice, and this was fine.

It was a great lesson in what happens when life doesn't go the way we plan it. If we stick to the plan (mentally), and resist reality (mentally), we end up suffering, and creating suffering all around us. If we can let the plan go, and completely accept what actually is, it turns out that we're totally okay. We're at peace, and we generate peace. Amazingly enough, we may even have fun!

I finally did make it to Springwater, just as retreat was getting underway.

It felt deeply good to be there in the silence and the vastness.

⚬

I visit with Toni, her husband Kyle and their son Remo in Toni's apartment after dinner the first night of retreat. Kyle, in a lavender shirt and dark blue suspenders, is frail and luminous. He is dying. He has Parkinson's and prostate cancer, probably won't live to see the winter. Remo is here for a few weeks from California where he lives. After dinner, Remo will drive Kyle back home. Toni stays in her little apartment at the Center during retreats. Kyle and Remo join us for meals.

Later, from a window upstairs, I watch Toni and Kyle walking to the car where Remo is waiting. Kyle is walking on his two canes, wearing a baseball cap. He and Toni stand in the sunlight by the car. Remo snaps a picture of them, their arms around each other. I remember snapping a picture of my father the last time I ever saw him.

Up at the pond at dusk, I listen to the chanting of frogs, which begins slowly at first, rises in a wild crescendo, then falls back into occasional arrhythmic twangs. Tiny little clouds float over the hilltops, the sweetest of clouds. It grows dark.

Walking back down the path away from the pond in the dark, Angel comes running to greet me. I recognize her bark. Then I see her emerging from the darkness, racing toward me. Angel is Jack's dog. He's one of the men on staff who has been here since the place was built. I call Angel the ecstatic dog. I squat down. Angel puts her paws on my chest, licks my chin in the dark, tail wagging like crazy, her whole body vibrating.

In the middle of the night, I hear the owl for the first time.

In the far north woods, on the last day of the retreat, I run into

Heinrich, the old man who lives next door. His face is full of light. It is as if I am seeing him for the first time ever.

"It's beautiful here," I say.

"Everywhere is beautiful," he replies, "but here it is very green."

We smile, and listen for a moment to the stillness of the woods, sharing this moment together, then each walk on in our separate directions.

Sharon asks me later what keeps me going in this spiritual life, despite all the imperfections and setbacks. What keeps me going is the small exquisite patch of sunlight on a tree in the woods, the delicacy of rain, the light in Heinrich's eyes, Angel's pure enthusiasm and love, the happy trees dancing in the wind, waving their big green leaves.

A symphony of sounds fills the air, and rich fragrances. Everything pulses, vibrates with aliveness here. The grass is filled with light and dark, with smell. It is humming and buzzing with crickets and wind. It is soft and moving. It is listening and breathing.

At dusk, an enormous red full moon rises up out of the hills. It fills the universe, shimmering in the pond like a flame. The air is humid— buzzing, crackling, sizzling with life. Springwater is a very erotic place. It makes me want to sing, twirl, make love, write books.

❧

I began to think about rejoining staff. Finally I decided to apply. They accepted me, but not without some hesitation and debate. That was a real jolt to my ego. I had always thought of myself as God's Gift to Springwater, Toni's possible successor, someone who had done a great job on staff. I always assumed they'd be thrilled to have me back. And some of them were, but others had reservations. I was known to be opinionated, at times irascible and argumentative, and I'd been hanging around with all these strange gurus. Sharon told me outright she thinks it won't be good for me or the Center if I come back. She says I've outgrown the place, I need to do my own thing.

I knew she was right. Coming back here now would be a way of avoiding something. It would solve my dilemmas about money, and probably eventually provide me with a ready-made avenue into teaching, but in my heart, I knew this was a false move, not the real solution.

But they accepted me. And I said yes. The plan was that I would return to Oakland, pack up, and be back here by fall. Almost immediately I felt deep sadness and regret.

❧

Rain sweeps across the fields. Pink lightning flashes in the sky.

I receive a letter from a woman in Europe who read my book. Her hands are deformed since birth. Her mother hid her, beat her, was ashamed of her. The woman survived. She married, had children, became an artist, and was even able to forgive her mother. It is a deeply touching letter. I am struck by the incredible beauty of each life exactly as it is: the pain, the mistakes, the acts of forgiveness and grace, the ways we survive and reach out to each other.

The rain is coming down in sheets. I write a letter to the woman with the perfectly formed hands.

The night is hot and humid. Mosquitoes are biting.

In the field the next morning, I saw an indigo bunting, a totally blue bird.

My friend Earl arrived from California for the next retreat. It is my birthday. Toni gives me two photos, one of her and Kyle, and one of the view from their house: an empty field with a few distant cows. And a card: "Hi dear Joanie," it says, "Have a wonderful happy birthday on this steaming, buzzing, lively land with all its amazing human beings and animals coming together for a short period of time. With love and wishes from the heart, Toni & Kyle."

Earl gives me candles and a note: "Let Your Light Shine." He said that my light didn't seem to shine here at Springwater the way it did in my meetings in California. I knew that was true. I needed to be on my own, free of any institution, at least for now, and maybe forever.

I sleep naked under the covers. It is my last night here. In the morning I take a final walk uphill. A red fox steps out of the tall grass a few feet ahead of me, trots across the path, disappears. A grasshopper sits on the petal of a yellow daisy. The sun is rising.

Once the airplane took off from Rochester, I had the strange sensation that Springwater was a dream. I knew I wouldn't be going back on staff.

❧

It's a sunny, cool but warm, crystal clear Bay Area day. My second load of laundry is in the dryer. The mockingbird is singing. Airplanes are flying over. The freeway is roaring. I already sent the email to Springwater, telling them I wouldn't be coming.

Seeing Is Freedom

Yesterday I gave a one-day retreat. Twenty people came. Afterwards I had dinner with several of the participants. I realized how much I love all these people, and I wondered why I would ever have wanted to leave and go back to Springwater when something so alive and interesting is unfolding here.

❧

At work, there is a patient who comes every week. I assumed that this man was severely developmentally disabled, since that's how he appears. He is brought by a family member and is totally dependent. He cannot find his way to the bathroom without guidance. He seems like a severely retarded person. Today, I found out that in fact he is a brain injury case. He was in a plane crash. He used to be a cardiologist. It was a strange moment, as my picture of him shifted. It was such a clear revelation of how fragile and temporary our entire persona is. A little tap on the head, and you're somebody else.

❧

I go to the marina after work, and walk alongside the boiling sea. Dried wildflowers and grasses stand brittle in the fierce wind. There are big rolling waves and surf breaking on the glistening rocks, splashing me.

A dog is leaping for his ball. His ears fly happily in the wind. The clouds, blowing past—have they solved the koan of money? And the flowers, translating light into air. There is tremendous energy and work every-where, yet there is no doer. The effort is effortless. The dance happens by itself. Sometimes, blessedly, the mind stops trying to figure it all out and simply enjoys it.

❧

Awareness is not a thing, Toni says to me on the phone. Awareness is the whole thing. Guru-chasing, finger-biting, wanting to see the whole thing—it's all the same movement. Don't get caught in wanting to see the whole thing, she said, that's the trap.

Everything that happens is conditioned. The *seeing* of it all is freedom.

Visit to Chicago

Summer turned to fall. I flew to Chicago to see Mom and give a workshop on awareness and waking up. Mom and I spent much of our time with Francine, Mom's ninety-year-old friend who lives in the same building, and with Terri, Francine's daughter. Terri is a successful businesswoman, a writer, and a student of Joko Beck. Francine is bald, in a wheelchair. She is dying. She looks like a bald Buddha. She is glowing, ready to dissolve. The four of us share meals. Terri and I help Francine onto the toilet. Later a priest comes. The four of us take communion together. I hold Francine's hand. I walk in the zoo with Terri. We talk of death.

Mom and I grow closer.

Chicago these days is very grounding. Something about the presence of death keeps everything very real. The rest falls away, or shines in its holy perfection. Terri and I are dancing this goodbye dance with our mothers. Colored leaves are on the trees and falling through the air. And our amazing mothers are also falling through the air.

Back in Oakland, I ended my meetings. I've had this compelling desire to let everything go, and finally it was clear that this had to go, at least for now. We had a few last meetings and a party for closure, and then it was over.

The Beauty of Death

On the phone, Toni says Kyle is deteriorating very rapidly. He is getting more unclear mentally at times, mistaking Toni for his mother, wanting her to be with him all night, not really comprehending what he's asking for, thinking he can do things he can't. At other times he's very lucid. Toni continues to be up a lot of the night with him. The nurse says he won't live more than three weeks, but they've said that before, and he's lived. Toni said she broke down sobbing once.

Francine died last night. I talked with Terri this morning on the phone before I went to work. Terri was at my mother's apartment. Naked now in the fire of Death: No name, no form, no body, no mind. Only the bare truth remains, always alive, always here.

The sun is out after a night of rain; everything is glistening with light. It is a mild November day. I talk to Kyle on the phone. He is quite coherent, though it is very difficult for him to speak, and I have to listen intently to understand him. We have a sweet last conversation. He wishes me a good life. We say goodbye to one another for the last time. The nurses now say he won't live more than a week.

Talking with him brought up a big wave of sadness in me.

This much I know, beauty is here, where we are, waiting to be discovered. When the mind is not preoccupied with its stories, and the heart is open, there is breathtaking beauty and holiness in the afternoon light on the side of a dilapidated building on a rundown street. When the mind is preoccupied and the heart is closed, we can be standing at the Grand Canyon and see nothing but a bunch of ugly rocks. Stories persist only because we find them entertaining. When they disappear, there is nothing here except awareness.

And then I get the call that Kyle has died.

⚭

Death opens a deep space.

Wild Man Packer was my nickname for Kyle. I used to kid him about the wild bachelor parties he threw while Toni was on retreat. We enjoyed this little joke over and over. I loved seeing Kyle laugh. He had a delightful, whimsical sense of humor.

Such silly little moments can seem trivial and inconsequential when we are preoccupied by grandiose self-centered dreams. But actually, these moments *are* our life. Death, in its finality, wakes us up to the absolute beauty of where we are.

Kyle was remarkably unpretentious and gentle. He loved Toni and the people at the Center and being alive. There was a lightness to him, a buoyancy, a light that was pure love.

Kyle and Toni had a very tender relationship. I can see them walking, hand in hand, together. In the last year, when his hands had to be on his canes, he and Toni were still walking side by side, more closely in touch than ever it seemed to me. He was Toni's best friend.

Vedanta

It is raining softly on the green world. A deer and her fawn walk right by my door, munching. The rain falls harder.

Later, a small lizard crawls across my doormat, poops, basks in the sun, which has just come out. A white buck grazes in the bejeweled green grass. The lizard turd glistens in the light. The lizard and I seem in communion, silently. The clouds are reflected in the puddles on the deck, where last night I watched the moon break through them. Bits of blue sky appear. The dark green trees surround me, their huge bodies so deep and still. The lizard is gone now. Only the turd remains, like an author's book.

Meditation is not something you do for an hour here and there. It is the exploration of a lifetime. Or differently put, it is the exploration of this moment. It is moment-to-moment. There is no path and no way. It is the space that allows everything to be.

At dusk the jackrabbits run out and play. Clouds blow past. A white deer gleams in the darkness. Everything slowly disappears, grows color-less, merges into darkness. A plane flies over. It is night.

The next day the sun is out. The sky is blue and utterly cloudless. Everything is sparkling with light, wet from the rain. The deer are run-ning in circles playing. The wind is blowing. The waving leaves make waving lights on my wall. Everything is dancing today, playing. Leaves are falling, yellow and gold. The cows are mooing. I heard what I thought were children's voices. It was a flock of wild turkeys. It is the morning of Kyle's memorial in Springwater.

Later that evening, the moonlight is spreading across the grass like an exquisite silver lake. The power of the moon—out here in nature—is so huge. In the urban landscape, it gets dwarfed, drowned out, forgotten. Here the moon is awesome. Everything is breathing. I sit outside in the tremendous *aliveness* of the nocturnal world. The moon lights the large trees.

In the middle of the night, when I wake up to pee, I see a hare bounding across the field in the moonlight.

At dawn there is ice on my steps. The field is frosted. I leave footprints in the frosty grass. And now the sun touches the tops of the first trees. The grasses are subtle shades of pink and soft green in the dawn light. I can still see my footprints.

Frost sparkles on the deck, on the roof, on the grass. I delight in the sheer joyousness of light. It has no purpose. It simply *is* glistening. Awareness beholds it all: the light, the urge to bite my finger, the beautiful bird on the deck, the bowl of steaming oatmeal, the hot tea, the images of Kyle, the thoughts of Springwater, the dazzling beauty of a single dewdrop, an old withered leaf.

The frost recedes from the field outside my room like the spreading lake of moonlight in reverse.

I am biting, agitated, restless. Unsettled. Wild turkeys run past. Clouds blow in.

At lunch, a bird dines with me on the tabletop, shares my rice.

A banana slug slowly crosses the road. In an empty green field, two black bulls are squaring off in some kind of confrontation. They are butting heads. One pushes the other back a few steps. Then the other pushes the first one back. Back and forth they go in their ritualized dance. It is almost as if they are making love.

Spotted fawns play nearby, racing this way and that, and a meadowlark sings. The old caretaker is working in the garden. She is the same age as my mother. A bald swami who is in his eighties is up on the roof making repairs, dressed in a pair of overalls.

The full moon rises later over the pink landscape, the soft folds of Elephant Mountain absorbing the light. White deer move silently through the swaying grasses.

⋅❧

I love the sound of the old caretaker's voice. Just her presence in the room makes me smile. It doesn't matter what she says; it is the light that infuses the words, a gentleness. She is unglamorous, not conventionally beautiful. But a light shines in her, beauty itself, something that soothes my whole being.

In the woods, sitting still, there is subtle joy in listening to the tiniest sounds. There is delight in the textures of light.

Yesterday, there was fingerbiting, caught-up-ness, agitation, enclosure, narrowness, contraction. Today there is empty space. The bodymind likes one experience and not the other.

Now a loud generator hurts my ears. It passes. Lunch happens.

Back in my room, a single frog sings to me outside my door. It seems about to rain. A ladybug lands on the window glass. The air is still.

At dawn, in the moonlight, two jackrabbits chase each other. The full moon is just above the trees.

The truth is not in the mind.

Oakland: Sun Face Buddha, Moon Face Buddha

On Thanksgiving morning, I am back in Oakland talking to Toni about Kyle's last days. She tells me of warming up the urinal with the hairdryer so it wouldn't be so cold. The morning before he died, Kyle called for a last breakfast with the Springwater staff, and they all gathered around his bed, and he told them to be good to Toni and not to hurt her. You can't outfox the fox, he told her. And then he died.

I come home from work one night in the pouring rain, and there is a message on my answering machine from the National Endowment for the Arts. I have been awarded a writing grant. I can't believe it. I run down the hall to tell Adele. It is amazing the energy I feel! I call my mother. She is thrilled. I call my friends. Everyone is thrilled.

And then my friend Elaine calls me. The teacher she's been with for the last three years has just given her the boot. Elaine can't stop crying. I am ecstatic, and she is devastated. We laugh at the shifting sands: Sun Face Buddha/Moon Face Buddha. All of it is built on such ephemeral stuff. Back and forth we go, up and down.

I quit my job and reserved the solitary cabin in the woods at Springwater for next April and May.

In the Dunes and On Retreat with Toni

Toni is coming to California early this winter, several weeks before the retreat. She has invited me to spend this time with her at a condo on the Monterrey coast that a friend has offered her.

It is a beautiful place, on the dunes, right on the ocean, with a pristine empty beach full of shorebirds and only occasionally another person.

Toni and I cook meals together, take long walks on the beach, spend quiet evenings by the fire. We are old friends by now. We live and play together easily. We enjoy one another.

Schools of dolphins swim by. Toni delights in our disappearing foot-prints on the sand. Colors wash up on the beach in the sunset light. I wade through tide pools and at night watch moonlight racing along the waves.

The moon is closer to the earth than it has been or will be again during our lifetimes. We watch it rise from behind the dunes. Toni takes snapshots.

"What is freedom?" I ask her one night by the fire.

She lives with the question for a whole day.

"Freedom is an empty mind," she tells me the next night.

Thought can't get there. She speaks of not allowing any self-deception, any subtle system, to seduce us. The empty mind is free of "yes, but," free of doubt.

I bite my fingers uncontrollably after Toni has gone to bed.

The universe is pinching itself. Every action, even the pinching, is motivated by the desire for peace. It's not a skillful way of getting it. But that's the underlying intention. Killing my enemy, exterminating the problem group, drinking myself to death, biting my fingers—it's all aiming (ultimately) at peace. But it's off the mark. It creates the opposite.

I am amazed one morning to find Toni standing on her head. She tells me she does it every morning.

"Why did you stop doing your meetings?" she asks me later that same day. "I was so happy you were doing that."

That comes as a surprise to me.

Back in Oakland, we celebrate Christmas together. And then the retreat begins.

～❧

Retreat is so simple, so deep, so quiet, so open. Nothing to seek.

Toni said in one of her daily talks during the retreat: "This morning—this moment—is absolutely new. It has never been here before, and it will never be here again. That's why it's so beautiful."

Walking in the morning, I come upon a man who runs and hides behind a bush. He doesn't see me. I realize he is hiding from his dogs, playing with them. He is very embarrassed when he realizes someone is watching him. But he is beautiful: his love for his dogs, his play, his face, his embarrassment. We laugh together.

Toni knocks on my door one evening after dinner, comes to show me a book about Trappist monks she is enjoying. She found it in the library of the retreat center, which is a Catholic place. She sits down beside me on my bed and slowly turns the pages of the book. It has photographs of Trappist monks and beautiful text. She leaves it with me.

New Year's Eve comes in the middle of retreat. It is the millennium, the turn of the century. We celebrate in silence. I go to bed at 10 p.m. and wake up in another era. New Years Day, 2000: Wind and clouds blowing in the sky, fast. Beauty is here when we stop looking elsewhere.

Toni's way is so simple. Nothing except what is. In her talks, she imitates the sounds of birds and raindrops and machinery: zzzz, cheep

cheep, ping, plop, woooosh! Zzzzzz. That's it! No explanations, no high-sounding terminology, no calling it "Consciousness" or "God" or anything at all. Just cheep cheep, bzzzzz, wooosh. Nothing more. Just this. Just listening.

I'm scurrying around one afternoon, thinking I need another cup of green tea, and then I stop. I sit down in the little cloistered courtyard. There is a moment of discomfort, of dis-ease, feeling that this isn't enough, I need something more, I need to get away, I need to keep moving, I need the cup of tea. And then there is stopping. And suddenly there is dazzling beauty in front of me—the light on an orange—the delicious, delicate sounds of the fountain—Wow!

There is, in this work, infinite subtlety, infinite delicacy.

Toni is so open with where she's at. She says she had never before felt such a deep grief, and now she understands much better what others have gone through and talked to her about. She talks about how she is working with the grief, how she misses being able to share things with Kyle, misses being able to please him, how she craves these things exactly like an addiction. She says that in total awareness, she can bring up the thought of Kyle, and no reaction occurs. But when there isn't that total awareness, she says the mind runs off into grief and sadness. She is not resisting the grief, nor is she indulging it. She is not denying it or trying to act a certain way to look enlightened. She is exploring, interested. She is very simple, very open.

After the retreat, I drive Toni down the coast to Earl and Tom's place in Carmel and spend a day there with the three of them before heading home. In the morning, Earl and Tom and Toni and Woodrow the dog stand up on the balcony waving me off, and I feel such deep tenderness for all of them.

Coming home, I am exhausted, as if I've been on a huge journey.

Difficult or Easy?
Is There Anything to Do?

There is absolutely nothing to attain except the realization that there is absolutely nothing to attain.

TONY PARSONS

That which is before you is it, in all its fullness, utterly complete. There is naught beside. Even if you go through all the stages of a Bodhisattva's progress toward Buddhahood, one by one; when at last, in a single flash, you attain to full realization, you will only be realizing the Buddha-Nature which has been with you all the time; and by all the foregoing stages you will have added to it nothing at all.

HUANG PO

If you say that you do not need to fan yourself because the nature of wind is permanent and you can have wind without fanning, you will understand neither permanence nor the nature of wind.

DOGEN (GENJOKOAN)

You must be energetic when you take to meditation. It is definitely not a part-time occupation. Limit your interests and activities to what is needed for you and your dependents' barest needs. Save all your energies and time for breaking the wall your mind has built around you. Believe me, you will not regret.

NISARGADATTA

Some teachers stress how simple waking up is. If it takes any time or effort at all, it's off the track, because it's already here. It's what *is*. Other teachers speak of a lifetime of subtle and arduous attention, vigilance, and practice. Could both be true? After all, who would deny the utter simplicity of what is? And who would deny the *apparent* tenacity and power of the mirage, the misunderstanding? Consciousness may be all there is, and the problems may all be imaginary, but when these habits and hypnotic trances are operating, there is suffering. It hurts. And that's what motivates us to seek a different way of living.

The mind thinks it has to be either/or, difficult or easy, practice or no practice. But perhaps we don't need to reconcile all of these different approaches and expressions. They all arise; they all have their place, and exactly the one you need now is always appearing now. Trying to reconcile or choose between them is a mind game, a distraction. The mind is creating an imaginary dilemma and then trying to solve it. And since the problem is imaginary, it can't be solved, so the game is endless. Round and round the mind goes in a frustrating (but entertaining) tail-chase.

At one moment in "my life," being a drunk was what appeared. At another moment, formal Zen practice appeared. At another moment, devotional gurus showed up. At another moment, the falling away of the entire spiritual obsession and the turning on of the TV happened. At another moment, apparently deliberate, conscious attention arises. Each is perfect. They aren't really in conflict, until the mind begins *thinking* about them, and thereby manufactures conflict out of thin air.

No one owns any of these arisings. No one suffers them. No one has to figure them out. No one is going anywhere. There is no "you" who has to somehow get this all reconciled and worked out, so that you can get somewhere other than here, now.

If meditation appears, and you enjoy meditation, then meditate. If letting the formality of it all go happens, let it all go. You don't have to make one right and the other wrong; you don't have to choose or "be consistent;" you don't have to explain how both can be true. Just let it all be as it is. Actually, that *is* what is happening anyway. Everything *is* being allowed to be exactly as it is. Everything *is*, as it is. The mind fights its imaginary battles, and the whole time, awareness (the nameless, formless unborn) is allowing it all, even the mental battles.

"Meditation" is a word, an idea. But what is *this*, right now?

That's not a question to answer with another word or concept. It's not a question for the mind to tackle. It's a question intended to stop the mind and open that listening stillness that knows nothing and needs no answers. In this open presence right now, is there anything that needs to be reconciled or understood?

In Zen, there's an old story about a contest to determine who was going to be the next successor in the lineage. The student who was favored to win wrote a poem about polishing the mirror so that it would reflect clearly, without obstruction. Then some renegade kitchen worker wrote a poem saying that there was no mirror to polish and no one to polish it. His was the winning poem, and he became the sixth Patriarch of Zen.

Most of spirituality (99.9%) is about a path, a practice of mirror polishing. The realization that there is nothing to polish may be its end result. I believe it was Surya Das who said that the point of all those visualization practices in Tibetan Buddhism is that you finally realize that you're visualizing *everything*. But to get to that realization, you practice. You visualize. You polish the mirror. You cultivate awareness. The path is a kind of *prescriptive remedy* designed to make the apparent obstructions more and more transparent as the illusory mirages that they are.

Advaita, on the other hand, is more like a *description* of what is. It is recognized from the outset that there is nothing to be done, that *this* is already it. Any appearance to the contrary is just that, an appearance. The only one who could "practice" is the character in the dream, and anything that was achieved by such a practice would just be part of the dream. Advaita steadfastly refuses to feed the dream or nourish the seeker. The mind hates this. But so long as we are looking for a way out, we are reinforcing the notion that this is not it, that something better is needed. And we are reinforcing the mirage of the seeker, somebody who is separate, unworthy and in need of improvement.

Still, if that is not realized, there is suffering. So, there are paths. As Dogen points out, what we call practice is as natural as the wind and comes from the same source. If practice is meant to occur, it will occur. When that is deeply realized, what practice remains?

If there is a path, it is utterly paradoxical for it goes nowhere, no one is on it, and nothing is outside of it. Zen masters speak of effortless effort and the gateless gate, trying to point to the pointless. It is truly an impossible job. No words can express it. Hearing the words, which are always dualistic, the mind gets stuck on different false ideas.

Truth is groundless. You can't land anywhere. If you think, *I'm nobody*—that's not it. If you think, *I'm somebody*—that's not it. If you think, *there's free choice*—that's not it. If you think, *there's no choice*—that's not it. If you think, *there's something to do*—that's not it. If you think, *there's nothing to do*—that's not it. Any idea we try to solidify and land in is a dream. The Zen master destroys them all, one by one. What remains when *everything* (and "nothing" too!) has been annihilated?

That is the truth!

"Show me the Holy Reality," the monk said to the Master.

"It just moved!" the Master replied.

The Zone

One night in Chicago, I turned on the TV and happened upon a pre-Olympic women's figure skating competition. Michelle Kwan, who won the gold medal that night, smiled as she skated, gliding through the air in utter bliss. She was in the zone, as they say. She seemed completely and utterly at ease as she twirled, leapt and spun around like a Sufi dervish. Her body performed amazing feats, but she made it look effortless. To skate like that, you have to abandon yourself completely. There is no way to "do" it. You have to completely let go.

Part of the beauty of it is the possibility of failure. It is held in absolute vulnerability. For every winner, there is a loser. There is the young woman who falls during a triple twirl, her dreams shattered in one second.

A year or so later, I was watching the women's figure skating competition at the winter Olympics. A sixteen-year-old girl named Sarah Hughes gave one of the most remarkable performances ever. Sarah was in the zone. And this time, Michelle obviously wasn't. Sarah won the gold medal.

Sarah had no fear of losing, since she was in fourth place and had no real hope of winning, so she skated "for fun," she said. She was clearly mind-blown by her own performance, and being sixteen years old, she was totally out there with her surprise. She kept saying over and over to her trainer, "Wow! I never skated like that in my life! Wow!"

That's the zone. *It is never a permanent state.*

Once we know "the zone" is possible, there is, of course, the urge to repeat it, especially when the whole world is watching and so much seems to be at stake. And yet it can't be *willed* into existence, because it is precisely the opposite kind of thing: a surrendering of all control. Words never quite catch it, since the necessary surrender in the case of these skaters also requires phenomenal precision, concentration, skill, discipline, rigorous training, presence and energy.

Any attachment to results is clearly problematic. Sarah Hughes thought she had nothing to lose; Michelle Kwan thought she had everything to lose. In the quest for enlightenment, the attachment to results is again the obstacle, and yet such attachment cannot be willed out of existence. It can only be seen through every time it arises. In fact, the very notion of enlightenment is the biggest obstacle, for it creates the illusion of a future attainment.

In the quest for enlightenment, we imagine that the "goal" is to be "in the zone" all the time. But if anything, it's more about seeing the fleeting, insubstantial, dream-like and impersonal nature of everything—winning, falling on our ass, being in the zone, being out of the zone—and resting as that which includes and transcends all duality.

And what is that? Is it something terribly mysterious and far away? Or is it the most obvious "thing" of all: bare being, present awareness?

And is this awareness a *particular* experiential state of mind, or is it the unbroken wholeness that includes and transcends all states of mind?

Enlightenment is not about having a sustained *experience* of any kind, or being in a *state* of uninterrupted mindfulness twenty-four hours a day. It isn't an achievement. It isn't personal. And yet, this is precisely how the mind imagines it. The mind is forever at the Spiritual Olympic Games, looking for the Gold Medal Realization. And for every winner in such a competition, there has to be a loser: hungry seekers gathered at the feet of mythologized finders.

The finish line exists only in the thought-generated mirage. Bare being is always free and complete. Even when the mirage appears, there is *really* no-thing there! The only "problem" is that there is some idea that "you" (a mirage!) need to be liberated from mirages. It's like trying to save a movie character from the movie! Joan does not wake up from the illusion of Joan; that would be absurd! There is no one *real* to be saved! The dream characters do not get enlightened because they have no separate, permanent, real existence, except in the mind. *The one who thinks she is having the mirage is part of the mirage!*

The dream character is not the dreamer; she's the dream. It's a lingering confusion of identity. It's like those people who come to Nisargadatta and say, "I see there is nothing at all. Now what do I do?"

How quickly the mind reasserts itself!

"Am I really here yet? Is this it? Is there more? What do I do now? Am I done?"

Absurd questions. Funny. Makes me laugh every time when the bubble breaks.

Awareness has no problems, no sense of lack. It is only the character we take ourselves to be who feels inadequate and frustrated, who seeks something better like "enlightenment." The truth cannot be found or seen in the way that you can find or see your car. Because you are not outside of it. It is not an object. It is not somewhere else. Simply see the illusory nature of the separation. See that the entire story, the main character, and all the ideas of what should or should not be, are made up. You are awareness itself, totally free, always present.

Even if the story comes back, even if there is identification with the character, even if there are old habits and upsetting emotions, even if the bodymind contracts in fear, awareness is unharmed in any way. The only damage is *in* the story. It's make-believe, like the fire in the movie. If the false keeps arising, who cares? Only the false.

All of it is the play of Consciousness. Enlightenment is not a one-time event that transforms "you" into a spiritual superstar. It's *this*, right here, right now: the sensations of acid indigestion, the screech of brakes, the faint aroma of someone cooking lamb chops down the hall, the direct experiencing of anger or hurt. Nothing at all! Not exactly what the seeker had in mind!

Why Make a Religion Out of It?

I was invited by Rami Shapiro, a radical Zen rabbi, to participate in a dialog project, offering commentary on selected passages of the Torah for posting on the Internet. I was supposed to be the Krishnamurti-like voice in the dialog.

Today I sat down to write my first commentary.

Torah: When the woman saw that the tree was good for eating, and a delight to the eyes, and that the tree was desirable as a source of wisdom, she took of its fruit and ate. She also gave some to her husband and he ate. (Genesis 3: 6).

I sit here looking at this text on my computer screen. The computer has crashed once already this morning. I hear the traffic on the freeway. Airplanes. The hissing of the computer. A faint voice. Breathing. Morning sunlight.

And I wonder, does looking at a text bring us into presence, this moment? Does it open us to that listening space which is un-mediated, immediate, direct, here and now? Does it re-turn us to God? Or does it lead us into ever more complicated convolutions of thought that fascinate the mind?

This is not a question to answer from knowledge, from opinion, which we can then argue for and defend. Rather, it is perhaps a question to live with.

Rami writes: "Torah is the heart and soul of Judaism. Its stories, laws, customs, and ethics form the fertile soil of all authentic Jewish expression. There can be no serious Judaism without Torah, and no serious Jews without Torah learning. If we lose Torah we lose our soul as a people. If we lose Torah we lose our integrity as a nation. If we lose Torah we lose our authenticity as Jews."

My response: It sounds like losing the Torah is the very best thing that could possibly happen.

I don't mean to be disrespectful. But it's my honest response. So, I share it. Maybe it means I really don't belong in this dialogue. Or maybe it's the beginning of the dialogue. I honestly don't know. We'll see.

Rami said in an email to me: "I am a student of (what word can you use in this regard?) Krishnamurti, and try to apply his insights to Judaism."

I truly wonder, what is Judaism or any religion? It seems to me it is a sense of identity with a particular (bounded) group or community, with it's history (i.e., the story of its life), and with a collection of beliefs, dogmas, concepts, and ritualized activities, which can perhaps be revised, but never too radically, and always in the context of whether the revisions are still in line with the authority of the past. Krishnamurti questioned all of this. Like Toni, his interest was the aliveness of this moment. He pointed to looking freshly–without authority, without conclusions–and seeing when internalized preconceptions and authorities block and distort that aliveness and immediacy of being. I wonder how would "Krishnamurti's insights" be applied to Judaism or any religion?

Toni wrote something in her book *The Work of This Moment* that has stayed with me: "People have said to me: 'Buddhism is not the problem. Attachment is.' But would there be any 'isms' at all if there was no need for attachment?" I used to think Toni and Krishnamurti were both much too rigid and narrow-minded on this point. I saw myself as much more inclusive and open-minded because I embraced the truth in many forms and considered all paths valid and beautiful. But right now, it seems to me that Toni and Krishnamurti simply refuse to move away in any direction from the utter simplicity of being here now without any boundaries or divisions.

I wonder what is gained by holding onto identities and systems like Judaism and Buddhism (and of course, Krishnamurti-ism if it becomes that!)? It all seems like an unnecessary complication and obstacle to simple being.

Am I included in Judaism? No. It doesn't feel like it. Judaism is something other than me, something I can perhaps appreciate, participate in, or dialogue with in a friendly way. And of course I could convert. But I'm not a Jew.

I think it was either Krishnamurti or David Bohm who talked somewhere of false universals. In our longing for wholeness, we try to find it by identifying with groups (I'm Jewish, I'm gay, I'm American, I'm a leftist radical, I'm a woman, whatever it is), and we get from that a false sense of belonging—false because it is partial, exclusive, and based on division and separation.

I see the Garden of Eden as our natural state of being, which is always here, but often obscured by the thought-movies that capture attention. In the Garden, we are not divided into Jews, non-Jews, Buddhists, Hindus, or followers of Krishnamurti. We are not busy interpreting and re-interpreting ancient texts. We are simply here: alive, open, present.

What is it in human beings that takes us away from our natural being and creates so much suffering and conflict? As I see it, what takes us away is mistaking thought, which is conceptual abstraction, for reality.

The root-thought is the idea of "me" as a solid, discrete entity, an independent agent who seems to be at the center of "my" life. So instead of simple awaring, moving, and being, there is the added thought of "me" who is *doing* this, "me" who is *experiencing* this, "me" who is *observing* this: "me" who is the listener, the doer, the thinker, the observer. This "me" is by definition a fragment—separate, incomplete, transitory.

As soon as we conceive of "me," we are (seemingly) expelled from the Garden. Then "me" begins to seek something to save "me," to return me to the Garden. We try alcohol and drugs, sex and romance, money and power, revolution, indulgence, renunciation, enlightenment, gurus, saviors, authority figures, and knowledge. We happily share each of these seemingly wonderful fruits with our friends. We turn each other on to our newest "answers." We eat them together.

Knowledge promises control. Knowledge boxes and labels and divides that which is inherently uncontainable, unknowable, indivisible, and unnamable. Knowledge conceives of the world in opposites, like good and evil, and longs to have one side of the imagined duality without the other. Knowledge creates history and expectation. It creates traditions and authorities. It creates systems and beliefs.

The systems get ever more complicated. We revise them and refine them. We have dialogues between them.

Finally we begin to wonder, what is it that we really want? What is it we are running away from? And who is doing all this?

We speak of God and the woman and the man and the serpent and the tree and the fruit. We speak of good and evil. But right now, are these anything other than words, images, labels invented by thought? If those words, those categories, all disappear, what remains?

Is thought scanning for an answer: another word, another category, another object of knowledge? Can that movement of thought be seen for what it is?

And then what's here? Listening space....sound of freeway.... breathing....tapping of the keys....listening...being....

Do we need the Torah? Do we need Judaism or Buddhism or any isms? Do we need Krishnamurti?

I'm not saying we should burn all the books that have been written or refuse to read them. I'm not saying we should live without teachers. I'm questioning our human tendency to seek salvation, and by seeking it, missing it, because it is always right here. I'm questioning our tendency to create authority, to move away from simple aliveness and from the possibility of truly open inquiry without any conclusions or answers. I'm questioning what we habitually do with teachers and the words they leave behind.

Is there any real value in the Torah (or in Krishnamurti)? If there is, what is it, and how should we approach it? Do the words in a book (whether the book is the Torah or Krishnamurti or Toni or Joan or who-ever), do the words open us to simple wakefulness? And if they do, why on earth would we want to make them into "sacred books" to be taken as our authority? I feel the deepest respect and appreciation for all the great spiritual beings who have lived and shared. I enjoy reading their books. But when I see myself turning them (in particular) into God, I see idolatry. I see the first mis-step. I see the seduction of the serpent. I see the seed of human history.

Rami seemed truly pleased with my commentary. But I never wrote another one. I tried. But try as I might, I just couldn't wrap my mind around those Bible passages. It took too much effort.

February Visit to Chicago

Mom sits in her gigantic hair curlers, like a visitor from outer space. I walk daily to the zoo, visiting the wild ones. I stand close to a lion, watching it breathing, only inches away, through the glass window.

The wind is howling, the icy February wind. The lake is partly frozen, heaving and rolling blocks of ice. The trees are bare. It is the season of death.

Terri has Francine's furniture in her apartment now; Francine's classy silver cigarette case and lighter are on her mantel.

I read some of my manuscript to Charlotte, my mother's oldest friend. They met each other before they were married. Charlotte is an artist. She tells me today that all her life, and especially as an abused and loveless child, she has survived by going out into nature. There, even as a child, she'd find love pouring out of the sky. She speaks of the beauty of a twig, a cloud, the people on the bus. "When you're down," Charlotte says, "you go out into nature and you connect—it's all love—every squirrel, every leaf." She says that the presence of love permeates all that we see. It is available to us in simple wonder, in nature, all around us, everywhere.

Even the traffic is love.

When it was time for me to fly home to Oakland, Mom was never so openly or deeply sad to see me go.

Vedanta: Early March—2000

A deafening chorus of frogs at twilight fills the air. A screech owl cries out.

In the morning, I walk on a carpet of wet leaves and pine needles. Everything is sparkling with light, and smells of earth and pine, and then there is the stench of death. I find a dead jackrabbit.

For one mad moment at daybreak the next morning the young deer and the jackrabbits are all racing around the field chasing each other, running in ecstatic circles.

When I come back to my room after breakfast, the lawn is full of plump quails feasting in the dew. The sky is blue. The sun is out.

In the afternoon, the deer were in the field outside my room, and many lay down to nap or rest. One buck went around meticulously to each deer that was lying down and butted it in the side with his horns, forcing it to get up.

Later, everything is very still except the mist moving through the tall pine trees on the ridge. A bird, a brown towhee, stands happily in a puddle outside my door. It owns nothing. It is "homeless." *Everywhere* is Home.

After a beautiful day, I have a night of fingerbiting, lying in bed in the dark unable to stop. In the morning I head out for a walk. The mind is racing. I'm picking uncontrollably at loose ends on my fingers. I feel despair because "I'm missing the awesome beauty of Now." I want to stop the racing mind, the picking fingers, and I can't.

It hits me suddenly that all experience is transitory, that I'm looking for something like a permanent orgasm. Not just a permanent orgasm, but the biggest possible orgasm of all time, permanently. Reality isn't like that. Obviously. The biggest orgasm of our life, by definition, happens only once, and lasts for what? A few seconds? A minute? Then it's over. Gone forever.

Suddenly, everything stops. Instantly, all problems are gone, absurdly inconsequential. Frogs are singing, water is trickling, leaves are glistening. Butterflies dart around me. Huge tall redwoods rise into the sky, so still, light on their barks and intricate bejeweled cobwebs.

Thought says: "This is it! This is enlightenment!"

Thought begins framing the story, so I can tell about it during my future satsangs. "I was at Vedanta, in darkest despair, when suddenly..."

Isn't this amazing? How there is utter despair, total caughtupness and contraction, and suddenly total joy? How did it shift? Isn't it amazing how the mind tries to make something out of it, something for me to own, something to hold onto, and how this movement of the mind dissolves completely in seeing?

A big lizard is doing his push-ups on the cement outside in the late afternoon sun. The blue sky is cloudless. Hot, like summer. Everything is so green.

The tiniest little cloud is floating over the top of Elephant Mountain. Late afternoon sun is sinking. Tiny white flowers bloom on the forest floor in the Buckeye grove. I hear the most delicate birdsong imaginable, calling and answering. I watch big black cows splashing through a puddle in the green field, drinking from it.

Now the evening sunset clouds are on fire floating over the ridge, as I watch from the window in my room.

I clean and pack up the next morning. I say goodbye to the old caretaker. "Have a good re-entry," she tells me. "Don't get the bends."

Old Age & Death

I'm off to visit my friend Heather in Point Reyes. Lucy, her cat, is twenty years old. She looks ancient. Every tiny movement requires enormous time. Heather says she loves seeing how Lucy is aging so gracefully, accepting each new limitation as it comes, accepting her current reality, whatever it is. Lucy delights now in the simplest things—just to step outside and sniff the air.

Heather and I take a walk in the rain. A great blue heron lands in front of us, floating down out of the sky to hunt for gophers in the field. Afterward, I have hamburger for lunch at the Station House Café. Could be one of those cows out at Vedanta. One of those huge beautiful beings, who love their calves with such tenderness, who splash through the puddles, who gaze at me as I walk past. I am eating a cow. What a strange mystery this all is.

The Journey East

I load up my ancient Toyota and drive out of California, over snow-capped mountains, on through miles of sage brush and tumbleweed, through snow storms, wind storms and rain storms, across Nevada and Utah and Wyoming, over the Continental Divide and into Nebraska. The landscape changes. Wild, uninhabited mountains and deserts give way to rolling green hills and tender, gentle farmland. The traffic thickens. Geese fly north by the hundreds above me. It rains for hours.

I drive into Chicago at last, into the massive traffic jam, and finally I reach the turquoise lake, and Mama waiting for me, the first crocuses blooming in the park. After two weeks, I continue east, arriving at Springwater for the April retreat. After the retreat I'll move out to the solitary cabin in the woods, where I'll be for six weeks, then back to the main house for my last month at Springwater, then back to Chicago.

I have the sense that I will not be returning to California, except to pack up my belongings. I want to be closer to my mother. I imagine I'll find a place to live somewhere in the Midwest. But until late July, I'm here at Springwater.

One night at dusk, listening to the rain, I hear the peepers for the first time. A thrill goes through me. These tiny frogs, celebrating the rain, herald the end of the long winter here and the coming of spring. I drink in the beauty, the quiet, the simplicity of this world. Wind races on the face of the pond, rippling the water. The ripples move through the tissues and cells of this body. Geese fly overhead, so low and close I hear the beating of their wings in the moonlight. The first lone bullfrog begins croaking, solo. He is alone. No one else has emerged yet.

Paradoxically, when it is seen that everything is constantly disappearing into and arising out of formless emptiness, it is also seen that each thing is infinitely precious and holy. Nothing has any meaning or purpose beyond itself. Every moment is a kiss.

Progress

Like the worms in the cow dung, the moment the cow dung
dries they are finished, however much progress they have made.

NISARGADATTA

The future never arrives. Like the mirage in the desert, the closer you get to it, the farther away it is. Of course, in the phenomenal manifestation, relatively speaking, there can be apparent progress and improvement. A person can learn a language, recover from an injury, get rid of an addiction, develop an athletic skill, win a gold medal at the Olympics, and move from total caught-up-ness in non-stop compulsive thinking to greater awareness and presence. Humanity can evolve from ox carts to jet planes, and from spears to nuclear bombs.

Such progress is always perfectly balanced by regress. Our dream of achieving the perfect society or the perfect me never quite materializes, because it is based on a fallacy: the idea that you can have a one-sided coin. There is no controlling what things come to us and whether or not we "succeed" at them. Thus, we don't always get the gold medal no matter how hard we train. Or we can't get rid of the addiction no matter how hard we try. Things that seem like progress (such as machines, technology, and nuclear energy) inevitably have a negative side to them, and seem to bring regress as well as progress.

And ultimately, all progress is wiped out by regress. The aging brain can no longer remember the languages it learned, the aging body gradually decays, the former Olympic athlete can no longer walk to the bathroom unassisted, and finally, the bodymind dies. Even the "mindful presence" that we have carefully cultivated disintegrates into senility and finally into nothingness. In time, the gold medal disintegrates into dust. Regress wins. At least for a moment. Until birth starts the whole thing over again.

There is nothing wrong with improving yourself on this level: exercising the body, eating a good diet, learning a new skill. It's enjoyable; it's fun. But if you imagine that success or failure is within your control, or that you will finally achieve The Perfect You, you will be greatly disappointed, as you will be if you depend upon progress and success as the source of happiness and fulfillment. Death wins every time. True happiness is not in the future. It depends on nothing at all.

Alone in the Woods

It is growing dark; the twisted dead tree outside the window is disappearing into the dusk—gnarled, half-eaten, beautiful. It is cold today, damp and bleak. I feel as if everything has been removed.

A crow rises up from the ground on its huge black wings, and floats down on a branch. All around the dead tree are living trees, but except for the scrawny pines, they are bare. It is early April.

I am living in a one-room cabin, nestled in the woods at the lip of a ravine, above a little stream. The cabin has electricity, but no running water. There is an outhouse with a composting toilet—quite grand and odorless. I walk to it in the rain and cold, breathing in the smells of wet leaves and earth. A bird is building her nest by the door of the outhouse.

It's a simple life here in the woods. Things slow down. I wake up, empty and rinse my pee bucket from the night, use the outhouse, brush my teeth, eat fruit, drink twig tea, sit quietly. I cook oatmeal on the hotplate and wash the pot without running water. Basic tasks, like washing the dishes or brushing my teeth, take time and attention. I am made aware of my impact on the environment, of how much I consume, and the amount of waste I generate in various forms. Springwater life has always made me more conscious of how we impact the environment, because when there is still a great deal of empty space and quiet (and time to appreciate it), you see very vividly the impact of a single car, or one new building, or one new telephone line.

Salt. Bowl. Raisins. I make a list of things I need from the main house, and then realize I don't need any of them. I throw the list away.

Out the window, everything is dead, about to be reborn. The view is stark, empty—the season of death and dying. It has been cold and damp and overcast for days. Bleak.

It is Lent, the season of repentance: changing the direction in which we are looking for happiness.

Meditation

At those moments when all is clear, it isn't that we finally "get it," but rather, that we finally stop trying. We relax. We see: there's no problem. There's no me. There's just what is. Just aware presence.

Then the mind begins spinning. It says, "I've got it!" It-less-ness becomes an "it." The mind tries desperately to hold onto "it," but this "it" is now only an idea, a memory, something dead. In this very effort to hold onto "it," the spacious freedom of it-less-ness *seems* to evaporate. The mind thinks, "I had it, but I lost it," and begins trying to get "it" back.

So we're at work, or in traffic, or at home, and the mind compares the *thought* of what is (not the actual present *experiencing* itself, but the mind's *idea* of it, the interpretation, the storyline) to the *memory* of this other experience, and the memory seems better. The mind tries to get rid of what it thinks is in the way: thoughts, tension, noise, whatever it might be. It tries to remember and repeat the steps it imagines it went through before to get to the other experience. It is a movement full of ambition, seeking a future attainment, resisting what actually is.

That very movement is the agitation that creates the illusion of bondage. That movement is doomed to failure, because the future never arrives, and *everything* that can be acquired will eventually be lost. No *experience* is permanent. Awareness is already here, containing the noise and agitation of efforting, unharmed by any of it. We need only see the futility of the effort, and turn attention to what is. When we stop trying to achieve what we think would be better, there is peace. That doesn't mean not doing anything; it means not seeking or being attached to *results*.

Awakening is about giving up the ground, as we do every night when we fall asleep, or finally, at the moment of death. We give up all our ambitions, all our worries, all our efforts. We give up the whole story of me, and we simply relax. We surrender. We allow ourselves to be swallowed. We allow ourselves to not exist. This is liberation.

The Birthday Party

It is Kyle's birthday, Toni's husband of fifty years who died last fall after a long and debilitating illness. Toni has invited all of us who are around now to her home on this Sunday afternoon at the end of April for a get together, a kind of informal memorial celebration. Monika, George, Martin, Heinrich, Bob Kenilworth, and myself are the guests. A candle is burning in the window when we arrive. Toni has tears in her eyes—she has just been on the phone with her son Remo. Monika has brought flowers, and a rhubarb cake she has made, sweetened with maple syrup. Toni serves fine coffee and black tea from Germany and a delicate peach sherbet along with the cake. We sit at the dining room table. The fine china cups are from Inga, Heinrich's wife and Toni's friend, who died of cancer. Inga left them to Toni. They are very simple, very round, very spacious, exquisite white teacups into which Toni pours the steaming hot coffee or tea.

It is a simple afternoon. Nothing spectacular happens. And yet, it feels as if everything is changed by it. Toni is full of delight. She shows pictures of Kyle, of my going away party when I left staff, of the grand-children. Her house feels deeply peaceful. I look out the glass doors into the vast open spaces of the landscape outside. Everything inside is arranged with such beauty and taste. The quiet and silent presence of the life that Toni lives here, and Kyle's passing that happened here, all permeates the place with peace and stillness. We all absorb it.

I am left in a deep place. Enlightened. Awake. Complete.

Weather

A week later I have several days and nights of fingerbiting. The mind is tangled in worried loops like a rat on a treadmill. Feelings of grief and terror sweep through the body. It rains for days on end. My fingers are bleeding. And then a friend stops by the cabin for tea in the late after-noon, and his presence is so gentle that my heart opens, and tears come, and everything is washed clean.

At dusk I am walking through the woods. It is raining lightly. The air is humid and fragrant. The peepers are chanting. A great blue heron flies very low right over my head.

Back at my cabin in the dark, the night's final blessing: the owl comes to visit. She is very close, closer to the cabin than she has ever been, hoot-ing in the darkness for a long time. I sit on the porch, listening. Rain is falling harder now, splashing, trickling, popping, rushing, and the owl is hooting.

Merton in his hermitage, thirty-five years ago, wrote these words: "Perhaps I have an obligation to preserve the stillness, the silence, the poverty, the virginal point of pure nothingness which is at the center of all other loves." *(Day of A Stranger)*

The next morning, the sky is empty and blue. For the first time, I have all my windows open and the heat off. I am barefoot, wearing shorts and a T-shirt. It is glorious. I feel very close to what is truly sacred out here in the woods. There is a conversion happening, here where life is deep and simple.

The trees are greening; the woods are changing overnight into summer. The trees in the north field have burst into blossom, the trillium and the May Apples are blooming in the woods. It's warm and humid, almost hot. A week ago the windows were closed, and I was snuggled under several blankets and a down comforter.

Suddenly I am no longer alone in the cabin. Gnats, mosquitoes, spiders, ants, and wasps have joined me. Everything is teeming with life, and I hear wind rustling the green leaves outside. The universe is croaking, humming, singing, buzzing. Everything is alive and growing. Large beetles pelt the windows at night like rain.

A thin crescent moon hangs in the sky, and at dusk a line of deer pass single file in front of the cabin only a few feet away, almost completely invisible in the gathering darkness, their feet crunching the dried leaves on the forest floor.

In the woods at dusk I find the disconnected jawbones of a raccoon, top and bottom, with the teeth in place. Nothing else remains. Not a trace. Suddenly I hear the owl, very close. She flies over me and lands just above my head on a branch. I gaze up; she gazes down. We commune like this for some time, a bat zigzagging back and forth between us, and then I move on. The owl follows me. She lands directly over my head again and cries out. This continues for some time, the owl following me, the two of us gazing at one another in the darkness, the song of the thrushes.

In the morning, swallowtail butterflies dart back and forth through the air. The tree by the pond has burst into white blossoms. I see the turtle, asleep in the cattails where the blackbirds are nesting.

Again there is rain and cold and darkness for days on end. And then sunlight, everything sparkling with light and happiness. And in the inner world, the same process: darkness that seems unbearable, and then clearings where there is only space and pure awareness. And then the darkness again. And the longing for the light to stay permanently, and for there to be no more darkness.

Can the inner weather be seen as impersonally as the outer weather, or do we imagine that the inner weather is my doing: my fault or my triumph?

The Beauty of Subtraction

Yesterday, I deleted everything I had written from my computer and my zip disk. I needed to make space for the unknown.

Immediately, I feel enormous energy, relief and freedom.

The greatest gift anyone ever gave me was nothing at all. Merton gave me this gift years ago when I read of his life in his hermitage, which he saw as a deliberately irrelevant, useless, extraneous life, a life given completely to "the silence, the poverty, the virginal point of pure nothingness." Zen gave me this gift of empty space, of silence. Toni gave me this gift. Springwater gives me this. Must we rush to quickly fill it up, to do something, to produce some turd? I am so tired of endlessly rushing to fill up the silence.

> *Do not worry about your life...Consider the lilies of the*
> *field....Strive first for the Kingdom of God and all these things*
> *will be given to you as well....Where your treasure is, there*
> *your heart will be also.*
>
> JESUS

Can we trust this? I want to find out.

Last Days in the Cabin

Endless days of rain and cold and darkness begin to get me down. I am resisting the damp cold, wanting the sun to shine. Then I go out into it, walking for hours in the wet woods, and it is beautiful beyond all words: the wet leaves, the wet bark, the steamy air. When we stop resisting and wanting *what is* to be different, we see only beauty. Again and again I learn this lesson.

The bird is sitting on her eggs in the nest by the outhouse door. Her head pops up occasionally to watch me come and go. Life is definitely not fair. Some baby birds get eaten, some don't. Some people live as bestselling authors, or as CEOs of successful corporate ventures, or as revered gurus. Other people live as child molesters, mental patients, battered wives, junkies, or convicts on death row. If you had a choice, which life would you pick? Do we have a choice?

The first fireflies are blinking in the dark fields at night. What huge joy fills me each time: the first peepers, the first frog, the first wood thrush, the first firefly. These simple delights, they cost nothing, and they fill my heart with boundless joy.

Today is warm. The sky is blue. Here you do not take such miracles as sunlight for granted! It is my last day in the cabin. I am packing up to leave. By late afternoon, the sun is slipping in and out of the clouds. The windows are open, but it is cool. A fly is buzzing. A cardinal is singing.

Together in the House

Life in the house, in the community, is far more difficult than life in the cabin, in solitude. A month goes by without a moment to write. I am exhausted, blown apart, broken open. The ground beneath my feet fell away. There was nowhere to stand, nothing to grasp.

It was a difficult summer. There was intense questioning going on about how Springwater was functioning. As always, I was right in the middle of the fray, full of ideas and opinions. There were endless meetings, conversations, talks, arguments, misunderstandings and reconciliations. I cried all summer. I cried deeply, uncontrollably. I fell into people's arms and wept.

On my last visit to Springwater, every time I talked of love, Toni would grill me, what did I mean by love? This summer, on her sofa, I cried, and we held hands. "All my life," I said to her, "I have searched for perfection, and really that just means what I want. And now I see, the only perfection is right here, as it is. It's all about opening the heart." Yes, Toni said, yes, yes, yes. Because it was *coming from my heart* this time. She was overjoyed when I said she was no longer my authority.

Driving to Rochester for a haircut two days before my scheduled departure, I saw vultures sitting on the body of a deer, freshly dead, lying on its side in a field.

Toni and I went down a dark hole together that evening. It was an old argument, Toni saying she has no power, me saying she does. I am in the woods afterward, full of grief and anger and the tight knot in my heart, thinking I'm done with Toni, and she meanwhile is at the pond searching for me, and the next morning she calls me, and I'm deeply touched that she cares and startled by my own lack of faith. We have a healing talk. I pack up my room and then walk alone into the north field at dusk. The wood thrush is singing. A stag in the tall grass leaps away. Two does and a fawn trot across the path. The dark wind enfolds me. I stand at the rim of dark green trees, looking down the magnificent empty path through the tall grasses, the last light dying in the sky. My heart is full of tears.

I have the sense that something has shifted, that I will not be returning to Springwater in quite the same way ever again. My life has been intricately bound up with this place, this community, and this way of working for a very long time now. I have long imagined myself ending up here again some day, perhaps being one of the people who carries on after Toni is gone. Toni is dear to my heart. I respect her enormously. She has been my primary teacher and is my friend. Yet something has changed.

I am no longer attracted to long silent retreats and motionless timed sittings. It all feels too structured, too formal, too serious in some way. Several times Toni has expressed reservations about spiritual teachers who joke too much, questioning whether there can be real presence when people are laughing that much. Yet I have found humor enormously liberating. I wonder, is there a subtle separation being reinforced here at Springwater between "presence" and everything else?

Toni's work is about shining the light of awareness on stories, thoughts, images and beliefs. It is about waking up to bare being. It is about seeing through the illusion of the separate self. The practice, though Toni would never call it that, is bare attention, silent sitting, open listening.

It seems to me that Advaita takes a step beyond this. In Advaita, there is no practice, not even the subtlest kind, and no attention or energy is given to the apparent human drama. All of that is seen to be merely a passing show, a dream that arises in Pure Awareness, like a wave arises in the ocean. The wave isn't going anywhere and is never really separate from the ocean. Likewise, our apparent human life isn't going anywhere, and "we" are never really separate from the unnamable vastness. In Advaita, some last trace of effort is erased. There is no "work of this moment" to be done. There is simply the recognition that everything already *is* whole and complete, and could not be otherwise. There is no need to be in *any* particular state of consciousness. The seriousness of the whole spiritual endeavor is gone.

Toni would question where all those words are coming from. Is it philosophy or is it direct experience? Toni always brings me back to the simplicity of this moment: the *actuality* of enlightenment! Advaita, *when I'm just slightly misconstruing it*, can easily get me all snarled up in seeking "final enlightenment" as a future event.

Sometimes it seems Toni and Advaita are just different expressions of the same essential understanding. At other times, the difference seems more fundamental, and I wonder if Springwater is going to be disappearing behind me as things do in this life.

When I first arrived here in 1988, coming from the world of traditional Zen, this place seemed radical and open, and in the most essential ways it still does. But now, after being in the satsang world and doing my own meetings for several years, this place also seems like a Zen center in many ways, bound by a tradition and form that is no longer my way.

By the end of the summer, it was clear to me that I don't need to change Toni or Springwater. I just need to let go of the place and go do my own thing. I'm on my own. And right now, that feels both appropriate and essential.

I pack everything into my car one last time and hit the road to Chicago. I've pretty much made the decision to live in the Midwest, somewhere near Chicago. I'll spend some time with Mom and look around for where that might be.

Chicago: The Mother, The Root-Ground, The Heartland

I'm back in my mother's highrise, utterly exhausted from my summer in Springwater. Not many people can understand why someone would be exhausted after spending the summer at a meditation retreat center in the countryside. People have very romantic ideas about what life is like at such a place.

After a week of rest and recuperation, I'm still exhausted, but I begin looking for where I might live. I check out Madison, Wisconsin and Iowa City, Iowa, two nearby places that seem quieter, slower, smaller, more my speed. But finally I decide on Chicago itself. I begin searching for an apartment.

Internally, the ground beneath my feet continues to crumble and dissolve. I am cast back again and again into not knowing. Baby sea turtles hatch on the beach and must make it to the sea. Some make it and some do not. It is all part of the biological flow, those that make it and those that don't. When I am identified with this apparently separate individual bodymind, then I am afraid I'll be one of those turtles who doesn't make it. I'll die on the beach. My life will be down the drain. This is a tragedy only to the illusory ego, not to Life Itself. Life Itself is an experiment, a play, an unfolding process of discovery and exploration, with forms constantly being created and destroyed. Permanence is not in the forms. There are many failed experiments, many discards, tragic only from the egoic point of view.

I think of that movie, *Close Encounters of the Third Kind*, where all these people were being called, and they kept feeling attracted to this shape, and this one man kept making the shape with his mashed potatoes on his dinner plate. It turned out it was a mountain, a place where the beings from outer space would be, to which these people were being mysteriously drawn. But the people had no idea why they were feeling compelled to play with their mashed potatoes. Their families thought they were losing their minds.

We see a dim shape, we *feel* it, we're not sure what it is. We're being drawn by something we cannot know. I'm being drawn by something I cannot explain or even understand. I might be a discard, a failed experiment, someone who never makes it to the space ship, a baby turtle dried up in the sand. Or I might be the new. It doesn't matter either way. We are swept along, used, used up. Sacrificed. Swallowed.

⁓

Was the cabin in the woods a dream? Here there are non-stop cars, trucks, traffic, sirens, horns, construction noises, screeching brakes, yelling people, the annual air show, fighter planes streaking through the sky. Everything is concrete and steel and fumes. I am exhausted, over-stimulated.

Mom and I walk to the conservatory in the park. We walk very slowly, which is the only way my mother walks now. She holds my arm for support. We enter the conservatory and move through ferns, orchids, succulents. We walk arm in arm through the steamy humid rooms, admiring awesome, fragile beauty. My mother is a lover of plants. Her apartment is full of plants. She talks to her plants. She bends over one of the orchids now and touches it.

Mom says she's glad I'm coming to live here, and she hopes we can be together at the end. Mostly she is so loveable, but occasionally she infuriates me, and occasionally I infuriate her. She is so totally unlike me in some ways. And who can push your buttons like your mother? But we seem to find our way through the rough spots fairly quickly and gracefully. We both know our remaining time together is short, too precious to waste.

⁓

I found an apartment and signed a lease. I call Adele to tell her. I begin sobbing on the phone.

The night before I leave Chicago, in this already fragile state of mind, a letter comes from my friend Betsy at Springwater cataloging all my faults in great detail. I feel myself bristling, beginning to defend myself in my mind against the charges, some of which are so totally untrue. It's like being punched in the stomach when I'm already down. How could she do something so totally insensitive? Eckhart Tolle's words come back to me: *If you're defensive, you're defending an illusion.*

If you're going for broke, the deepest truth is all there really is.

Packing Up

On the flight back to California, I was seated next to the abbot of the San Francisco Zen Center. Now I am back at Adele's, my home for these last four years, scheduled to fly back to Chicago in a month. Between now and then I have to hire movers, pack up my life, and say my goodbyes to California and all my friends here.

I feel like I am going out into the desert, metaphorically speaking, by moving to Chicago. I am leaving home, going to a strange land, a land without gurus, the land of my childhood, where everyone has now grown old. Sometimes I feel terror, sometimes grief, and deep down, a sense that all is well, that this is exactly the right step to be taking.

⚜

I visited my friend Jarvis Masters in San Quentin. He is an African-American Buddhist writer living on death row who has transformed in prison from a violent young man into an extraordinary being. He lives under conditions that are unimaginable and has since he was arrested as a teenager for armed robbery. He is now almost forty, I realize. His seemingly endless appeal process continues, and I pray that his life will be spared by some higher court, but the truth is that he may eventually be executed. It is unfathomable to me to think that the State of California would deliberately kill this man. He is truly a beautiful person. I began corresponding with him over a decade ago when I learned of his case and heard that he was participating in a retreat with Toni Packer that I was on. Jarvis was keeping silence and following the retreat schedule as best he could in his cell. He took up meditation while in prison, and considers Toni his first teacher. I was moved by his story and by the transformation that had occurred in his life. Jarvis also began writing while in prison, and his first book, *Finding Freedom*, was published in 1997. He practices Tibetan Buddhism, and his primary teacher, Chagdud Tulku Rinpoche, has visited him in San Quentin, as have a number of other Buddhist teachers including Pema Chodron. I have had the privilege of visiting Jarvis a handful of times in the years since we began corresponding.

The other visitors at San Quentin are mostly women and children visiting husbands, fathers, brothers, and sons in prison. Many drive for miles to get here, women with multiple little children in tow. We all stand in line for a long time. We are allowed to have a few dollars, a few keys and our ID on us, nothing else. We are searched and inspected. Women whose dresses are too short are turned away. We pass through many gates and doors that close and lock behind us. Finally we reach the high security visiting room. We surrender our ID and keys to the guard at the last door.

The room has a long row of telephones, spaced only a few feet apart. Each prisoner is brought to a cell on the other side of the glass. The glass is thick and scratched. The prisoner is brought into the cell in handcuffs. After being locked in the cell, he backs up to the bars, and the guard removes the cuffs. They will be put back on in the same fashion before the door is re-opened. The telephones are black and they weigh about three pounds. They are ancient. My arm grows tired and then painful holding it. You can hear the conversations on either side of you. They can hear you. You have exactly one hour. Armed guards stand behind you. You are face to face and only inches apart on opposite sides of the glass, talking through these black telephones. It is oddly intimate (much closer than you'd normally be to a friend you were talking to), and oddly separate (the glass, the telephones, the guards). Nothing is private.

Imagine what it would be like to have your only contact with your spouse or your father or your child occurring in this manner. Imagine the pressure, the difficult emotions that could flare up without hope of resolution, the restlessness and upset of the children, the different forces pulling on the mother. I can only begin to imagine it. But here I am, visiting once again with this beautiful being, face to face. And then I am released back into the sunshine, walking along the sparkling water.

San Quentin sits right on the Bay, at the edge of the water, in the shadow of Mt. Tamalpayas, but Jarvis has seen neither. He has never walked in the woods or on a beach. He grew up in an inner city household of drugs and violence. He was in San Quentin before he ever had a chance. He is accused of being part of a conspiracy to murder a prison guard years ago. They know he didn't kill the guard, because he was locked up in his cell on another tier at the time, and they know who did it. That man got life without parole from a different jury. Jarvis got death.

❧

I went to satsangs with several different teachers while I was in the Bay Area, soaking up as much spiritual juice as I could before I left for Chicago. As it turned out, it was a huge blessing that Chicago was off the guru-circuit. The spiritual desert was exactly what I needed. But at this moment, it felt a little like I was about to step into an abyss.

I met Tony Parsons, not to be confused with Toni Packer, at two local events he did. He's this delightfully ordinary fellow from England, probably in his late sixties, with a roguish and irreverent sense of fun, who says there is absolutely nothing to do and nowhere to go. He transmits the sense that absolutely *everything* is okay just as it is. His eyes twinkled, and he gave me a kiss and told me it was obvious that I was "about to pop." And indeed, I felt like the last traces of illusion were dissolving in his presence. Right there on the spot, I signed up for his retreat this coming spring in California. I purchased an airline ticket. Knowing that I would be back so soon made it less heartbreaking to leave all my friends.

There is something wonderful that happens in the presence of someone who is clear and awake, and in the company of others where that space is opening up. There is an undeniable energy that happens when people gather together in that way. My heart was attracted to these gatherings like a hummingbird to a flower. But at the same time, I knew that this energy was not dependent on anything. Telling myself the familiar story that I'm just about to pop, that I need another retreat to make that happen, that Tony has something I don't, all of this felt like the very lifeline that kept the illusion of bondage alive. In fact, it *was* the illusion. Still, it seemed irresistible at that moment.

Finally everything I own is in cardboard boxes except the furniture. On a rainy morning, the movers load it all into a truck and drive away. Two days later I say goodbye to Adele, load my suitcase into the rental car, and drive to the San Francisco airport where I board my flight to Chicago.

Homecoming

The Heart Land

It is a balmy October night when I arrive in Chicago to stay. The trees are ablaze with color. A few weeks later the movers arrive, and my new apartment is piled with boxes. The fiery autumn colors give way gradually to bare branches and the first snowfall.

After I got to Chicago, I began to wish I wasn't going on this trip to California to see Tony Parsons. I felt so happy just to be in my new home. I was tired of travelling. I felt quiet and settled in a way I never had in my life. I didn't really feel any desire or need to go on a retreat with Tony. I began to think seriously of canceling the trip.

I am on my own at last. I have come home.

No Escape

It was forty-below here last night; my windows were coated with solid sheets of ice, the inside of the windows that is, making trees and sky totally invisible. The branches of the two locust trees that are right outside my windows were bathed in red light at sunrise; the clouds were on fire. I sat here in my bliss chair in my nice warm tree house and watched. My bliss chair is a big leather armchair that faces the windows.

Now the sun is out and the windows have almost completely melted. The sun returns, a little more each day. I am doing a great deal of absolutely nothing, watching the smoke rise up from chimneys and blow across the sky.

❧

The snowdrifts in the street are shoulder-high. Chicago is a magical white wonderland. Something deep inside is settled and knows it is home. I listened to an old tape of Joko recently, and she says: "There's nothing that needs to be cured, not when we know who we are, not when we're home." That idea that something needs to be fixed *is* our mistaken belief, the root of our suffering. The search *is* the suffering. As Mel put it to me long ago: "Our suffering is believing there's a way out." I've stopped looking for a way out.

❧

Two mourning doves have been roosting in the tree all afternoon. At sundown they get up, stretch, ruffle their feathers, gaze around. One is further out on the branch. He walks back up the branch to his mate. They stand face to face in momentary communion. Then both turn to face the West, and at the same exact moment take flight together.

It grew dark, and I canceled out of the Tony Parson's retreat.

A heaviness lurked around me when I woke up. I recognized it. It was a familiar claustrophobia, the sense of being stuck here, "here" in a very generic sense. I relaxed into it, opened, saw through it. The problem evaporated. I evaporated. The sun came out in the winter sky. Amazing back-lit white clouds drifted past my window. A vacuum cleaner hummed. And I knew I am always home.

I walked in the park enjoying the sunlight on the snow.

Next morning, I wake up again to depression, to the lurking sense (and sensation) of something unbearable and lonely. I don't run from it but just let it be. This is so simple, but it has taken years to allow this to happen. When these scary feelings come, the compulsion to find a way out is so strong. Immediately the mind begins scanning for salvation: a book, a drink, a guru, *something*. Just to stand still and completely allow it to be as it is, to let it unfold itself with no agenda at all, no attempt to manipulate or fix—it's so simple. It's amazing how easy it is. And it's amazing how the terrible specter that had been imagined dissolves in the light.

Rage

Next thing I know I am filled with rage, first over the new Bush administration, his cabinet appointees, the whole thing, and then over my loud neighbor who plays her radio all night, then over the incompetent phone company that can't fix my line correctly. Content doesn't even matter; it feels like a primal rage. For awhile last night and this morning, there was deep presence, spaciousness and love. But then the rage came again. I stormed around my apartment cursing under my breath. Now, I feel tired and nauseated. I want to cry, but it hasn't come out yet. I start biting my fingers again.

My neighbor next door is nearly deaf, and she plays her radio all night long at very loud volume, right on the other side of my bedroom wall. She listens to a frenetic talk show that is non-stop, bullet-fast talk, literally all night long. I hear every single word. Most of the talk has been about the disputed presidential election, and now it's all about Bush, the new president-elect. I haven't slept much since I moved in. I tried writing her a nice note on a beautiful card. She didn't respond. I can't sleep with earplugs, but I've tried pillows on top of my head. I still hear the radio, and I can't breathe. The maintenance man helped me nail rugs to my wall to buffer the sound, and he talked to her. She denied playing the radio. Nothing worked. I never thought I'd be happy for traffic noise, but here I'm always happy when it's not too cold or windy or snowy to leave open a window, because the traffic noise helps to drown out the words, and then I can sleep. Some nights are worse than others. Lately it's been especially bad. I feel rage at my neighbor. I bite my fingers.

This morning I have a headache. I'm tired. I want to cry. But the sun is out. And I'm still alive. I hear the doves cooing. They've been in the tree all morning, in falling snow. Seeing them, my heart opens.

One night, after being in vast empty space, I went to bed fully enlightened. I was in bliss. I was just drifting off to sleep when the radio went on, even louder than usual. I snapped. I began pounding on the walls. My neighbor pounded back. I screamed "SHUT UP!"

The next morning I felt terrible. I wrote her an apology. No reply. I feel like I'm walking over hot coals, the burning heart land.

No Pop: Zero

For a long time there's been this recurring tendency to compare my story about my experience to other people's stories about their experience, and then imagine that there are bigger awakenings to be had. Finally, here in my living room in Chicago, it has become so obvious and clear that this very process of comparing and evaluating and seeking something bigger *is* the apparent obstruction, *is* the me-structure. I could have *said* all of that five years ago, but now it is crystal clear in a way that is irrevocable and obvious. If that sounds like a "pop," believe me, it wasn't! There was no pop. No bang. No moment of truth. Zero.

It's just clear as can be: here is *all* there is. There is nothing bigger, except in the mind, in imagination. The seeking for something else has vanished. I don't seem to care if someone else has had a bigger bang. The very idea seems ludicrous.

Seeking and comparison have stopped before and then come back again. So maybe tomorrow I will be booking myself into another retreat with yet another guru. I really don't know. But what's new is that now it doesn't seem to matter in the least one way or the other. Before, when the seeking and the doubt would abate, there was always a fear that it might return. Now I'm not afraid of that possibility. Let it come, if it does.

❦

I watched the sun set from my bliss chair. Clouds turned pink. Birds flew past the window. Airplanes flew past. Clouds turned blue. Snow fell furiously, big snowflakes. The ground is covered in white again. Night has come.

The anger is gone. It might reappear, or maybe it won't. It was coming in waves. Fingerbiting had been completely gone for longer than ever before, but it came back with the anger and is still happening. I do notice that the habit is going away for longer and longer periods and that it comes back less severely when it does. Something is shifting. Right now, I feel only tenderness toward my neighbor. I am finding an increasing acceptance of whatever shows up: biting, no biting, enlightenment, delusion, whatever it is.

I write when the urge comes and don't force it otherwise. It may eventually become a book, or maybe not. It doesn't matter to me either way.

The windows were covered with ice again last night, and temperatures went below zero. But today the sun is out, snow is melting off the lawns, and the trees have that reddish tint that they get in the spring. I often hear a cardinal and once saw it, a streak of red, flying past my window. Another time I saw the female perched in my tree.

I feel groundless and grounded. I sit happily in my bliss chair and watch out my windows: the smoke, the birds, the planes, the empty sky.

Beginning of Spring

I'm down with some terrible flu. I haven't been this sick in years. Last night I lifted the window shade to see how much snow there was and instead saw the full moon. The thick clouds opened at that very moment.

Last week it felt like spring was coming. The snow had melted away and the trees were just starting to bud, so when I looked out the window this morning and saw snow on the ground again and another gray day, it was too much. It all began to get to me. Now it is raining, sleeting, and the wind is howling. And then the sun is out and everything is calm. Geese fly over, and again spring is in the air.

Life seems to be doing something (amusing itself, teaching itself, who knows what) through all of us, and apparently our foibles, addictions, dependencies, anxieties, depressions, and confusions are all part of the show, along with the awakenings. None of it is really "ours". I am often reminded of Gertrude Stein's last words on her deathbed: *All my life I've searched for the answers, but what was the question?*

~&

The snow is melted off the south side of the street but remains on the north side. It is half winter, half spring. A tiny gray cloud moves slowly across the sky. A moment ago snow was pouring down in huge flakes, blowing wildly in all directions, even falling upwards, whirling around. Now there are just a few lingering flurries. In the distance I hear the train whistle, and the voices of children in the street.

When my mother told me she'd given up chocolate for Lent, it struck me as an interesting practice, to remove something from your life that you normally use a lot, not forever but for a limited period of time. So I decided to give up spiritual books for Lent. The first day felt like withdrawal. Then it became a huge relief. It feels like growing up.

~&

I was terribly sad this evening, and I turned off the computer, sat down in my bliss chair, stopped resisting the sadness, and lo and behold, as soon as I stopped resisting it, it wasn't there anymore!

I had a deep and quiet evening and a deep sleep, in which I dreamed I went to live forever at Springwater. I woke up to find everything white again and snow falling everywhere, another blizzard.

So, there are openings and there are closings. The closings pass when they come and so do the openings! Today flowers are blooming in the melting snow.

Zelda

My friend Zelda is telling me on the phone about how she was in the grocery store in Berkeley shopping, and she meets this woman—a stranger, from Persia—at the lettuce, and they begin to talk as they sift through the lettuce leaves with their hands. The woman is dark-skinned and heavily made-up, and she tells Zelda that she is a poet. Zelda is thrilled. I can picture Zelda, the aliveness of her face, the way she would smile like a Sufi at the Tavern. The woman recites a poem for her. Zelda reads it to me on the phone.

Later in our conversation, Zelda tells me, "I've never had a spiritual experience."

This is a woman who kisses trees, who brings home poems with the lettuce, who writes love letters to her friends, who talks to squirrels. This is a woman who hosted my weekly meetings and occasional daylong retreats in her home, welcoming everyone with flowers and blankets and laughter. This is a woman who sang operas professionally, a woman with big hands and big feet and bright red lips, a woman whose heart radiates God. This is my dearest of friends. She *is* a spiritual experience, and she imagines that she has never had one, that she's probably too old, that it's too late now.

She sits there utterly awake—radiant and radiating light, laughter bubbling up out of her heart, and tells people she's never had a spiritual experience. She can say it with total deadpan. She believes it! It's absurd!

And this is what we all do! This is what happens to us when we believe and get lost in the mind and what it tells us. We are confused by *thinking*, which tells us we're too old, we're not getting it. It's what happens to us in this culture of spiritual experiences and achievements. We keep looking for the experience somebody else described, and missing the aliveness that is right here now.

But before all these stories (I've got it, I'll never get it), before any word that tries to capture the un-capturable, before it even occurs to us to think that there's something to get or something missing or someone to get it—in that first virginal instant of simply being here—everything *is*.

It is *this* that requires no thought to understand, no effort to get, no path to come to. It is utterly inescapable, utterly obvious, here right now.

From *this* place, life is a miracle. *Everything* is sacred.

Once the mind gets tangled in trying to get it, trying to find it, trying to evaluate whether it has it—life is a knot, a mess, a torture. Nothing is sacred, because nothing is seen. We're busy looking for something else.

Enlightenment is *what is*.

＊

I'm sitting in my bliss chair, the late afternoon light is turning the branches of the big trees out front a beautiful dark golden orange, and suddenly a big plump robin lands on the branch right in front of my window, red breast glowing in the orange light, the first robin I've seen this spring. My heart leaps with joy. It's spring!

Meeting My Neighbor

Early one Saturday morning, in the lobby of my building, I meet my next door neighbor, Mrs. Szostkowski, the woman who plays her radio all night long. She is probably about eighty, originally from Poland. After the night I exploded and pounded on the wall, the maintenance man got the landlord involved. Eventually, through the landlord's intervention, my neighbor turned the volume down to a level where I don't hear the words, at least most of the time, and I can sleep. It has improved my life greatly. But the maintenance man has told me that ever since my first note to her, my neighbor has hated me, so I've had an uncomfortable sense of bad vibes.

More recently, several things have led me to suspect that my neighbor may not fully realize what she's doing. This has given me more compassion for her than when I thought she was deliberately being inconsiderate and deceitful. I rarely see her, but when I first moved in, I was struck by her lovely smile. I kept hoping that one day I would run into her in the hall, and everything would be resolved in a face-to-face encounter.

This morning it finally happened. I'd been out for an early morning walk, and as I come into the lobby, there she is. There is no one else around.

I wave at her, and she waves back happily.

"Who is this smiling at me so early?" she asks.

"It's Joan, your neighbor."

"My neighbor?"

By this time we are face to face, beaming at each other, and she is trying to place me. She puts her hand on my cheek.

"Joan in 413, the one who wrote you the notes," I say.

"413?" She's trying to figure it out, trying to make me someone she likes, because obviously she likes me.

Finally she gets it. "Oh, you're the one I don't like! The one who wrote me the notes." But by this time she has been smiling at me, placing her hand affectionately on my heart and on my cheek.

We talk more. She notices my missing arm and tells me about her struggles with cancer and macular degeneration.

"The landlord told me you were very nice," she says, "but I told him, 'She attacks my wall...how can she be nice!?'" My neighbor's palm is on my heart as she speaks.

We laugh together.

A month later I run into her again, and she has no idea who I am.

Doing & Not Doing

To work in the world is hard, to refrain from all unnecessary work is even harder.

NISARGADATTA

Spring is back. Until I feel snowflakes hitting me as I type, blowing in the window. Now it is snowing so hard I can't see the other side of the street.

Snow is everywhere. It has a kind of mad energy—these last spring snow storms—the flakes are huge and blow in all directions, up and down and sideways. I actually love it, as sick as I am of snow, and as ready as I am for spring.

I feel little ambition to do anything more than be quiet, sit in my armchair as much as possible, watch the birds and the clouds, talk to the folks in my building when we pass in the halls, visit my mother, nothing much. I sometimes have the *thought* that I should be doing something more. But nothing seems to come. Any movement that starts to arise toward something else simply doesn't feel genuine. It drops away, and I just keep sitting quietly, watching the clouds.

At some point, the need for money will force my hand, since sitting in my bliss chair doesn't pay the bills. Then again, maybe it does, since I seem to be quite well supported by life at the moment, and in fact, always have been. It just feels a little uncertain and unpredictable! Once I got a fortune cookie that said, "You will be paid thousands of dollars daily for doing nothing."

The trick is to truly do nothing. It's harder than it sounds.

There is immense pressure from society to produce, to advance, to achieve, to accomplish, to perform. We are driven to "make something of ourselves," to "contribute to the world," to "be helpful," to "actualize our potential." Most people never even question this compulsion or the self-image that underlies and propels it. To do nothing goes against the grain; it's heresy. But there is actually great beauty in lying fallow, being quiet, especially as the world at large speeds up. As you see through the illusion of the entire movie, the game of achievement and success loses its meaning and its allure. You become increasingly aware of the empty hole we are always trying to fill, and you grow more willing to leave it alone or dive right into it. You see through the ideals about what *should* be happening and instead attend to what *is* happening. You allow action to emerge on its own, in its own good time, which is what happens anyway.

This morning in the locust tree, I saw a cardinal, a chickadee, and then a woodpecker. Along with the first blooming flowers, the boy birds have been chasing the girl birds, and the boy squirrels have been chasing the girl squirrels (there may be some deviants as well, it's hard to say).

The other day in a big puddle I saw many birds taking bathes. They seemed quite ecstatic. But this was all before the blizzard.

Now, we're back to winter.

One way or another, life does support us to do exactly what it wants us to do. Whether the money comes from a job, a generous friend, an inheritance, the sale of a manuscript, or a grant from the government, it is all coming from life itself.

I know that eventually some doing will emerge out of this not doing. And I can feel some fear of that, some holding back perhaps, because when you actually do something that you have imagined doing, the real thing is inevitably imperfect. It falls short of the imagined version, which was flawless. For the perfectionist mind, that is daunting. I had all kinds of doubts about writing my first book, then about publishing it, then about offering meetings. All of that worry turned out to be a joke.

There is something vital and alive that arises in actually *publishing* the book, *offering* the meetings, or *building* the retreat center. Possibilities unfold in the actual *doing* of something that cannot unfold by merely *imagining* it. The actuality creates venues for exchange, investigation, exploration, and realization. New elements come together. It's a kind of improvisational play that reveals life to itself, a play of Self-discovery. And the funny thing is that the apparent flaws and loose ends turn out to be a key part of the whole process, the grit that becomes the pearl.

We think that what we are doing is about "me" and "my life," but it is always about something much larger. It has long fascinated me how everything in my life that initially seemed like my own private and isolated experience turned out to be a social movement. When I was a child, I thought I was probably the only person in America attracted to Buddhism. I was sure I was the only girl who felt a resistance to the role I was supposed to play as a female. I was the only little girl I knew who wanted to wear pants and climb trees. And then, when I felt attracted to women, I knew I was *really* alone. A few short years later, there was a feminist movement, a Gay Liberation movement, and Buddhism was spreading across America like wild fire. I could give so many other examples. Our seemingly private attractions and problems are always a shared phenomenon. We just don't always know it. And when we don't know it, we can feel very alone.

Down to the Bones

I began to take an interest around this time in the Feldenkrais Method, a form of awareness through movement work that is very much about curiosity, interest, exploration, discovery, and above all, awareness. It works through the body, through the bones and the nervous system, below the level of the conscious, thinking mind, and it touches every aspect of our lives. You do a lot of rolling around on the floor.

From the usual point of view, my life these days could look fairly absurd. Rolling around on the floor doing a bunch of strange movements and sitting in my bliss chair watching birds and squirrels—how was all this going to result in my being able to pay the rent and put food on the table? Had I lost my mind? I sometimes wondered. But then, remembering the lilies of the field and the great mystery, I would relax and just keep rolling and sitting.

Baby Boss

At ninety-one, Mom insisted on getting web-TV for email, against my advice. She had never used a computer before, and it seemed to me that this would be no small challenge given that her eyesight is terrible, her hands shake like leaves in a windstorm, and her short-term memory is going rapidly out the window. For the first few days, I wondered if she'd be able to get it. I found it painful to watch my always-indomitable mother being defeated.

I found myself telling her how great she was doing while thinking to myself that she was going to fail. She kept snapping at me to shut up. I realized suddenly that this was a perfect mirror image of how she related to me as a child with one arm—the difficulty she must have felt seeing my vulnerability, watching me being frustrated by something—her fears that I wouldn't make it lurking under the always encouraging overt message—and the double-message that gave me, the craziness of it. And now it's all happening in reverse as she turns into the disabled one, and I become the caretaker.

I was wrong, too. She loves having email. She's firing off messages to people all over the world. She deletes a few by accident every now and again, and when she can't get it to do what she wants, she starts randomly pushing every button she can find on the TV remote. For weeks she had all her TV programs in Spanish, and neither of us could figure out how to get back to English. But somehow it all works out.

I sent her a card once that pictured a 1940's housewife shrunk down and seated in a high chair with a huge baby in a diaper towering over her. Mom loved it. Ever since then, she calls me Baby Boss. We talk openly about the role reversal and our different feelings. It's a dance, and we're doing it quite gracefully, although every now and then I step on her toes, and she barks at me. But that's okay. We joke about it and grow closer.

I call her every day and visit at least once a week. We go to parties and weddings. We celebrate holidays. We visit her old friend Charlotte and her other friend Jane, who has Alzheimer's and is in a nursing facility now. We go to the park together. Or we sit and talk in her apartment or mine.

Journey to Hell

Yesterday I stood in line for five hours at the Department of Motor Vehicles to get my Illinois driver's license.

"Welcome to Hell," the DMV-employee at the door said to me as I entered.

For years I have dreaded this moment whenever I contemplated the possibility of relocating to a new state and having to apply for a new driver's license. But in all these years, it had never once entered my mind that it might be *this* state. When I was first licensed to drive, it was here in Illinois, and they slapped all kinds of restrictions on me because of having one hand. California removed them all without my even asking. And now, here I was, back at the DMV in Illinois, fearing the worst.

As the line snaked and inched toward the counter, hour by hour, we all observed that there was one particular civil servant who hassled everyone he processed, and at full volume too, so the whole room could hear. Most people in line were immigrants, and this guy was especially grueling on those who failed to understand English. There was another older guy working further down behind the counter, a sweet Jewish-looking guy named Morris, who looked like a guru. I prayed that I would get Morris. We all prayed that we would not get the man who hassled everyone.

At the exact moment that I reached the front of the line, the man who hassled everyone went on lunch break. Morris waved me forward. I ran towards him in a state of near-ecstasy.

He smiled sweetly. He definitely saw my arm because I had it on the counter several times holding down papers I had to sign. Finally he asked, Did I have diabetes? No. Was I epileptic? No. Did I have any disability that might impair my ability to safely operate a motor vehicle? No. That is, after all, the truth. He smiled sweetly. I was sent on to the cashier.

I passed the written test, although by then, after five hours and no lunch, I wondered if I would be able to remember how many feet in front of the approaching vehicle you should lower your headlight beams, and how many months they can suspend your license for DUI. But, thank God, I remembered everything except the shape of the slow-moving vehicle sign. I passed.

"My God, you're still here," the woman who had welcomed me to hell said as I turned in my test. I was photographed. An Asian woman who had stood near me in line offered me a muffin as we sat on the blue plastic chairs awaiting our licenses.

And finally, they handed it to me: an unrestricted Illinois Drivers License. Happy and relieved, I headed home.

I am struck by how deeply we can be touched, and how much can be transmitted, by everyone we meet: the woman with the lovely sense of humor at the doorway to the DMV who welcomed me to hell, Morris the Guru who processed my application, the nameless man who hassled everyone (who was himself in such obvious pain, and in whose eyes I saw glimpses of love and humor), the stranger from Asia who offered me a muffin.

When the Senses Fail

My mother's hearing has been in steady decline for the last decade. Even with her hearing aids, she misses a great deal of what happens now. She pretends a lot. And she goes to things even if she can't hear them (lectures, plays, parties, whatever). She figures maybe she takes it all in on a subliminal level. The words are just froth on the surface of events. "Nothing is really all that important anyway," she tells me.

Sometimes, her hearing loss makes for some interesting conversations. One night, she and I are having dinner in a Japanese restaurant. A car with a loud booming stereo system passes outside in the street. The bass vibrates the whole restaurant. I see Mom adjusting her hearing aids.

"Did you hear that noise?" I ask.

She nods, still adjusting her hearing aids.

"It was coming from a car out in the street," I tell her.

"It's okay," she replies, "We have our umbrellas."

Another time Mom tells me she's going out with her friends Amy & Blanche. "I couldn't really hear what Amy said, so I'm not sure what we're doing, but we're going somewhere. They'll pick me up in the lobby at six o'clock." What will she wear if she doesn't even know where she's going? She doesn't give it a second thought. My mother proceeds blithely through life, without a worry, never doubting that everything will work out.

The Mysteries of Ecology, Economy, and Exchange

Start a huge, foolish, project,
like Noah.

It makes absolutely no
difference what people
think of you.

RUMI

There was a shift. I can't say when or how it happened. After a long period of lying fallow, doing nothing, not knowing what would emerge, or if anything ever would, there was a change. The book is pouring out of me. There is tremendous energy. I feel like I'm going down rapids. It's exhilarating. I'm thinking about offering meetings again.

The long winter is finally over. Oh, the miracle of those first tiny green leaves this morning. They weren't there the day before. And the little bells of the ice cream truck.

Here you don't take spring for granted. It is a miracle. You feel like falling to your knees and kissing the ground. Everyone is ecstatic. Temperatures have soared into the seventies. We're all running around in shorts & Hawaiian shirts. There is so much energy in the air and inside me. A huge full moon is rising over the playground on the adjacent corner; it is still light out; the streets are full of people. Exquisite birdsong fills the air along with the shrieks of children.

The grass is greening up; flowers are blooming. Mom and I went to the park and watched ducks.

Three squirrels are working very hard to build a nest in the tree right outside my window, but there are no leaves yet, and without leaves, the twigs they diligently snap off and carefully carry to the selected site simply fall to the ground. Every day they try a different crotch of the tree, and they work very hard, and every day the pile of twigs at the base of the tree gets bigger. It's a kind of Myth of Sisyphus operation, but fortunately their squirrel brain apparently lacks the complexity to find it upsetting. They just plug away. And when they've done enough for one day, they sleep blissfully in their new non-existent nest just a few feet from my window. One was dozing there this afternoon, a smile on his face as the wind gently rocked the tree branches.

There's a lesson in this, it seems to me. We humans are each given a task to do, and it comes to us in the form of an unmistakable urge to do something. Often our twigs fall to the ground. But our human brain is forever filled with ideas about what we think we are supposed to be accomplishing. We compare ourselves to others, to past memories, to some ideal picture. We feel despair, frustration, humiliation, rage, anguish, and defeat. A few metaphorical days like these squirrels are having, and we humans would be plunged into some form of suicidal or homicidal behavior.

But the squirrels just keep plugging away. They have no story, no self-image, no ideas about what they are supposed to accomplish. They're just snapping off twigs, maneuvering them up and down the branches and arranging them, they know not why. The sun is out, the breeze is blowing, the birds are singing, it's a lovely day.

The Kiss of the Beloved

No words can explain the color red, the blooming flowers in springtime, the green leaves wet with rain, the white clouds floating in the blue sky. You can't analyze a kiss or a dance; you can only dissolve in its mysterious currency. Every sound, every smell, every taste is holy: the song of the bird, the roar of the traffic, the hum of the vacuum cleaner.

The Kingdom of Heaven

I'm walking through the park one morning and two Jehovah's Witnesses come toward me, an older Black man and a younger one, both dressed in suits and carrying Bibles. The older one does all the talking.

"Have you read the Bible?" he asks me.

"Parts of it," I reply.

"Do you know what it says about the Kingdom of God?"

"It says the Kingdom of God is within."

"It says a new age is coming, the handicapped will be healed, there will be peace on earth, abundance for all. God's Kingdom is coming."

"It's here," I say.

The young man smiles.

"You don't believe in the future?" the old man asks me.

"This is it," I reply.

I wish them a good day and walk on. The young man is still smiling.

The Beauty of All-Consuming Fire

A ladybug lands on my window. I buy flowers and take them to Mom. We go for a walk. We see multitudes of butterflies. One lands on Mom. Good fortune.

The magnolia trees are blossoming. And the exquisite redbuds. It's eighty degrees outside and smells of warm earth. Yellow forsythia is everywhere. There is more and more green out the window.

A friend of mine in California has just been diagnosed with a very fast-moving cancer. Ella is in her sixties, a vibrant person whose life is in full bloom.

I feel sad and unsettled by the news. Then, out of nowhere, I feel a joy welling up. This morning, in the wild summer wind, I feel the beauty of Ella dying, of the earth dying, of everything and everyone dying. I feel the beauty of impermanence, of all-consuming fire. This morning I know that everything is grace. When we stop identifying with a limited form, there is no death. Death is a celebration.

The trees have exploded into green; tulips are blossoming. I hear the little bells of the ice cream vendor and the train whistle that I love. I see cardinals, and lately flickers. At the zoo in Lincoln Park, my friend David and I watched the pink flamingos. They moved in slow motion like a dream. In the park down the street baby Canada geese follow their mother, swimming behind her, waddling on the grass, little yellow fluff-balls sleeping in the sun. It is raining now, and two mourning doves are roosting on the wet green branches of my tree.

❧

Today, when I popped in on Mom, she briefly said hello, and then kept right on with her web-TV and after that leafed through a clothing catalog. Usually she's very happy to see me, but every now and then it's as if I am as familiar as the furniture. It's kind of sweet, being that familiar.

My friend Elaine tells me that her mother, who has Alzheimer's and is in a home in Georgia, simply hangs up on Elaine now right in the middle of Elaine's sentences if she is not interested in what Elaine is saying. Elaine takes it all so beautifully. She says it makes her laugh. She'll be saying something she thinks is so important, and then, click.

It's rather beautiful what happens as the social graces begin to slip away, and a kind of pure honesty takes over.

❧

The sky goes suddenly dark as I begin to write this, and it starts to rain. Last night, after my friend Ella in California had died, but before I learned the news, I had intense dreams. They were all about facing various unwanted things and letting go. In the first and most striking part of the dream, I was handling Ella's face, as a sculptor might handle clay. She was dead, and it was somewhat gruesome. The process in the dream was about letting go of all resistance. When I woke up, I got the word: she is gone. It is dark outside now, raining hard. Lightning flashes in the sky.

❧

Wordless in the wake of death, at the feet of old age, in the bloom of spring, sometimes there is deep peace, and sometimes I feel a sad, hollow feeling, and tears come into my eyes. I've been discovering the nearby nature areas: woods, oak savannas, tall cottonwood trees with their seeds blowing off. Today with Mom, we visited her best buddy of recent years in a nursing care facility. Jane used to live in Mom's building and the two of them did everything together, until Jane got Alzheimer's and had to go to the nursing home. We ate lunch off plastic trays: jello, rice custard, soup.

The locust tree out front is full of squirrels chasing each other around, squealing and racing up and down the branches. And there are little yellow birds, maybe warblers. They have appeared in exact synchronicity with the dangling yellow flowers on the tree, which offer perfect camouflage. They are visitors, migrating through.

Mom said today, "It's so wonderful to realize that nothing really matters! It's so freeing."

The News

Outside, the freezing desert night.
This other night inside grows warm, kindling.
Let the landscape be covered with thorny crust.
We have a soft garden in here.
The continents blasted,
cities and little towns, everything
become a scorched, blackened ball.

The news we hear is full of grief for that future,
but the real news inside here
is there's no news at all.

RUMI

When I moved to Chicago, I bought a television, my first ever. For many years I have hated television. I always wanted to get one of those bumper stickers that says "Smash Your Television." That's how I felt. But when I moved to Chicago, I bought a TV. I got it mainly for the VCR, or so I thought. I planned to watch spiritual videos. But then I began watching the news every night. The last time I really let the news into my life, I was overcome with righteous anger, and I became a radical leftist, determined to save the world. After I woke up from that dream, I shut the news out for many years. It was too painful. I didn't want to feel that grief and fury again or get caught up in the world drama. I didn't decide consciously to let it all back in again, but it began to happen after I bought the TV. I've noticed that there is no impulse anymore to save the world. Watching the nightly horrors, I rarely get upset the way I used to, and when I do, it doesn't last long. There is a kind of equanimity now, an acceptance that didn't used to be here. The news seems like a movie, a conjuring act by the newscasters with stories and emotions blowing past like wisps of cloud or smoke in the wind.

Next thing I knew, I started watching an occasional program, whatever I happened to tune into: *NYPD Blue, Friends, Will & Grace, Oprah, Nightline, Drew Carey, The Bachelor, Who Wants to Be a Millionaire?, ER, The West Wing,* whatever it might be. I was amazed by how much had changed in the almost four decades since I had last watched television with any kind of regularity. The news anchors used to be white men, every single one of them. Now they are every gender and race. And in the sitcoms, dramas and interview shows there are lesbians and gay men! The lesbians are having babies! There are even transsexuals! There are interracial couples and single parents! People get divorced; babies are born out of wedlock. Women are lawyers, doctors, cops. Black families live in mansions that they own. Heroes are complex and flawed, not all-perfect. The last time I watched TV with any real regularity, it was *Leave It to Beaver, Father Knows Best, I Love Lucy, The Jack Benny Show, The Lone Ranger,* and *Dr. Kildare.* It was another world. I had never heard of transsexuality. Or for that matter, ecology. Another thing has changed, too. It's strangely jarring at times to realize that the actor I find so attractive, the one I could happily imagine myself coupled up with, is young enough to be my daughter or son.

Before long I had a DVD player. Not only was I watching TV shows and the news; I was watching movies, too. It was as if I had rejoined the world after a long absence but with an entirely different perspective on the whole thing.

> *I go to the market place with my wine bottle and return home*
> *with my staff...*
> *I use no magic to extend my life;*
> *Now, before me, the dead trees become alive.*
>
> from the last Ox-Herding Picture, as rendered by Nyogen Senzaki
> and Paul Reps in Zen Flesh Zen Bones

Rolling on the Floor

After days of carrying twigs up and down the branches, the squirrels have finally succeeded in building a nest in the tree right outside my window. It has bits of paper and plastic in it, too. In the evening I watch them hanging out on the branches and then disappearing into their nest at twilight.

This morning a bird hovered at the window glass watching me type.

Rolling around on the floor in my Feldenkrais class clarifies why I have been less and less attracted in recent years to prolonged periods of motionless sitting. I have never felt so free, so out of my mind. I haven't sat on a cushion in months. It also clarifies why I am less and less attracted to verbal discussions. I love dropping out of the mind, out of the verbal realm altogether. It makes me wonder how I might organize meetings out of this emerging perspective. I'm just rolling around on the floor with the questions, and even the questions roll right on out the window.

We roll around doing funny movements, and somehow in the process life gets transformed. It is turning me upside down and inside out. I know less and less every day.

The Feldenkrais Method is not about being successful in the move-ments; rather, it is about learning from the inside out. Sometimes it's about learning how I react when I can't do the movement that is being described. The method is never about imitating or trying to duplicate an ideal. It is about listening to your own inner truth, to what is.

It's hot and muggy and sunny, going up into the nineties now. A pair of mourning doves has been roosting on the window ledge right outside my bedroom window. It even looked like they were going to build their nest there as they began arriving with twigs, but apparently they decided against it, and they moved the twigs they had gathered elsewhere. But they still roost there, right outside my window.

Latin music floats up from a passing car, firecrackers are popping, cicadas are humming, the train is whistling, the little bells of the icecream vendor are tinkling. There are fireflies at night. Winter seems oh so far away. It is green and steamy.

Oroborous

Studying Feldenkrais, I got the idea to exaggerate the movements involved in biting my fingers. When I felt like biting, I would bring my hand to my mouth and go through the motions of ripping a huge piece of flesh off one of my fingers with my teeth. I wouldn't actually be biting into my flesh at all, but I'd imagine that I was, and I'd go through the motions, exaggerating them greatly. I paid attention to what was pleasurable about it and to every detail and nuance of it. I discovered it was very pleasurable!

One time, I began to pretend that I was devouring my whole hand, and then my whole arm, and finally my whole body. There was nothing left! Except everything! I was everything and nothing. It was an ecstatic moment.

Sometimes when the biting happens, if there is total awareness, complete attention—no attempt at all to get rid of the biting or make it stop, no judgement of it, just complete attention—then it's an amazing thing. Biting is as beautiful as watching the doves or the sunset. It's just sensations, nothing more. It's empty of meaning. And in that total awareness, it ends. Effortlessly. It just stops. But it doesn't matter anymore either way.

Summer in Chicago

It's still early, but already sizzling. Traffic is streaming by in waves of sound. Indian music drifts up from the street. You can see the humidity in the air; it's so dense. It's exactly a year since I made the decision to move here.

They've issued heat warnings on the news for days now. Heat kills more people than earthquakes, floods, hurricanes, tornadoes, volcanoes, and all other weather disasters combined. One year in Chicago, over four hundred people died in a single week. The weatherman warns us to stay indoors and not go out. Everyone is asked to conserve power. Actually, I kind of enjoy the intense heat. It's a primal experience. You're reduced to the level of a plant. The mind can't function. You just sweat.

I was out past midnight last night at a wedding with Mom. I knew the bride when she was a child. The wedding itself was downtown in Grant Park, all of us seated in the blazing sun. After the wedding, they had hired double-decker tour buses to take the guests to the posh downtown hotel where the dinner was held. After an hour of cocktails, we were seated at tables in the ballroom where an elaborate multi-course dinner was served: salad, passion fruit sorbet, mushroom stuffed filet mignon, Chilean sea bass, vegetables, potatoes, white chocolate icecream in some kind of shell with fruit sauce, champagne, and wine.

There was a jazz band, a horde of waiters in white gloves. The man next to me at my table said he thought there were four hundred people there. The same man told me a very funny long story, went out for a cigarette, came back and told me exactly the same story again. Mom said she heard nothing the whole time but noise.

There were speeches, toasts, the cutting of cake, the snapping of many pictures, the bride and groom dancing. The wedding guests were from all over the world. Many languages were spoken. The officiating priest was from Brazil where he runs a ministry for street children. I consumed alcohol, sugar, and filet mignon in wine sauce.

There was a great thunder and lightning storm the next day. The sky got very dark, thunder was crashing, lightning bolts ripped across sky, trees were whipping around every which way in the wind, rain poured down. I sat in my bliss chair and watched.

And then the heat wave continued with even more humidity.

Walking to Indian Boundary Park at sunset, a woman in a billowing pink sari is walking toward me. The park is crowded. On the next bench from where I sit, an old woman is reading a book in Russian. Adolescent ducklings swim around the fountain in the pond, darting in and out of the spray. I walk over to the playground where there is another water fountain that children play in. A young mother holding a baby walks into the spray. The baby, arms outstretched, looks up in wonderment at the falling water.

What Exactly *Is* Spirituality?

Do anything, but understand that nothing is true.

RANJIT MAHARAJ

There is no more dangerous illusion than the fancies by which people try to avoid illusion.

FENELON, ARCHBISHOP OF CAMBRAI

For a long time, there has been no meaningful difference between what occurs when I'm "meditating," and what occurs when I'm just "living my life." The boundary disappeared. I find no real difference between what happens in my bliss chair and what happens as I walk through downtown Chicago.

In the last year, I've stopped sitting formally, but I still sit quietly in my armchair whenever it arises naturally. There isn't any sense of holding still or deliberately "meditating." All attempts to cultivate awareness and "be present" and *get* something (like "enlightenment") have fallen away. There's just what is.

There used to be an image or an idea about what "awareness" or "awakening" ought to look like, an image that didn't include fingerbiting, emotional upset, mental confusion or obsessive thinking. That fell away.

Studying Feldenkrais, along with reading more about the brain and neuroscience, makes me wonder if thought is as much the operative factor as I have been assuming it is. Feldenkrais assumes it is not. Obviously, thought has great compelling power when believed. But I'm increasingly discovering how much of life happens outside conscious awareness, and how thought may be more like after-thought than anything causative. I wonder now if insight into thought is as essential or as central to waking up as I have believed it to be. I'm also increasingly "aware" of how many different ways the words "consciousness" and "awareness" get used, perhaps because no one is really at all sure what they mean or what they are! They may turn out to be something like "ether" in the old science!

Toni responds: "Yes, yes, 'consciousness' and 'awareness' are like the ether of old science—wonderful metaphor. In that case, all concepts are, aren't they?"

Finding the Absolute in the Relative

I feel an overall sense of confidence, relaxation and well being. I don't bog down in difficult feelings when they arise. On those days when my book doesn't seem very good to me, I just keep going. Recently, when a friend was angry at me, being very judgmental and critical, I felt this remarkable absence of reactivity. I simply listened. There was no defensiveness, no anger, no hurt.

❧

Sitting in my bliss chair, I see the squirrels who are nesting in my tree kissing each other. Sometimes they groom each other. Sometimes they stretch out on a branch with all four legs dangling down and lie there, utterly languid. Sometimes I don't see them at all for days.

Sweat drips down my face. In the night I wake up and can't breathe. It is so hot there is no air. The morning brings thunder and lightning and torrents of rain. We had floods. There were eight feet of water on the highway; people were escaping out their car windows and swimming to safety.

I walk in the park at sunset. A mother is blowing bubbles into the air, and a flock of little children are chasing the bubbles. More children run over from nearby, bubbling with delight. They belong to all races. The older ones can catch up to the bubbles and pop them, but the littlest, a toddler, stands tottering in absolute awe, following one and then another bubble with her eyes, twirling, staggering, reaching out, taking a few quick steps, utterly wonder-struck. The icecream truck plays its simple tune over and over in the background: *Turkey in the Straw*. I walk around the house humming this tune.

Monster heat continues, twenty-three people dead in Chicago so far. The heat index is up in the hundreds, the humidity unbelievable.

❧

I have come to feel a deep love for our so-called humanness. The urge to transcend it completely, to leave Joan out of this book and write only the "purist" truth, has given way to a deeper truth which includes every-thing, *even Joan!* And *that* turns out to be the cosmic joke: the pure book I wanted to write, the one that spoke only the absolute truth, is actually *this* book. There is no other book. *This* is the purity. *This* is the absolute. Finger-biting, stormy weather, heat, cold, sun, rain—white gulls flashing past my window, a dazzling moment of beauty, gone in an instant.

Everything is God

The first leaf on the tree outside my window has turned bright yellow. Other trees in the neighborhood are starting to turn. It is raining and cooler. Fall is in the air.

I've been in Chicago for a year now. It's the first year in decades that I have not left home and traveled somewhere else. Something has settled. I always imagined myself "settling" in some quiet, spacious, rural place, something more like Springwater. And here I am in Chicago, a big, noisy, polluted city, the last place I imagined myself. And yet, it is so deeply right, at least for right now.

Everything in my life seems perfect: the years of getting drunk and stoned, the years of political activism, the years of meditation, the years in satsang. No one part seems any more holy than any other. It could not be otherwise.

It's as if, for so many years I've been seeking salvation, and it suddenly dawns on me that there is no need of any such thing. There is no one to save. Nothing means anything; it all just is. And that isn't depressing. It's all "meaningless" the way a dance or a flower is meaningless. It doesn't *need* any meaning.

Sometimes everything glows with beauty and light. Sometimes everything seems flat. Sometimes there is vast space. Sometimes there are thoughts. Sometimes there is contraction. Sometimes there is expansion. I'm not chasing any particular state, trying to get it to endure forever. Experiences of all kinds arise. They pass. Somehow, in its raw ordinariness, Chicago is the perfect ground to recognize the obvious: What is, is. It really is that simple.

Most remarkable of all, I've noticed that I don't want to finish first anymore in the Spiritual Race to the Imaginary Finish Line. The race has dissolved into thin air.

The beauty of writing a book is that you don't know what it's about until it's over. It's like watching a photograph slowly appear in the developing tray. At first just a few amorphous shapes, and then slowly, out of nowhere, a coherent picture emerges. And it's all a magic trick, like the photograph. It's just an image inside an image inside an image, a photograph of nothing at all.

At night there is heat lightning, the sky lighting up and flashing, the cicadas buzzing at a frenzied volume doing their bhajans.

Walking in the morning, I see green leaves shimmering with light. Fruit hangs in the trees. I stand at an intersection, waiting to cross the street. A big truck rumbles past me, leaving a huge cloud of smelly exhaust. The exhaust is the Beloved just as much as the shimmering leaves. It's all beautiful. It's all God.

I'm home.

The Grande Finale

September 11, 2001

If there is anything—any person, any behavior, any circumstance, any situation, any place, anything that you do not see as God, that's where the work is. The world is exactly as it should be. Everything is God. Everything is good. The only time we suffer is when we believe a thought that argues with what is. When I argue with reality, I lose.

PARAPHRASE OF BYRON KATIE

This is the time
For you to deeply compute the impossibility
That there is anything
But Grace.

HAFIZ

If a fish is born in your aquarium and you call it John, write out a birth certificate, tell him about his family history, and two minutes later he gets eaten by another fish—that's tragic. But it's only tragic because you projected a separate self where there was none. You got hold of a fraction of a dynamic process, a molecular dance, and made a separate entity out of it.

ECKHART TOLLE, *The Power of Now*

Love your enemies and pray for those who persecute you, so that you may be children of your Father in heaven; for he makes his sun rise on the evil and on the good, and sends rain on the righteous and on the unrighteous.

JESUS

Sooner or later we may discern the palpable difference between just being here as we are, openly attentive, and the state of entanglement in a web of fantasy about being somewhere else. Can we directly experience this difference without a need to elevate or disparage either state? Every state of being speaks for itself.

TONI PACKER

You see, there are NO choices. What is, is. When you know that, it's over....There is nothing terrible. Shall I say it again? There is nothing terrible. There has never been anything terrible....It's all about you're destroying my dream. That's all...There has never been evil and there never will be.... Evil is a story of how you think nature should be...

BYRON KATIE

Whatever is happening is always happening only in the mind that perceives it.... All there is, is Consciousness. Consciousness is all there is.

RAMESH S. BALSEKAR

To the awakened mind the end of the world is no more or less momentous than the snapping of a twig.

JED MCKENNA

I am writing in a lightning storm in the middle of the night. The President has just announced America's Holy War Against Terrorism. President Bush says God is on our side; "the enemy" says Allah is on theirs. It is a little over one week since hijackers used commercial jetliners to attack the World Trade Center and the Pentagon, two symbols of US economic and military might, two symbols filled with ordinary human beings like you and me.

I flew to California the day before the attacks happened. I watched the towers collapse live on the TV in Adele's living room. It seemed at that moment fundamentally no different at all from the violence and suffering I see every night on the TV news, only now it was here in America. It was something I had long expected, although the magnitude and brilliance of the attacks was beyond anything I had imagined.

Adele was lighting candles and rushing out to embrace our neighbors. People were phoning us, all sounding tearful and shaken. I felt oddly peaceful.

In fact, at the risk of being burned at the stake, I will tell you that I even felt some excitement and satisfaction at seeing the buildings collapse, perhaps because the World Trade Center and the Pentagon have mostly symbolized "evil" in my mind. I am, after all, a former Sixties radical. But I think it was for a deeper reason.

The status quo was breaking apart and something infinitely truer was being revealed. It was a moment of tremendous love. The normal routine, business as usual had been utterly shattered. People were jumping out windows, falling into the arms of strangers, crawling down smoke-filled hallways. The fragility and preciousness of life was palpable, unmistakable. And for those who could see it, the mystery on the other side of death was shining through. Like a volcano, an earthquake, or a hurricane, this was a celebration. Not the usual kind of celebration. Not without enormous pain and heartbreak. But a celebration none-the-less, a cosmic celebration.

Please don't get me wrong. I was not happy to see ordinary human beings suffering, nor would I wish this on anyone. I am not *condoning* the attacks, nor trying in *any* way to invalidate or deny the pain and loss that was experienced. I'm only telling you in all honesty that a rush of excitement was one of *many* instantaneous reactions that arose in this bodymind at that moment. It happened.

Furthermore, I understand why there is anger at the United States, and I understand what motivates so-called political terrorists. It was no mystery to me why some on the Arab street were reportedly celebrating. They had their reasons, too.

I even found myself feeling angry that others around me were so upset. Why didn't Americans get this upset every day when they watched the news? Why wasn't everybody lighting candles and calling each other up then? The United States had been blowing up civilians all over the planet for years. What about them? What about the fifty thousand people (mostly children) who die *every day* of starvation? What about the hundreds of thousands of Iraqis the US has killed with bombs and economic sanctions, and the thousands more we probably *will* kill? What about the Palestinian people living under brutal US-backed Israeli occupation? What about the innocent civilians we nuked at Hiroshima and Nagasaki, and napalmed in Vietnam? What about the cruelty and bloodshed, the unfathomable pain all over the whole planet? Why wasn't everyone holding candlelight vigils every minute? Why now? Did only American lives really matter?

I found it painful to hear people describing the hijackers as evil, satanic, cowardly madmen. Because I knew they were not. I knew they were just people, exactly like those in the Trade Towers, people who loved life and gave theirs up for what they believed to be right. We love to turn our so-called enemies into devils because the truth that they are just like us is too unbearable. I took it *personally* in a funny way that people hated the hijackers. I know from having been in the radical left years ago that people do this kind of act because they believe they are doing good. Now the US will turn around and drop bombs on them for the very same reason. Who are the terrorists?

Seen through their own eyes, all terrorists are freedom fighters. They have come to the conclusion, often after years of peaceful work, that armed violence is the only way. This isn't really as incomprehensible as people pretend. President Bush came to this same conclusion when he announced his war on terrorism. It's a very common conclusion.

September 11 pushed deep and different buttons for all of us in America, often triggering clashing responses. If my conditioning had been different, if I had been identified as a patriot rather than as an outsider and a rebel, if I had been living across the street from the Trade Towers, if someone dear to my heart had been in there that morning, an entirely different set of reactions might have occurred. No reaction is right or wrong. They all happen, for myriad reasons, and none of it is personal. It's all what is. Grief, terror, joy, numbness, anxiety, anger—many waves of energy.

However you saw it and whatever you felt, it was a raw time in America. The US was no longer invulnerable. We all saw the possibility that this government could be decapitated in a single attack, that this nation could fall as empires have fallen throughout history. This was only the beginning. American civilians would be dying. There would be more attacks. Moreover, perhaps "evil" was not endemic to the US as some of us in the radical left and the counter culture had long assumed. Perhaps we hadn't noticed before how much there was about America that we loved and appreciated. Perhaps reality was more complex and messier than any of us had wanted it to be. For many, it was a time of reassessment.

I could see immediately on the morning of 9/11 how compelling the drama of it all was. We love these dramas. We may not want to admit that, or even see it, but we do. It sells newspapers as they say because *finally* something exciting is happening. We love excitement and suspense and even horror. Adele left for work that morning, and I immediately switched off the TV.

I was disappointed and a little bit irked that this was happening on the first morning of my much-anticipated vacation in California. I had woken up that morning steeped in the beauty and quiet of where I was, very much looking forward to a leisurely breakfast with Adele, a day of visiting with friends. War was not what I had in mind, and I didn't want to get sucked into the drama.

As the day wore on, it became clear that the hijackers were Islamic fundamentalists. I faced the specter that the US government was going to be brought down not by radical leftists or deep ecologists, but by right-wing religious zealots. An even darker age lay ahead if any of us survived to see it.

I left the radical left because I stopped believing that terrorism was the solution to terrorism. I stopped believing in the black and white picture of good guys and bad guys.

Is bin Laden evil? Is America evil? Is anybody evil? How does it affect us when we see something or someone as evil? What if no one is evil? What then? Is seeing beyond evil perhaps the beginning of being able to love and understand and heal? When you're awake, the whole concept of evil simply makes no sense at all. But when you're dreaming, it looks very different.

The Israelis and the Palestinians both think they are the victim, that the other is the aggressor, the real terrorist. They each have compelling and understandable reasons to see it the way they do. Countless people on both sides have been killed, maimed, terrorized, left homeless. There is an enormous reservoir of pain and hatred. Can such vicious circles end?

Will we put an end to terrorism through anger, hatred and violence? Can we bomb it out of existence? Is there any other option? I honestly don't know. There may be situations where violence is actually the least violent and most sensible option. I do know for sure that when the mentality behind it is hatred, vengeance and black-and-white thinking, it will in some way serve to perpetuate and strengthen the root of the problem rather than dissolving it.

Ultimately, there is no solution for the world and no need of one. The horror is horrible, the pain hurts, *and* at the same time, on a deeper level, all is well. Despite the fire that is raging in the movie, the screen remains undefiled. The world appears and disappears inside awareness, and awareness is not at war with anything. The heart of things is at peace.

Moreover, when you start looking into it deeply, it becomes very difficult to find the separation between light and dark. Enormous beauty and compassion have come out of the terrible experience of Nazi Germany. The horror of the Vietnam War created huge suffering, and it also created Thich Nhat Hanh and a social revolution in US society. It changed the course of history in so many ways, some favorable and some unfavorable. The apparent misfortunes in my own life have been the sources of my deepest wisdom, insight, compassion, humor, and strength. And yet, if I were choosing my life, I'd leave them all out. Perhaps that's why we're not consulted. We'd write a very flat script.

This is the fallacy of positive thinking and visualization—we never visualize ourselves with cancer, losing an arm, being a drunk, biting our fingers all night, our child ending up in a wheelchair, our bank account at zero, the world suffering yet another war. We visualize some all-one-sided, happy picture that misses the richness of life as it actually is. We visualize what can never actually exist: a one-sided coin, up triumphing permanently over down. But that's not how it works. Up cannot exist without down. They are always in perfect balance. Neither one really exists.

Perfection never exists the way we imagine it in the mind. The only real perfection is *exactly* what's here right now. That doesn't mean I like everything that happens, and it doesn't mean I don't act to bring about something different. I wouldn't hope for anyone to have a bomb dropped on them, or for any child to be born disabled, and if I could snap my fingers and have a new right hand, I'm sure I'd snap those fingers. If asked to choose between a million dollars or the loss of both legs, I'd pick the million dollars without a moment of hesitation. But I know from my own life experience that loosing both legs could be incredible grace, and that having a million dollars could involve profound suffering. Life happens. Ultimately it is beyond the scope of the mind to evaluate.

From our human perspective, it would be a terrible thing if there was a global nuclear war that wiped out all life forms on earth. But from the perspective of the totality, it might be just one more tiny event, clearing the way for something new to emerge. From the point of view of the dinosaur, their extinction would seem like a dreadful mistake. From the point of view of the polio virus, the Salk vaccine would look like genocide. From the perspective of the universe, the disorder is all part of the larger order, in which there is space for all possibilities, for experimentation and mistakes, for play. There is room for everything in this dream, even the horror.

This doesn't mean we might just as well drop a nuclear bomb on our neighbors or let our children get polio. But it does mean that we no longer imagine that we know what's best for the universe. We no longer imagine that we have to (or could) "save the world," or that it would surely be a "good thing" if we could. We simply respond to life as best we can, doing whatever life moves us to do.

❧

In the wake of 9/11, I was angry at the American war mongering, the patriotism, the flags flying everywhere. My anger was, of course, essentially no different from the anger of those who wanted to go and bomb Afghanistan, or those who rushed out to attack their Arab-American neighbors. All hatred arises from the sense of separation, and it keeps that sense of separation alive. It hardens and divides us.

Can there be a waking up from anger and hatred?

What enrages us most is invariably something that reminds us of ourselves in some way. It is a mirror image, reflecting our own shadow.

Perhaps Osama bin Laden is the mirror image, the shadow, of America. Bin Laden is the wealthy global freedom fighter who has willingly sacrificed a life of riches and comfort to fight for what he sees as the highest good. He is willing to use brute force to bring to its knees what he perceives as evil. I've noticed that he and President Bush are using a remarkably similar vocabulary.

And if bin Laden is the reflection of America, what about the reflection of Joan? What about the flag-wavers, the warmongers, the gung-ho patriots, America itself? I begin to look at the aspects of me that resemble what I see in America: spoiled, greedy, arrogant, thinking I should get my way and dominate everybody and be number one, believing myself to be innocent and good, self-righteously waving my various ideological flags.

Today I've been walking around here in Chicago amidst the flags, allowing my heart to open to the love and the pain of those who fly them. I've been looking into the mirror, seeing all my own forms of flag waving. And finally, I've been seeing something very tender and precious.

I've been discovering the beauty of America. We solidify ideas, like "America is bad" (or the opposite) and then can't see past our own constructions. I see very clearly at this moment how all images and ideas prevent fresh seeing. There is no world out there, no solid or enduring objective reality that we are all looking at. Rather, there is only the seeing. What we see is what we get. And what we see is what we do. The seeing *is* the action that emerges out of it.

Perhaps a country is not so different from a person, each of us with our neurosis, our warts, our shortcomings. Over a lifetime we learn, if we're lucky, to love each other, and most challenging of all, to love ourselves as we actually are, not as we wish we were. Perhaps I am learning to forgive and love America—imperialism, corporate greed, George Bush and all.

As long as we continue to see evil and cowardice in one another, instead of love, however apparently twisted and misguided its expression may be, and until we understand the hurt and fear that motivate *all* acts of war, all of them being acts of terror, it seems to me that we will only continue to perpetuate the endless cycle of hatred, misunderstanding, attack and retribution that, as Gandhi said years ago, will leave the whole world blind. Given the weapons now in existence, I sense that this world will come to a fiery end in our lifetime if this lesson cannot be learned. Ultimately, it doesn't matter.

The world, like the body, will die sooner or later. We care for it as we care for the body, as best we can, but we don't need to save either one. And ultimately we can't. They won't be saved. All forms eventually disintegrate.

And that isn't a tragedy. Death is at the very heart of life. Forms are temporary. When we mistake the form for what underlies and animates it, we are always, sooner or later, disappointed. What happened on September 11 was a big disillusionment. And in that, there is grace.

There is beauty in death, in the massive dissolution and crumbling of forms. There is a tremendous freedom at the heart of it. It's not unlike the koan of being born with one arm, having to find beauty and perfection in something that the world regards as a tragedy, a wound, a mistake, a sorrow. I have found that beauty.

We have a tendency to think of humanity as something separate from nature and separate from God. We tend to regard what humans do as an aberration from the rest of the universe, a kind of cosmic mistake. But obviously, human beings and everything we create (can openers, billboards, atom bombs, concentration camps, retreat centers) are all part of the natural world. Ultimately, it is *all* Consciousness Itself. *What else is there?*

Species come and go. Whole populations are wiped out by natural catastrophes. Solar systems are born and explode. The entirety of human history is only an instant, a momentary flash in this vastness.

Does this mean that there is no place for sorrow? No place for transformation? No place for discernment and correcting apparent mistakes? *Everything IS, including our responses:* the impulse to stop war, to help the poor, to clear up confusion, to save the whales. It's *all* happening. It's inseparable. No one is doing any of it. It happens by itself. *Everything is grace* when we recognize it as that. Grace is in the *seeing*, not in the situation.

Okay and not-okay, good and evil are meaningless evaluations after the fact. The *actual reality* of each instant of what we now call "the holocaust" or "9/11" was something else entirely from the *story* that thought and memory has put together. Right now, both "the holocaust" and "9/11" are figments of our imagination. That doesn't mean they didn't happen. It means that right now, they happen *only* in imagination. This is true not only of 9/11 and the holocaust. It is true of *everything*. By the time we even perceive something, it is over. Our perceptual mechanism captures only a tiny fragment of what is. The human mind can't possibly understand or judge it. The human perspective is far too limited. The vastness of unconditional love embraces it all. Unconditional love sees no other. Everything, as it is, is the truth. It *is*.

The Most Ordinary (and Extraordinary) Retreat

I was in California on September 11 to attend a weekend retreat with Tony Parsons, the teacher from England whose retreat I cancelled out of last spring. On the spur of the moment, on sudden impulse, I had decided to go. I wanted to see Tony again, and I wanted to experience a retreat where nothing at all was imposed. As it turned out, it was the perfect place to be in the wake of 9/11.

Tony did not seem to regard the attacks as anything more serious than a fleeting dream. He said that these kinds of things will always arise as long as the illusion of separation is believed to be real. I resonated with what he said, but it upset and outraged a few of my friends.

It was lovely to be with Tony. He doesn't want to be a guru, and I'm no longer looking for one. The search is over. I was there, as he put it, simply to bask. It was wonderful to be on a retreat where there was no schedule, no imposed silence, no meditation, nothing special. People played badminton and took walks. We gathered with Tony three times a day for dialog, had three meals a day together, and that was it. Even that minimal schedule was made up on the spot. There was no plan at all in the beginning. There was no tape recorder, no video camera, no sales table. It was absolutely simple. Tony poked fun at every sacred cow in the spiritual scene. He was very available. People took walks with him, ate meals with him. He told us to phone him up if we felt like it. Just an ordinary guy. And at the same time, not ordinary at all.

The retreat was held in the redwoods, and with no planes flying overhead, it was astonishingly quiet. We were far away from the media hysteria that was consuming most of the nation. We had no TV or radio. It was an enormous blessing. We had only reality.

＊

Returning to Adele's when the retreat was over was a return to the drama. I found her in a semi-dark room, surrounded by flickering votive candles, on the phone with someone discussing trauma and healing. There was a heaviness and a sense of crisis in the air. I wanted to be back at the retreat where sanity prevailed. I felt angry at Adele for being caught up in this hysteria. And soon I was caught up in it myself.

A World of Scary Thoughts

Returning to Chicago was a nightmare. By then, it was exactly one week since the attacks. There was a steady medley of patriotic songs playing over and over at the Chicago airport. I felt myself getting angry. Flags were on display everywhere. They were already on display here in Chicago before this happened, but now it was beyond belief. Every other house was flying the flag. Cars were sporting them, sometimes several per car, big ones. They were on every store, in every window. Children were carrying them. Homeless people were selling them. It was patriotism gone wild.

I hated the flags. To me, at that moment, they symbolized cutthroat imperialist greed, a culture of grotesque materialism that was destroying the planet, and now a false sense of unity that depended on having an enemy for its energy. Their proliferation everywhere spelled fascism to me, not freedom. My heart hadn't opened to them yet.

The weather was cold and drizzly and bleak. The cicadas had died out. My editor in New York rejected the original manuscript for this book. I missed California. I felt like I was in an alien land. Newspaper headlines spoke of the American people being ready to go to war, ready to fight dirty, as if we have been fighting clean in the past. There were articles in mainstream newsmagazines arguing in favor of using torture (as if this, too, was a novel idea).

I watched the TV. Tears filled my eyes again and again. So many acts of kindness, community and self-sacrifice were evident in the wake of these attacks, so much love and generosity. My heart began to soften, even to the flags.

There is an undercurrent of visceral fear I detect in myself knowing what may be coming. The specter of a world ravaged by fundamentalist fanatics armed with weapons of mass destruction, ready to commit suicide for the cause, while the US and Israel grow ever more brutal and self-righteous, the thought of having to suffer excruciating pain or watch loved ones suffer it, not to mention economic catastrophe and environmental devastation, all of these are definitely scary thoughts. Right now, right here, that's all they are, thoughts. Still, the undercurrent of fear comes and goes.

My stomach is unsettled. I feel vulnerable. Feeling the shaky feelings, crying. Seeing how the soft open space turns hard and solidifies in the terrorist mind (my own). Another chilly sunless day.

Meeting My Neighbor After the Attacks

It is raining, and I'm coming home with groceries. I spot my neighbor, the one who plays her radio all night, in the parking lot, clinging to the hood of a car and trying to get up the curb.

"Hello, Mrs. Szostkowski, can I give you a hand there?"

She takes my arm.

"Ah," she says, "You live up on the fifth floor." In my building, the fifth floor is occupied by Catholic nuns.

"No," I say. "I'm your neighbor."

"Oh yes!" she says, "You're the lovely one. You don't complain anymore."

We are walking together now, arm in arm, in the rain.

Miracles do happen. Love does arise, mysteriously. Perhaps we will all awaken from our dream of good and evil, an eye for an eye, and discover that we are all really Catholic nuns.

The Other Possibility

I was over at Mom's apartment, waiting for her to get dressed, and this book was on the table so I picked it up: *Will the Circle Be Unbroken? Reflections on Death, Rebirth, and Hunger for a Faith* by Chicago writer Studs Terkel. Studs had written a beautiful inscription to my mother. He's about her age. It's a collection of interviews with people. I random-ly opened it to his interview with Mamie Mobley, the mother of Emmett Till, that fourteen year old Black boy who was brutally killed back in 1955 while visiting Mississippi. He was her only child. She describes inspect-ing his mutilated body after it was brought back to Chicago in a box. She describes the odor, the mutilation. This woman had incredible fortitude. She examined that body slowly, with unflinching care, and her spirit was not broken. She saw Jesus with his wounds. She heard the Spirit. She was a schoolteacher, and the Spirit told her to teach. She did.

Bombs aren't the only response to violence. There is another possibility. It is the path of Christ, and I'm not speaking of Christianity, I'm speaking of Christ. It is the willingness to die into love. It is a radical path, demanding everything. Ultimately, it is the only path, and even what appears to be going in another direction is all headed into that same Great Death.

It is a sunny windy October day here. The leaves of my trees are turning bright golden-yellow, dancing in the gusting wind, making amazing moving patterns of light and shadow on my wall. Mom and I went to the botanical gardens.

In the midst of war and internal upset, there is the deeper recognition that nothing needs fixing. Everything is fine. Even if that includes the fiery end of the so-called world. And even if Joan is feeling terror and not peace at that moment. Even that is okay. I've developed an almost tender fondness for the flags that are waving everywhere and for America.

I've decided to start offering monthly meetings. I sent out fliers.

The Bombing Begins

The bombing of Afghanistan has begun. I wept. Football crowds cheer the news. It is my mother's ninety-second birthday. I hear geese flying over, winter coming. It is a cold, sunny October morning.

The Feldenkrais training has resumed, with day after day of intensive body awareness work, touching and being touched, the war as a backdrop, menopause playing tricks with my hormones. Emotional tides swept through me, old feelings of hopelessness and despair rushed to the surface. I went back on caffeine; I bit my fingers.

There is really nothing to "do" about all our "neurotic" human patterns, whether it's fingerbiting or dropping bombs. I put that word *neurotic* in quotes because our way of regarding these things as afflictions, failings, and mistakes is a big part of what makes them seem so problematic and unbearable. It has been a tremendous relief to realize that none of these things are personal, none of them really matter, not ultimately.

Then perhaps it is possible to meet these arisings with simple presence devoid of any agenda. This is a radical possibility. Whatever action arises out of that aware space won't imagine that it is saving me or saving the world.

Feldenkrais thinks in terms of making the nervous system and the brain aware of different possibilities. The old habits may recur at times, especially under stress, and that's okay. The new possibility is also there. The habits and difficulties we all face are microcosms of the larger habits that the world is caught up in (so evident now). They teach us humility because "I" can't just go in and fix them at will. They teach us compassion because if I can't do that, then no one else can either. They provide an excellent laboratory to explore absolutely everything. And ultimately they are the doors through which we may discover that which is undisturbed by *anything* that appears. It has been said that our greatest problem is our greatest gift, and I have found that to be true again and again.

The body and the world will always be imperfect, however much they may improve. But there is something (no thing) that is untouched by chewed fingers, sleepless nights, and the devastation of war and famine.

Awareness accepts everything, even the end of the world. Acceptance doesn't mean we don't act. A baby is born, and we feed it. We don't ignore it because "it's going to die eventually, so why bother?" We respond intelligently. The response is obvious and natural. It flows from awareness. It *happens*—mysteriously, on its own, out of nowhere.

Snow Flurries

It has been cold, we've had snow flurries, the trees are mostly bare, and there has been a great deal of rain and cold and heavy winds this last month. I left home one morning, and my trees were full of beautiful yellow leaves, and when I came home that evening, they were completely bare. The wind had stripped them. One day the grackles tore apart the squirrels' nest and carried it off in pieces.

America is changed. People await the next attack and wonder if the mail will bring anthrax or something more deadly. Economic collapse is in the air although we are still (by and large) living in astonishing affluence and comfort compared to the rest of the world. There is a strange mix of things in the air. Shopping is held up as an expression of patriotism, there are awesome acts of generosity and a heightened sense of community, and many people seem to be re-evaluating their priorities, looking for something deeper.

The Zen Master from Iowa

Believe me, there cannot be too much destruction.

NISARGADATTA

In terms to do with the world, this is utter madness. What I'm talking about is the courage to give up, to die, to let go.

TONY PARSONS

Seek for the source of the doubter, and you will find he is really nonexistent. Doubter ceasing, doubts will cease.

RAMANA MAHARSH

If and when you understand...you will throw up your hands and give up everything, since you are convinced that it is all unreal.

NISARGADATTA

The pre-publication review copy of a book came in the mail asking for my endorsement: *Spiritual Enlightenment: The Damnedest Thing*, by Jed McKenna. Apparently a memoir, this provocative book is the story of a few days in the life of Jed McKenna, an iconoclastic, homegrown,

Advaita-Taoist-Zen master with a thriving farmhouse ashram in Iowa.

I sat up into the wee hours reading it. It was compelling and delightful, but also in some way unsettling. This wasn't the kind of spiritual truth that would sell. It wasn't something you could translate into a lucrative coaching business or offer to the mainstream as "stress reduction." Jed had no urgency to help people or save the world, no missionary zeal, no ambition. This was truly a book about nothing.

In that sense, I loved it. But there was something about the way Jed talked about enlightenment that bothered me. He was absolutely *sure* that *he* was enlightened. In his words, he was "done," a butterfly who could never again be a caterpillar. As I read the book, the nagging, doubtful thought that "I" wasn't quite all the way "there" yet popped back up. The mind began to imagine that "I" was a caterpillar struggling to become a butterfly.

This whole story was so old by now, so threadbare, so transparently absurd. The whole notion of totally and permanently enlightened people was a complete oxymoron. And yet, suddenly here it all was again, still believable. I was not thrilled to have this whole nightmare reappear just as "I" was about to start offering meetings. But like it or not, here it was.

Jed appeared to have in spades what "I" again seemed to lack: complete confidence, doubtless certainty. If "I" was *really* awake, the mind argued, then obviously this doubt and confusion wouldn't be happening. It seemed that for Jed, the illusion had dissolved permanently and absolutely, never to return; whereas, "I" was apparently still capable of getting re-hooked and re-hypnotized. And *that* story, *that* "I," seemed real.

The mind was turning in a familiar vicious circle, chasing its own tail, gnawing on itself, unable to stop, tangled in the illusion of the character who struggles to get out of the movie, the "me" who longs to wake up from the dream of "me." And of course it can't do it, for how can an illusion wake up from an illusion? This is the slipperiest of all the Magician's tricks: the Enlightenment Movie, in which the imaginary me sets out to destroy itself and escape from the movie in order to preserve and exalt itself and get into an even better movie, the movie that pretends it is not a movie.

But true enlightenment isn't about a better movie or a better role.

It isn't about *you* escaping the dream, waking up, having mystical experiences, "living mindfully," or "being present." It isn't about *you* getting somewhere. Awakening is nondual awareness; the unattainable, inescapable, ever-present absolute; the unbroken wholeness that has no opposite. It is outside the frame of consciousness and the entire apparent phenomenal manifestation. Consciousness and all of manifestation is *in* it, not the other way around. Enlightenment has nothing to do with succeeding *in* the dream, whether as a corporate tycoon or as a seeker after enlightenment. It's the end of *all* of that, or more precisely, the end of taking all of that to be real. It happens to no one. It doesn't actually *happen*. It *IS*.

❧

Jed left me with one very wonderful question: What is true? Right now, if this whole story of me and Jed dropped, there was nothing left: just bare presence, the simple truth.

But the mind kept picking that story back up, picking the scab, re-opening the wound. The review copy ended a little differently, and there was an address for Jed. I wrote him a letter pouring out my imaginary dilemma, hoping he could save me, thinking maybe I would drive down to Iowa and see him. But he never wrote back. I felt humiliated and embarrassed. Then finally, I began to laugh.

It dawned on me at last that Jed was a fictional character. This was a novel, not a memoir. It was the great revelation of Oz. Jed McKenna and his ashram in Iowa evaporated into mental mist right in front of my eyes. The guru behind the curtain was fictional, and so was "I". The whole thing was make believe, including the "I" who "keeps getting re-hooked."

❧

And even if this is forgotten again, even if the mind knots up and "I" appear to be chasing my own tail, even if the rope looks like a snake and scares "me" to death, awareness can sit back and have a good laugh, enjoying the show, enjoying the trick it is playing on itself: Look, there goes Joan, doing her little doubting and seeking dance again, isn't that sweet. Instead of, Oh My God, *mea culpa*, how could "I" be such a stupid idiot! It is realized (by no one) that "I" am a dream. The whole thing is just a show. There is no one left to take delivery. The apparent dilemma is no longer serious or real.

True liberation includes and allows it all. Nothing is left out, not even illusion.

There is no one to awaken and nothing to awaken from.

~❧

Life is very good at sneaking up from behind and playing tricks on you. There you are, thinking the search is over for good, happily writing a book about awakening, when all of a sudden, BAM! Some book about enlightenment comes in the mail out of the blue. You open it up, and a crazy Zen master from Iowa comes tumbling out with a big stick and confidently announces that *he* is a butterfly. Instantly you start dreaming that *you* are a caterpillar. The Zen master hits you over the head and yells, "You're not real! You're a fake!" as Toto pulls back the curtain.

The joke is, there's no one here. Just empty space, non-dual awareness, the unconditional love that can't possibly be enlightened or unenlightened.

Offering Nothing

My monthly meetings have started. People have appeared. I am interested in exploring whether there can be silence in a group without the constraints of formal "meditation." I'm interested in exploring without roles, without conclusions, without the mythology of attainment, without a system or an answer. I'm interested in something simple, direct, immediate. I have no idea what will happen. It's a mystery, an adventure. The desire to *be* an authority and the desire to *have* an authority are ever-more tansparently silly. Whenever I think I have to offer *something*, I panic. When I remember that I am offering nothing at all, everything relaxes.

❧

Mom and I attended another memorial service for another former neighbor. I saw two of my childhood playmates, now white-haired and middle-aged, whom I hadn't seen in maybe thirty years. Their father, the deceased, had requested "God Bless America" as the finale of his service. So there I was, former leftist radical, on my feet singing "God Bless America," tears in my eyes, my mother at my side.

Afterwards, it started to snow.

The Wheat Kernel

There is no such thing as an enlightened person for who is it that can become that which already is?

There is simply seeing and not seeing. Seeing does not come about through something gained but rather through an illusion lost.

What you are looking for is that which already sees.

TONY PARSONS

Toni Packer told a joke once during a retreat. I put it in my last book, but it bears repeating. The joke is about a man who thought he was a wheat kernel. As a result of this delusion, he was put in a mental hospital. After awhile, the psychiatrist felt that the man was cured, and so he was released. On his way home, the man saw a chicken crossing the road, and he ran back to the mental hospital in terror. "I thought it was clear to you now that you're not a wheat kernel," the psychiatrist says to the man. "It's clear to me," the man replies, "but I wasn't sure it would be clear to the chicken."

The joke illustrates the difference between the complete absence of an illusion and a partial insight or the presence of a belief. For most of us, the idea that we are a wheat kernel is absent. It simply isn't there. We don't have to remind ourselves of this fact, nor do we need to think twice about whether or not to flee if we happen to cross paths with a hungry chicken. The whole problem just doesn't exist. And the truth is that we are not a wheat kernel, even if we think we are.

We could say that enlightenment refers to the absence of the illusion that there is a separate self. That absence is the actual truth, the natural state, and therefore; it requires no effort to maintain. Any effort is part of the illusion.

When the illusion is absent, it's absent. When it's not absent, a dedicated and spiritually trained mind may try to mimic that absence. The effect is like the man who ran back to the mental hospital. Intellectual understanding or partial insight is quite different from direct seeing or the absence of illusion. Direct seeing is immediate and complete. It *feels* spacious, transparent, and simple—like a huge relief, a relaxation, the lifting of a burden. The absence of an illusion has no qualities at all. Intellectual understanding, by contrast, *feels* opaque, pinched, complicated, and unsatisfying. It takes time. It is always striving, battling, efforting, straining.

Under pressure, beliefs and partial insights tend to collapse. When faced with the metaphorical chicken, "you" run away, and then feel terrible about blowing "your" enlightened self-image as someone with no self! (Pretty funny!) Whereas when the illusion is absent, no one does anything, and no one needs to think about it. It's a non-issue.

Sometimes the mechanism that would get upset over something is simply not plugged in; for example, when my car was stolen, or when I was stranded at the airport for several days on my way to Springwater. The potential upset just wasn't there. At other times, the mechanism *is* plugged in; for example, when I mistook the cricket at a satsang for somebody's pager and got upset. In that case, when the truth was finally *seen*, the upset dissolved instantly and completely. But if I had not actually *seen* the cricket, and had instead been trying to convince myself that it was unspiritual to be upset, the effect would almost certainly have been an inner conflict between my *real* feelings and my superego agenda for how

I *should* be. As we've all experienced, it never works very well when we *pretend* not to be upset, or try to *act* like we're not in order to uphold some image of ourselves as an enlightened person.

So, the mind asks, how can I unplug the illusion? How can I see directly? How can I become completely certain that I am not a wheat kernel? The answer is that "you" cannot "do" direct seeing, and the "I" that wants the illusion to go away *is* the illusion.

Okay, the mind continues, so if you still sometimes take your life personally, get upset over crickets, or run away from metaphorical chickens, does that mean you are unenlightened?

Who is this "you" that we are speaking about? That is the real wheat kernel.

When the story drops away, the truth is quite obvious and undeniable and simple. Seeing is happening, hearing is happening. It is all happening on it's own, emerging out of nowhere. The eye can never see itself. It's too close, too all-inclusive to locate. You *are* this seeing-listening-being, this awareness in which everything *is* allowed to be.

Without the words, there is no thing. Not two. Just *this*.

Rise up and walk. You are not a wheat kernel, a caterpillar, or a neurotic seeker. Nor are you a fully enlightened butterfly. These are insubstantial dreams, word-creations, wisps of cloud, no-thing at all. *You* are the seeing, the listening space, the timeless NOW, the spaceless HERE, the single eye.

A Visit with Mrs. Szostkowski

I've been taking care of my next door neighbor's cats while she is away over the Christmas holidays. Not Mrs. Szostkowski, the one who plays her radio all night, but my neighbor on the other side—Joyce, a retired nurse, who has had me over for tea.

One morning, I am coming out of Joyce's apartment, locking the door behind me, and there's Mrs. Szostkowski in the hall. She asks me if I am on my way to the hospital. I realize she has mistaken me for Joyce.

I tell her I'm not Joyce; I'm Joan, her neighbor. She glances toward my missing hand. Her face lights up in recognition.

"Ah, yes, of course!"

She beams. We are holding hands now. She invites me down the hall to see her apartment. Next thing I know, I am in Mrs. Szostkowski's living room. She offers me cookies. I meet her Senegal parrot. She tells me of living through bombing raids in the Second World War, and how she does not want any more war. I see that she has a photograph of President Clinton on her wall and a painting of Jesus. She asks me if I am a Catholic. We begin talking about God.

She shows me the radio in her bedroom, the one I still hear sometimes in the middle of the night, although it is much better in the last year, and I have learned to sleep through it when it does go on and the volume goes up. It is an old-fashioned radio, on her night table, positioned right by the wall that divides (and joins) us at night.

As I am leaving, Mrs. Szostkowski gives me a bag of cookies for my mother and tells me to come visit anytime.

Winter / Spring

I am teaching English and basic writing skills at a city college. My students can barely write a sentence. Many have English as a second language. Most are adults returning to school. They have children and jobs. I don't know when they find time to sleep. I'm afraid some of them don't. They are Black, Latino, Polish, Palestinian, Filipino, Bosnian, Indian, Pakistani. They write papers that touch my heart, hinting at what they have lived through. They dream of bright futures and a peaceful world.

❧

Two doves are outside my window this morning kissing. Breast to breast, they are locking beaks, pecking at each other's necks, and for a moment the male mounts the female. Then they stand separately, side by side, fluffing, pecking at themselves, then they kiss some more. She flies off, and he follows. It is the first day of spring.

❧

There was a last spring snowstorm, and now the sun is out. White clouds drift aimlessly across the blue sky. Traffic roars on the street below, and the first tiny green buds are beginning to appear on the trees. The seasons follow each other, one after another, in endless succession. I am the space in which it all unfolds in a single timeless instant.

The leaves appeared and the spring flowers. The squirrels rebuilt their nest. The old man at the end of the hall died. It is strange to think that I will never see him again, that he is gone. He was a sweet, gentle man. Every time I saw him, in the hall or on the elevator or at the mail-boxes, I felt happy. He and his wife always left a card at my door at Christmas and at Easter.

Referring to Kyle a year after his death, Toni said, "It's like a dream." I wasn't sure if she meant his long illness, or their whole life together, or what. But the entire past is indeed dream-like, filled with dream characters who once seemed so real.

Truth or Illusion?

Experience takes place only in the present, and beyond and apart from experience nothing exists.

RAMANA MAHARSHI

I was channel surfing last night, and I landed on Oprah. She was doing something about people who had been severely injured on 9/11, and I watched for awhile. The part I saw was about a woman who had been badly burned over her entire body, doused with burning jet fuel at the World Trade Center. She was still in the hospital. She had been through excruciating pain. Her fingers were partially burned off. Her face was burned off. She had to learn to walk again, to use her hands again.

The images on the evening news are relentless: wailing Palestinian women kneeling in the rubble, bleeding Israeli bomb survivors, starving Africans eating dirt and dying of AIDS, anguished parents whose children have been kidnapped, a nine-month old baby girl who has been raped. The pain is real enough. Bodies hurt. Hearts are broken.

Perhaps the essential question is not to debate philosophically whether these people are illusory or real, but rather to wonder if it is possible to see the illusory in the beliefs and ideas arising right now. Is it possible to let old grievances go? Is it possible to discern the difference between present reality (presence itself) and stories (even so-called "true" ones) arising in imagination? Is it possible to recognize what is undeniably real, but utterly undefinable?

Unconditional love expresses itself in the firefighters, the nurses, the physical therapists, Oprah, all of us who see the show, the burned woman fighting for her life, the freedom fighters in the occupied Palestinian territories, the settlers in Israel fleeing their memories of the holocaust and the pogroms, the young American men dropping bombs on Afghanistan, and yes, even in the hijackers bravely flying their captured planes into their targets full of ordinary people. It is an amazing web, astonishing and incomprehensible, horrific and beautiful, terrifying and tender.

I've grown tired of all the righteous ideologies, the comforting explanations, the consoling beliefs. Just to be alive is enough, just to see what is as it is, without explanation, without a solution, without needing to deny the pain or wallow in it. Suffering can only end here.

Drop the story of past and future and what remains?

Is Anything a Tragedy?

How do we respond to suffering when it arises? Is it really a tragedy that someone has burns all over their body, or that someone else has cancer and their body falls away? I'm not saying it is or it isn't. But can we drop our assumptions?

We often imagine what someone else's suffering must feel like. But there is a tremendous difference between the actuality of something and what we imagine. I have long realized, for example, that people's *ideas* of what it must be like to have only one hand are very different than actually *having* one hand. People over-estimate the difficulties in most ways, but sometimes under-estimate them in others. Their fantasies are nothing like the actual experience.

Or take another example. I was once in a bad car accident. I was with a group of friends, in a van, returning at night from a camping trip. We were traveling at sixty or seventy m.p.h. on a freeway, and I was seated *between* the two front seats, on the engine case, next to the driver. Obviously I had no seat belt. Suddenly the van began to swerve, and I realized we might crash. I felt fear. Adrenaline flooded the body. And then, as soon as it became clear that we actually *were* crashing—*as it was happening*—there was no fear at all. Time was suspended. The body responded automatically. I was studying martial arts at that time, and the body instinctively went into a tuck. I was pure awareness. The van went off the road—rolled, flipped, and spun. I was tumbling around and around inside the van as this was happening. I watched it all from a place of complete neutrality, a place entirely untouched by it. I remember wondering, very matter-of-factly, if I was going to die. But there was no fear of dying. There was absolutely no pain and no fear. There was total presence. Someone *imagining* the accident, and *imagining* what I must have been feeling, would suffer much more than I *actually* did in that moment. In fact, I was not suffering at all!

The actual experience of those who died on 9/11 may have been one of tremendous peace, perhaps even ecstatic bliss. For it is not uncommon at moments like this to realize, not intellectually, but directly, as I did in the van crash, that who we are does not get hurt, that life itself does not die. Energy does not die. Forms come and go, and in fact, this body is *constantly* dying and being reborn. Only the mind creates the *idea* of a solid *thing* that has endured throughout an entire lifetime. The only "thing" that has actually been here the whole time is presence, the emptiness at the heart of all the forms, the space, the ground. The rest is only a pattern, a habit, a mirage, a dream.

Death is only a loss for those left behind. The one who dies has nothing real to lose. So can we begin to question our habitual, socially constructed reactions to death and apparent misfortune? I'm not suggesting we repress or deny grief, nor am I prescribing a correct response. There is no "correct" response. But it may be the case that some of our knee-jerk responses actually *create* a great deal of unnecessary suffering.

I know from my own experience what happens when people pity me because I have one arm. There I am feeling totally fine, totally whole, totally happy, and suddenly someone else is looking at me with great sorrow, and saying how sad it is. That's not my experience at that moment. That's *their* experience. And they're laying it on me. Seeing their pity, suddenly I no longer feel okay. I absorb their trip. It's contagious. It brings me down. Whereas when someone sees me as whole and beautiful, that's also contagious. I become beautiful. What we see is what we get. When we see what is as God, it *is* God. That's the mystery. That's the alchemy. It's all in the seeing.

Realizing that everything is God does not mean, as people often think it does, that we lose all sense of discernment, discrimination and responsibility and rush off to the nearest shopping mall and start gunning people down. If I really see everything as God, I don't want to gun people down. If I did something like that, it would be because of some powerful compulsion (made up of genetics, conditioning, neurochemistry, social circumstances, and thoughts believed to be real), *not* because of any insight into the nature of reality.

In fact, I would say that kindness and the ability to respond intelligently are the natural actions of clarity. What we *call* evil is a reactive mechanism that comes out of conditioned habit, inattention, unseen or uninvestigated beliefs, and who knows what genetic, neurological or biochemical factors as well. "Evil" is an inherent possibility in any complex, living design. In a larger sense, all such "malfunctions" are Consciousness

Itself, and calling them "malfunctions" or "evil" is a human judgement. They are part of a larger tapestry which we cannot see all at once, and therefore cannot judge. Good and evil *appear* very different to us, and yet they are both aspects of the One Being, perfectly balanced at all times.

Still, we know intuitively that Hitler is not expressing clarity and God-realization. We *feel* the difference in our own lives between spacious openness and defensive anger. When there is clarity, we don't behave like Hitler. *And we don't hate Hitler either.* We might even kill Hitler in order to save ourselves and others, but we will not do it out of hatred and vengeance. Clear awareness recognizes wholeness even when everything *seems* torn apart and broken. Awareness embraces *everything*. We don't pity the victims and hate the perpetrators. We don't even see such a division, or any such roles. We know that we contain it all.

The mind can so easily get lost in philosophical dilemmas. There is no need to *think about* whether Hitler or disabled children are perfect or imperfect, good or bad, caused or uncaused. When there is simply thoughtless awareness, the intelligent response is obvious. It's responsive to the moment. It's not a philosophical dilemma. It's clear. There's no prescription for enlightened action. It emerges out of the whole situation. It's choiceless. Ethics doesn't need to be cultivated, and in fact, can't be cultivated. Cultivated ethics won't hold up under pressure. When you really *see* somebody, you don't put them in a gas chamber. It's not a moral dilemma. It's obvious.

Hitler doesn't happen out of an open heart and an open mind. Hitler is the result of deep attachment to a belief system, a sense of "us" and "them." Hitler was sure he was right. Hitler knew who needed to be exterminated.

I find the roots of Hitler-consciousness in my own mind whenever I think I know who is wrong, or who needs to be gotten rid of. And I also find the roots of Christ-consciousness in my own heart, at least occasionally. And I know which one of these two feels like poison, and which one feels like the deepest truth. I know which one breeds more Hitlers. I know the Hitler-mind within us is very strong, and that opening the heart does require something like a crucifixion. I also know that both Christ and Hitler are aspects of one reality that includes and transcends them both.

Hating the rapist or the child molester is a response that may arise although only if we believe in the illusion that they could have done something different. Could they? Does hatred take away the suffering and resolve the problem, or does it further exacerbate it? In this moment, will the cycle of hatred and confusion continue or stop? Is there a choice?

There is a very moving story in Helen Prejean's book *Dead Man Walking* about a man who found his teenage son shot in the head. The man knelt by his son's body and said the Lord's Prayer, and as he came to the part about "forgive us our trespasses as we forgive those who trespass against us," he hesitated. And then he realized that yes, he *could* forgive whoever had done this. What a tremendous moment of grace. Forgiveness is a possibility, even under the most horrible circumstance. And then we begin anew. For this man, and for everyone he touches for the rest of his life, this will be a blessing.

That is not said in order to project an ideal response. Losing a child is a deeply painful experience. But in fact, the body is not permanent. It is utterly vulnerable and momentary. We have the *idea* that children are not supposed to die, that crime should not happen, that everyone is entitled to a safe, happy, healthy, prosperous life ending peacefully in old age. This is our idea. Is it true? We suffer when we cling desperately to ideas that don't match reality, when we think life should be other than it actually is.

When we are faced with the death of someone we love, especially perhaps a child, or with some massive violence, as in a war, then we are brought face to face with a profound mystery, an opening into a larger dimension, an invitation.

Will we miss it by getting lost in ideas of evil, blame, guilt and revenge that reincarnate the suffering?

Or will we fall into the mystery itself with an open heart?

If my friend Jarvis on death row can change from a violent young man into a beautiful awake being, if I can change from a gutter drunk into the author of this book, *then so can those I dislike or find repugnant, whose views or actions I hate.* We never know when someone might wake up. Can we give each other the space and the possibility to change? Can there be a noticing that this space is always already here?

Thousands of people are buried alive by earthquakes in Central America and India. We feel badly for them, but we feel differently when a young man blows up the Federal Building in Oklahoma City, or when people hijack airplanes and fly them into buildings. We think that the people who die at the hands of other people are victims of something more personal than those who die through an "act of nature." The actions of Timothy McVey, Adolph Hitler, Ariel Sharon, Yasar Arafat, George Bush, or Osama bin Laden are not usually seen as acts of nature, because we think of these people (and ourselves) as having some kind of independent will, independent of nature or God. Is that actually true? The atrocities committed by our fellow humans seem to us to be the result of some kind of misunderstanding or malfunctioning that we think might be avoidable, or might be in our power to change, unlike the earthquake, which is clearly beyond human control.

Thousands of people dying, perhaps slowly and painfully. In a sense, nothing is happening except that forms are breaking down and new forms are emerging. We make up a story around it and call it a tragedy. And yet, as sensitive beings, when we see such suffering, how can there not be sorrow? And in the case of the human-generated suffering, a natural curiosity to find out if there is any other way for human beings to function. What makes us do these kinds of things, and can it be otherwise? Is there another possibility? And if there is, what is the source of it?

I Is What I Is

One night during the dog days of summer, I went to Andy's, a Chicago jazz club, to hear Franz Jackson's band. My friend Dan plays bass with them. My mother and a couple of her friends went too. Franz is turning ninety this year and was just back from a European tour! He plays saxophone and sings. The piano player, Joe Johnson, is in his eighties. The drummer is in his seventies. The three of them started playing together about fifty years ago, and Franz has been playing jazz in Chicago since the late 1920's. He is like a guru, serene and happy, completely at ease and unperturbed. If he forgets the words, or sings the wrong verse, or can't get a sound out of his saxophone, he just goes right on, enjoying the show. If he gets tired, he yawns. Nothing needs to be covered up; whatever happens is perfectly okay. He has an album called *I Is What I Is.*

Mom was totally into it. She was calling out requests and clapping along. At one point Franz was singing *"Life is a Cabaret."* It was an epiphanic moment for me, a moment that changed my perception. I saw how life is indeed a cabaret. Consciousness is singing and dancing, snowing and raining, chasing it's own tail and waking itself up. Coming home, the lake was churned up by the wind, full of waves and whitecaps. The lake was as excited as I was. Everything was playing.

The Mystery

It is hot and muggy, lush and green. The cicadas and grasshoppers and crickets and tree frogs are frenzied—buzzing, humming, clicking and rattling. The nights are hot and full of sound. Everything sweats in the primal heat. Thunder and lightning storms pass through. Half the country is on fire, the worst fire season in history out West, forests going up in smoke.

I've found peace with my actual life. I've grown fond of the Joan character. Is everything neatly resolved? Not at all. But what *has* changed is that it no longer needs to be. If anger should arise, or confusion, or some old habit, it would only be another cloud in the sky, another momentary expression of what is, another face of the mystery.

Life As Play

There's a show on TV called "Friends" that I watch occasionally, a ditzy sitcom about a group of six friends in New York City. They each have their personality quirks, and occasionally they irritate and upset one another, but through it all they love each other. One of them, for example, is a high maintenance, obsessive-compulsive type who worries about stains on the furniture and can't stand to have anything out of place. Another, who lives with her for awhile, spills and rearranges things. Like friends everywhere, this little group drive each other crazy at times, they trick each other, and they love each other. And we laugh watching it because it's so familiar. We know these people. We identify. We've played all the parts ourselves at one moment or another. We've lived out our own versions of these same scenarios.

The problem is that when it's us, in so-called real life, we take it all very seriously. We really believe that our friends should change their ways, and we believe even more fervently that we should change. Especially as we grow more self-aware and begin to see more and more clearly all the petty, egotistical, compulsive, crazy things we are always doing, we feel mortified. We don't want to be that way. We want to be perfect. Flawless. Beyond reproach.

But when we watch this TV program, we laugh. The personality traits of the characters are endearing, not horrifying. It's quite obvious to us that the goal of the show is not to get all the characters to be perfect people (whatever that might be). We enjoy their idiosyncrasies, their quirks, their differences, the ways they rub up against each other and set each other off. It's funny. It's heartwarming. It's a good show.

As we grow more and more able to see our own lives in this same way, as play, we can begin to appreciate our differences, our quirks, our supposed flaws, our humanness. We can begin to see them as endearing instead of horrifying. We can appreciate the fun behind the moments of irritation and upset. We don't so quickly lose sight of the love that is underneath the entire play. And we don't lose sight of the playfulness of the play. And even when sometimes we *do* lose sight of it—getting all upset and self-involved and caught up in our drama—we recognize that *that's* part of the fun, too! It isn't about being perfect, or getting it all neatly resolved, or being above it all and never again absorbed in the story. It's a good show. Getting caught up and tricked by it from time to time is all part of the fun. It's not a problem to be solved; it's a play to be enjoyed.

Think of it! There are stories inside of stories, multiple and alternative stories, characters inside of characters, an infinity of mirrors, a net of jewels. Consider the magic of movies and novels and plays, night dreams and day dreams, the multitude of interlacing dramas that are apparently going on in this world from the microscopic level to the astronomical, infinitely great and infinitely small, a drama that no two apparent individuals see in exactly the same way. You are enjoying a million points of view, an infinity of experiences. You are enjoying telling yourself the story that you are bound, the story of being "you" and "me." It's a wonderful play.

When we recognize that it's a play, we're free to play. We approach our apparent problems and dilemmas in a different spirit than when we imagine that we have to win the game and achieve some ultimate perfection and save the world. We realize we're fine just the way we are, foibles and all, and so is the world.

The Man with the Yellow Gloves

When I lived at the Berkeley Zen Center, there was an old black man in the neighborhood who used to direct traffic every morning during rush hour. He wore bright yellow gloves and stood in the same place every day, at the side of a busy thoroughfare, making wild hand gestures to "help" the traffic. He was "crazy." He'd call out, "God bless you! Have a beautiful day!" to the passing commuters as he gesticulated wildly. He was out there every morning without fail, rain or shine.

After many years, people knew him and looked for him. People would honk and wave at him as they passed, and he would wave back, blessing them and making circles with his arms. I'd always be out walking my dog in the morning, and he'd wave and call out to me, "God bless you! Have a beautiful day!" And I'd wish him the same. He was a radiant man, completely out of his mind or completely sane, who could say.

Many years later, when I was living at Springwater, we saw him on the national news one night. He had "retired." The city of Berkeley had honored him in a special ceremony. The mayor had thanked him for his years of dedicated service to the community. The ceremony made the national news.

Tears filled my eyes. God bless Berkeley! And God bless the crazy man in the yellow gloves! He was a real Zen man. He saw a job that needed doing, and he did it. It didn't matter that it was a make-believe job, that his hand signals were meaningless absurdities, that nobody paid him a cent. He saw what needed doing, and he did it. For many years, he brought happiness, love and good cheer to the morning commuters on their way to work. In fact, he *did* serve the community!

He gave free blessings to everyone. He showed up, rain or shine. He lived and worked outside the world of logic, inviting us all to wake up to a deeper reality. His was a gratuitous blessing, a miracle that, in the end, touched the heart of the whole nation.

I will never forget the man in the yellow gloves. He continues to bless me, even now.

The Current of Love

There is a fellow at the place where I do my xeroxing, he's probably in his sixties, a totally ordinary guy, but whenever he is helping me, I feel so happy. I love the sound of his voice. I want to ask him, "Are you a guru or something? Is that what you do when you're not here?" I'm sure he'd look at me with dismay. But there's something about him, an energy; I don't know what it is. I love standing next to him. I love watching how he pushes the buttons, how he lines up the pages.

I feel the same way about the owner of a small bookstore I frequent in California, and about one of the check out clerks at Dominicks, the nearby grocery store, and about one of the old caretakers out at the Vedanta Center. There are certain people whose presence I find enormously soothing and pleasant to be around. It's something about their vibration, their essence. These people could be talking about how to repair a toilet, and I would be mesmerized.

The grocery clerk has a big gray beard, and the first time I met him, I was checking out and wished him a beautiful day, and he replied, "Every day is a beautiful day." He gazed deep into my eyes. I think he's a secret guru, too.

The essence of life isn't confined to the forms. That's why in the old Zen stories the monks are always getting tricked by some little old lady selling vegetables at the side of the road. The monks secretly consider themselves really special, elevated, spiritual people, and they think the old lady is just an old lady. But of course, she turns out to be a Zen master in disguise. Life is like that.

Recently Mom and I went to visit her close friend who has Alzheimer's and is now in a nursing home. Jane had deteriorated considerably since we last visited her, but she is still totally happy and sweet and cheerful, as she always was. Actually, Jane is one of those people I love to listen to, just because of her energy. As we sat conversing, it struck me that Jane's mannerisms were the same as always, her conversational style was exactly as it had always been, the inflections in her voice, the way she told a story—it was all exactly the same. The only difference was that now the content no longer made any sense.

But it didn't matter. Mom and I just played along, and Jane played along. The content never *really* makes any sense anyway, and the content is never really what matters. What matters, I realized at that moment, is the current of love that is under the content, the exchange of energy, the dance itself. The content is just bubbles on the surface. For some of us with sophisticated mental lives, that content can get very complex and can seem terribly engaging and important, as if we really are ironing out the meaning of life and exchanging vitally important ideas. But truly, it's all just sounds. What really matters is the love.

Maybe things like Alzheimer's and senility are actually a gift because they allow us to realize that. Funny, because that's usually our worst fear, that our mind will go. But we are not the mind. We are the formless, timeless unborn—unconditional love. *That* is untouched by Alzheimer's or death, and *that* can be deeply felt in the check out line at the grocery store, in a small bookstore, at the local xerox place, in a nursing home—in the midst of the most ordinary transactions. Suddenly we see and feel below the surface. We touch God. We recognize that there is only God.

The Price of Enlightenment: Giving Up Everything

When the mind wants to break its link with the world it still holds on to one thing.

KABIR

Make no effort either to work or to give up work; your very effort is the bondage.

RAMANA MAHARSHI

As long as you see the least difference, you are a stranger to reality. You are on the level of the mind.

NISARGADATTA

When such dualities cease to exist
Oneness itself cannot exist.
To this ultimate finality
no law or description applies.

SENGTSAN, *Hsin Hsin Ming*

Often, over the years, I've thought I had to get beyond fingerbiting, caffeine consumption, guru chasing, or *something* that I was apparently attached to, in order to *become* enlightened. I should eliminate everything in my life that might have a trace of ego to it: my writing, the meetings and workshops I was offering, my website. I should give away all my money (back when I had some to give away). I should find some humble job stacking grocery shelves and "be nobody, doing nothing." Maybe if I did all of that, maybe *then* I would be an enlightened somebody at last!

But the price of awakening is *everything*. It has nothing at all to do with giving up some *thing*. Enlightenment is not about *becoming*. It is not about transformation. It is about death. It is the end of the whole illusion of improvement and separation and time. Above all, it is the end of the "somebody" who would "get" enlightened. Not that such a one has ever really existed. The whole problem, the whole search is imagination. Enlightenment is the default state, our natural being, what *is*. It has never been absent.

Some twenty years ago, I spent a few days at Tassajara, a Zen monastery in California. I was new to Zen practice. A Zen monk, who happened to be the abbot of the Zen Center at that time, said that "unenlightened people are simply people who refuse to admit that they are enlightened." In response to that, someone asked him if there was any difference between an abbot and a thug. The monk said there was no difference at all except that an abbot knew that he was also a thug, whereas a thug did not realize that he was also an abbot.

Some years later, I remember someone asking Gangaji during a satsang what the difference was between an enlightened person and someone like Archie Bunker.

"What if I said, none at all?" Gangaji replied.

A huge amusement swept through me.

It's taken twenty years, a split second, from that moment at Tassajara until now, when I can finally say that it's true. There is no difference at all.

Hearing this, the mind will rebel. It will go crazy. It will argue, kick and scream, insist and resist. But contemplate this truth deeply. There is no real separation. This *is* it.

Many fellow-seekers over the years went off to Japan when I was in the Zen world, and India when I was in the Advaita world. It seemed as if the genuine, authentic goods were over there in some Asian country. But I never went to Japan or India. I had the deep sense that the genuine, authentic goods are right here.

Many fellow-seekers changed their names. They took on new and exotic-sounding Japanese, Tibetan, or Hindu names. I considered the possibility. Suppose I metamorphosed into Ananda. No more Joan. A fresh start in life! Think of how good it would sound on my flier: Satsang with Ananda. But again, I couldn't do it. Re-naming this character couldn't possibly be the key to waking up.

I longed for a single teacher or guru with whom I would have total and complete resonance. And I found many wonderful teachers with whom I resonated deeply and had profound and meaningful relationships. But in the final analysis, there was no single one among them of whom I could honestly say, this person is my one and only. Appropriately, the last teacher I tried to make something out of turned out to be literally no one at all! When it came down to it, I was on my own.

I longed for a big awakening, one of those dramatic shifts where the divine hypnosis (along with all my neurosis) falls completely away forever. Never mind that "forever" is only an idea with no actual reality (other than Now), and never mind that all experience is transitory, and never mind that the "me" who wants all of this is a mirage. Other "me's" apparently had this kind of total, permanent Big Bang event, and this me wanted it, too. I was like the proverbial fish in the ocean who is thirsty and searching for water.

When I first started offering meetings, I felt second-rate. Not when I was actually with people, and the meeting was happening. Then there was just awareness, and it was beautiful. But later, when I was alone and the mind would start rolling, I would sometimes begin to worry about my legitimacy, my motives, my qualifications. I had never been to India. I had no single guru or teacher who had given me their blessing and implored me to carry on their lineage. I hadn't had a Big Bang awakening experience. Plain, old, ordinary Joan was still here, her life as messy and imperfect as ever. Why was she even offering meetings? (She wasn't, of course, that was the illusion).

When this movie was playing in the theatre of mind, it seemed momentarily real and believable. But who was watching it? Who was acting in it? Who was writing the script? Who is writing these words right now? Who is creating *all* of this? And is it real?

Gradually, I began to see that Joan's apparent imperfection was actually an enormous blessing, not a huge mistake. Because if I had gone to India and found a single teacher with whom I had absolute resonance, and if I had turned into Ananda and had an enormous explosive experience and been completely transformed into somebody else, then I would be one more person convincing everyone else that this is what is necessary. I would be one more person up on a pedestal looking very special and unique. I would be one more reason why you, as you are right this second, are not whole and complete.

Instead, my koan and what I have to offer is the realization that truth is here now. You don't ever have to leave Chicago, metaphorically speaking. You don't need a great guru. You don't have to turn into Anandaji. You don't need to stop smoking, watch less TV, meditate more, do another retreat, or anything else first. Nothing needs to be acquired, gotten rid of, or transformed. And you definitely don't need a big experience. As the old Zen koan says, ordinary mind is the way. There is nothing *real* that needs to be transformed. You are already completely it.

The "I" *looks* real sometimes, and the illusion becomes momentarily absorbing and believable, just like when you turn on the TV. But that movement in and out of dreamscapes is no longer problematic when no one is taking delivery of it. It just happens (to no one).

The whole idea of enlightenment fades away.

Springwater Journal Entry

Waking up this early spring morning, the hillside out my window is covered with robins. After breakfast I walk to the pond and find it is liquid for the first time in months. What a rush of pure joy in my heart.

I find a big frog floating in the cold water. I touch his back, and he doesn't move. I think he is dead, frozen. I sit awhile and then rub his back again. Suddenly his eyes open; he blinks, turns and swims away. Awakening from his long winter sleep.

How does winter become spring? A warm day, then a blizzard. Another few warm days. Another blizzard. Back and forth, until one day it is fully spring and no longer winter, although you can't say exactly when it happened.

Finally I see, "winter" does not *become* "spring," except in the mind.

Attaining Nothing

If you need time to achieve something, it must be false. The real is always with you; you need not wait to be what you are. Only you must not allow your mind to go out of yourself in search.

NISARGADATTA

There is no 'I' to get enlightened. That's illusion. There's only being here with what's here without division. Eyes open. Eyes and ears open, to let everything reveal itself as it is. And maybe feel this Love. In loveness with life, as it is.

TONI PACKER

Enlightenment is not something you achieve. It is the absence of something. All your life you have been going forward after something, pursuing some goal. Enlightenment is dropping all that.

JOKO BECK

There is absolutely nothing real in the way. What appears to be in the way is that you imagine yourself on the way somewhere.

SCOTT MORRISON

The general notion of the sustained transcendent experience is a construction...The radical abandonment of spirituality in its entirety is the first step of a life of inquiry freed from the demands of attainment, an exploration not restricted to the archaic notion of enlightenment....You are still asking about a point of transformation. You are positing a period of life before this point, which is in one state of mind. There is the point of transformation, and then there is the rest of the life, which is lived in a fundamentally different way. This is the enlightenment myth...I don't see a difference in my being now, before, or ever....It isn't a realization. It is the exhaustion of the idea of spirituality.

STEVEN HARRISON

You need no more experiences. The past ones are sufficient... It is not experience that you need, but the freedom from all experience. Don't be greedy for experience; you need none.

NISARGADATTA

There is no reaching the Self. If Self were to be reached, it would mean that the Self is not here and now, but that it has yet to be obtained. What is got afresh will also be lost.... You are the Self; you are already That.

RAMANA MAHARSHI

The mesmerizing seductiveness of the dream is seen in the long-standing belief that, <u>someday,</u> (if the Dreamer only plays his cosmic cards right), he will, eventually, "awaken." But, in truth, the so-called "Enlightenment Bus" that he's been waiting for will <u>never</u> show up for him. Why? Well, in expecting that some <u>future</u> awakening may occur for him somewhere in time, he's only reinforcing his belief that the very same Consciousness he is seeking is not 100% <u>fully</u> present for him...right here and right now.

CHUCK HILLIG

Would there be any quest for enlightenment if it weren't for our sense of time?...Our craving for experiences is a resistance to simply being here, now. It's the hum of the airplane. The fog. The wind blowing gently, the rain dripping, breathing, humming, pulsating, opening, closing, nothing at all....It's such a relief to realize we don't have to be anything.

TONI PACKER

People often ask me if I'm an enlightened being. I don't know anything about that. I am just someone who knows the difference between this hurts *and* this doesn't. *I am someone who only wants "what is."*

BYRON KATIE

With some realization comes imperceptibly, but somehow they need convincing. They have changed, but they do not notice it. Such non-spectacular cases are often the most reliable.

NISARGADATTA

To enjoy the world without judgement is what a realized life is like.

JOKO BECK

Enlightenment is nothing.
Delusion is the greatest wonder.

JED MCKENNA

Realization is already here. All that is necessary is to get rid of the thought 'I have not realized.'

RAMANA MAHARSHI

"The day I became enlightened" simply means the day I realized there is nothing to achieve, there is nowhere to go, there is nothing to be done. We are already divine and we are already perfect—as we are. No improvement is needed, no improvement at all.

OSHO

Awakening doesn't mean that you awaken. It means that there is only awakening. There is no you who is awake, there is only awakeness. As long as you identify with a "you" who either is or is not awake, you are still dreaming. Awakening is awakening from the dream of a separate you to simply Being Awakeness.... The word enlightenment points to who you are. Who you are is not a state that can be gained or lost. It is not a spiritual experience. All states and experiences come and go. Who you are is the permanence existing right now regardless of states and experiences.

ADYASHANTI

The understanding cannot disappear because it has not appeared! The understanding is What-Is. Understanding is Consciousness. Understanding has always been there. What has appeared is the misunderstanding. The misunderstanding will go and the understanding will remain exactly where it has always been....Enlightenment is the original state."

RAMESH BALSEKAR

If you WILL conceive of a Buddha, you WILL BE OBSTRUCTED BY THAT BUDDHA!!! And when you conceive of sentient beings, you will be obstructed by those beings. All such dualistic concepts as 'ignorant' and 'Enlightened', 'pure' and 'impure', are obstructions.

HUANG PO

Seeking to duplicate the so-called enlightened condition of other characters in the play is a distraction from your true nature... You are already completely wide awake and aware right now.

NATHAN GILL

Dilemma and Seeking Are Not A Program For The Actual Future Realization Of God, Truth, or Happiness, but They Are Merely A Means For Preventing Present Realization of God, Truth, or Happiness....Real God Is That Which Is Always Already The Case. Therefore, Real God Need Not Be Sought. Real God Is Only Avoided By Any Kind Of Seeking.

ADI DA

*Stop thinking of achievement of any kind. You are complete
here and now, you need absolutely nothing.*

NISARGADATTA

*If you cannot find the truth right where you are, where do you
expect to find it?*

DOGEN

*I truly attained nothing from complete, unexcelled
Enlightenment.*

THE BUDDHA

Moshe Feldenkrais titled one of his books *"The Elusive Obvious."* That
kind of sums enlightenment up. No such "thing" actually exists "out
there." It is not a destination or an event. Zen master Dogen said, "Those
who have great realization of delusion are buddhas; those who are greatly
deluded about realization are sentient beings." It's all in the seeing. You
can see the false, but not the true. Or put differently, *everything* you see
is true; nothing could possibly be false.

Right now, look and see if you can find anything *real* that needs to
wake up, that needs to be other than it is. You can find *thoughts* ("I'm not
enlightened yet," or "This can't be it."). And you can find *sensations* (like
those generated by such thoughts: sensations of contraction, urgency,
tension). These thoughts and sensations create the *sense* (the image and
the story) of "you" as "somebody" who is "not awake yet," somebody who
is "on the way" to "enlightenment." All that's really going on is thoughts
and sensations. Is there anything real that needs to wake up?

Of course we have all heard many accounts of enlightenment, and
there are many people claiming to be more awake than anybody else.
This helps to reinforce the credibility of the mirage. We evaluate,
compare, and rank people in our mind, lining them up in a make-believe
continuum from Most Awake to Most Deluded. But notice that right now
the whole continuum exists only in the mind, in imagination. All of these
apparent characters are nothing but Consciousness, *pretending* to be
divided up into enlightened and unenlightened, lost and found, me and

you. That's the dream.

These days, in the dream, enlightenment has become a buzzword, a commodity, a sales pitch. Teachers boast of enormous awakenings almost like men in a locker room comparing the sizes of their penises and wanting to be the biggest. People make fantastic claims about what the awakened life is like. Sometimes they say, "There is no enlightened person," but then they tell you their enlightenment story! They tell it every time they do an event. They post it on their website. Some talk about levels of enlightenment. Some offer training programs where (for a fee) you can rise through the levels, and others promise you enlightenment in a weekend workshop. There are myriad conflicting definitions of enlightenment, and no one agrees on who has it and who doesn't. How are we going to know which version of enlightenment is real? Or who really has it? Does *anyone* really have it? Is "it" *something* to be had?

People rush from satsang to satsang hoping to get it, or hoping to get some favorable version of it anyway, consuming endless spiritual books and tapes along the way. In all of this searching, they are overlooking the only real enlightenment. The search is all about avoidance and postponement. It misses the mark. Or it *pretends* to anyway. The mark is actually impossible to miss. It's unavoidable. It's all there is.

I don't doubt that a few rare characters *(in the dream!)* do experience a huge single event of radical and irreversible transformation where the illusion of separation falls away suddenly and dramatically, never to return with any tenacity or credibility. I also don't doubt that a host of other characters have manufactured this kind of experience out of thin air, convincing themselves and everyone else of its reality, because they felt it was what they were "supposed" to experience, especially if they planned to teach.

And then we have Suzuki Roshi, who compared awakening to going out for a walk in the mist. You get wet only very gradually and imperceptibly. This has been my own experience. I've never had a single, dramatic event of life-shattering magnitude after which everything was completely different, other than *this*, right now! For many years, I longed for this kind of ultimate breakthrough. I felt inadequate because I hadn't had it. But in all of this, I was worrying about the wedding plans of the child of a barren woman. That was Nisargadatta's way of saying that we were talking about an illusion and its illusory offspring: Joan and her experiences.

This was not an explosive realization, as I hope you've understood by reading this book. In fact, that's one of the main things I want to convey in this book. *Enlightenment is not an event; there is no enlightened person.* It didn't happen to Joan Tollifson at two o'clock in the afternoon on January third. There were no flashing lights, no plunge down a long dark tunnel, no change in vision comparable to dropping acid or being permanently high on ecstasy. It was not like a big orgasm that lasted forever. Joan's bad habits, shortcomings, and personality quirks did not magically disappear. She is not "in the zone" 24/7. It is simply an instantaneous and timeless falling away of the illusion that enlightenment is something else, that Joan is real. And therefore it is certainly not about *Joan* getting more and more "clear," or less and less prone to confusion. *It has nothing to do with Joan.*

Are those false ideas gone for good? Could they arise again? Who cares?

There may or may not be explosive events "for you." Once seen through, the mirage may or may not come back. Most likely, it will come back. Either way, it doesn't matter. Dramatic and irreversible events are not needed. If they happen, fine. If they don't, fine. You're not a caterpillar turning into a butterfly. That's an analogy. In truth, there's no caterpillar and no butterfly and no "you" to be one or the other. There's no line to cross. That's all part of the dream.

I once asked Toni Packer if she'd had one of those final, permanent, irreversible, big bang awakenings where the little me disappears never to return. She replied, "I can't say I *had* it. It's right now."

This is the only permanence, the only forever there is! This is the eternal present: being itself. No *experience* is permanent. No *state* is permanent. It is not the *individual* who wakes up because the individual is a mirage. Here is always here. You *are* here. It's not that "you" are in a place called "here," and could be in some other place tomorrow or yesterday. But rather, "you" and "here" are two different words that point to one and the same presence. You *are* here. If you are trying to get "there," you can be sure that you will never arrive, because the destination, the journey, and the one taking it are imaginary. You *are* here. There is nothing else, except in the mind.

You may say, well that sounds good, and intellectually I agree, but in fact I *feel* that I am someone, and that this someone is not home, not there yet, not fully awake. But you will *never* be "there." *There* is an idea in the mind. You *are* here. Still, you may insist that you can see "others," like Ramana, who are clearly awake in some way "you" think "you" are not. This *seems* very convincing. *It is a very convincing illusion.* And this is precisely the illusion that enlightenment sees through. But that "seeing through" is not an event that happens "to you." *You* are the illusion! The One Mind is all there is. *Everything* is Consciousness. Consciousness is doing the whole thing, including you, including Ramana. It is doing what looks like confusion, neurosis, and evil. It is *all* there is. It's not that you might eventually *become* that, if only you can get rid of your false beliefs, your neurosis, and your hypnosis. You *are* that! Right now. *Always.* Without interruption. Without any *possibility* of separation.

Seekers want to seek, rather than be. There's this promise of something spectacular that might happen to "me" in the future, and that seems so much better than the screaming children, the seemingly unbearable ordinariness and imperfection of mundane, daily life. Of course, it is unbearable and "ordinary" only when we aren't really seeing it. In that inattention, dreaming of something better, we endlessly postpone enlightenment. We put it off. We deny it. We pretend this isn't it. We look for it tomorrow, or in someone else.

The very idea that you are ever apart from it and have to find it, or that it has limits of any kind, is the illusion. The Absolute has no opposite. Nothing is outside of it or inside of it. It is One without a second. It only pretends to be divided up or lost. When seeking ends, everything is enlightened, even delusion. Everything is flooded with gratitude. Life is no longer about searching for a personal attainment; it is play, exploration, celebration, uncaused joy. Nothing needs to be different from how it is. *You* are choosing absolutely all of it.

Enlightenment is a word, an idea, a myth. It points to the one undeniable and indivisible truth that is right here reading these words. What is it? Enlightenment is not knowing. It is being.

Ordinary Mind is the Way

*Maybe we have some big spiritual experience, maybe we
dissolve and merge into the One, maybe our consciousness
expands infinitely across the universe and beyond, maybe we
have a kundalini light show. Each time the tendency is to
think, 'This is it.' Of course, truth is that which does not come
(which should have been a big clue—it only took me fifteen
years to catch on) and does not go. All of those experiences
came, had a life span, and went away. The tendency of
mind is to think, 'If I could just grasp on to that experience,
extend it infinitely through time, then that must be what
enlightenment is.' Of course, the truth is so compassionately
ruthless it keeps saying, 'No, no, no my dear, that's not it.'*

ADYASHANTI

*I sought 'enlightenment' as an escape from what I saw as the
problems, trials and boredom of ordinary life. The ordinary life
continues but is now seen in, and as, present awareness. The
'spiritual' search is over. Life is just as it is.*

NATHAN GILL

*The spring flowers, the autumn moon;
Summer breezes, winter snow.
If useless things do not clutter your mind,
You have the best days of your life.*

Ordinary Mind is the Way,
The Gateless Gate, Case #19

*i used to sit for hours trying to get something. now i sit for
hours in love.*

MIKE STILER

We've come to the last chapter, the grande finale, and we've come no
distance at all. Here we always are. Nothing is left out of this amazing
presence. America is poised for war as I write. The economy appears to

be crumbling. The News warns of impending biological and chemical attacks. Downtown Chicago has been declared a no-fly zone. Joan still bites her fingers at times. The mind of Joan can still knot up. All of this *is* allowed to be here—not by Joan—but by *that* which I am, *that* which you are. Non-dual awareness is always awake and embraces everything. It sees only itself *everywhere*, doing and being everything, even pretending to be a person, and then:

Trying to be a perfect person, trying to get all the ducks in "my" life lined up and in order.

Pretending to be unenlightened, and then:

Trying to *see* the source of the I AM, trying to *see* non-dual awareness or Truth. Feeling frustrated. Trying harder.

Trying to *experience* non-duality, trying to *feel* that the chair on the other side of the room is me. Feeling frustrated. Trying harder.

Trying to *duplicate* the enlightenment event that so-and-so described in his book.

Trying to eliminate "my" bad habits, "my" inabilities, "my" failures, "my" neurosis. Trying to eliminate all sense of me, all sense of personal doership.

Trying to turn into somebody else.

Trying to *understand* the truth, trying to *get* it. Feeling frustrated. Trying harder.

Terrified of being ordinary and imperfect, wanting to be extraordinary and special. Seeking enlightenment. Imagining "myself" flip-flopping between having "it" and losing "it."

Trying, seeking, trying, seeking. Wanting, fearing. Trying not to try. Seeking not to seek. Wanting not to want. Feeling frustrated. Trying harder. Trying not to try harder. Evaluating, comparing, hoping.

Thinking: "Now my life is a disaster, but *someday....*"

A moment from now, or ten years from now, *someday...*maybe, hopefully....it will be better.

Sound familiar?

All of this is not some huge problem that needs to be corrected, some terrible mistake that "you" are responsible for and need to fix. It is simply arising, along with the bird song, the traffic, the clouds, the wars, "the full catastrophe," as Zorba the Greek called life. In the words of Tony Parsons, "Duality is unicity playing duality." The perfection, the extraordinary miracle of what is, as it is, is self-evident. Obvious. Ever-present. Omni-present.

The Unbroken Wholeness pretending again to be a person:

"Are you sure this is really it?" the mind asks itself. And then: "For *me,* the miracle still comes and goes." And then: "Someday 'I' will live permanently in the miracle, and I will be able to tell everyone that I am enlightened, and I will be happy and okay and perfect and extraordinary at last! And *then* I can finally relax!"

What a wonderful joke!

Again and again, the divine giggles.

＊

A bird dives through the wind torn sky. The fan whirls. Leaves blow from green to yellow. In the wrinkles of the brain, seasons pass.

Every apparent life has its perfect trajectory, and the journey down the Yellow Brick Road to Oz is every bit as vital as the return to Kansas. It only appears to be a linear unfolding in the story. Actually, it all happens NOW. And what is discovered behind the curtain in Oz is not some exotic foreign treasure because in fact, the truth is simple. Obvious. Right under your nose. It has never been absent. That's the great joke about Oz or so-called enlightenment. It's right here!

＊

In my second year in Chicago, I never left. I traveled nowhere. I lost the ambition to be a spiritual teacher, although I continued with my monthly meetings. I stopped reading spiritual books and started reading novels. I read Salman Rushdie's *The Ground Beneath Her Feet*, Margaret Atwood's *The Blind Assassin*, Michael Ondaatje's *Anil's Ghost*, Arundhati Roy's *The God of Small Things*. I watched movies and TV shows instead of spiritual videos. I found truth exquisitely revealed in such films as *American Beauty, Frida, The Matrix, Leaving Las Vegas, The Hours*, and *Magnolia*. The eye of a first rate novelist or filmmaker is not unlike the awakened eye of awareness, a neutral eye watching the grand sweep of events. I enjoyed these "profane" expressions of truth because they made no attempt to deny pain or provide some ultimate solution. They were willing to hang out with actuality in all its many unsettling faces. And the actual is where I find God.

Right this second, the buzzing, humming, rattling drone of the cicadas, the roaring of the planes overhead, the rhythmic whoosh of traffic, the piercing sirens, the rustling leaves, the sunlight streaming through the window and falling across my desk, the breathing of everything, the vastness of being. All of this is what I am. All of this is God. God is the unconditional love that accepts it all, the vibrant mystery expressing itself in everything.

Exertion and relaxation, aspiration and acceptance, choice and choicelessness, self and no self—the words melt away; the imaginary boundaries collapse. There is only the utter simplicity of present awareness.

The answers we make up are all superfluous. What matters is the love, the immediacy, the *suchness*, the no-thing-ness that has been called the Self, the Tao, the Heart, God, and even—in Zen—a dried turd. *This* is never lost, and so it can never be found. The mind overlooks it again and again because it is invisible. And yet it is showing up everywhere, as trees and cars and lamps and televisions and dogs and pencils and grocery clerks and suicide bombers and heads of state and blades of grass. It is utterly obvious, but if you are looking for it, you'll go on seeking the image in your mind, and overlooking the invisible jewel that is visible everywhere.

❧

I go to see Mom a few days after her ninety-third birthday. She is hiding behind a corner in the hall. When I step off the elevator she springs out. "BOO!" She yells. I nearly have heart failure. She is laughing with delight. The next day on the phone she says, "I was so pleased with how that turned out!" Later she says, "I love my head. It's a vacant lot."

One of these days she'll go up in a puff of smoke, and I'll be left wondering if she was ever really here, or if I dreamed all this up.

A month later, as the leaves were blowing off the trees, we went to another memorial service. My Godmother this time. There is something beautiful about services for the dead and about being back in my home-town, surrounded by the ghosts of my childhood grown old, slowly dying off. Each moment, each life is Perfect Beauty.

A single leaf floats past my window. The trees grow bare. It begins to snow. It is winter again.

~❧

I wrote this book as part of my own process of waking up. Or more accurately, these words appeared out of nowhere. Before the words even hit the paper, they are untrue. Truth is always moving. The words are like clouds blowing across the sky, pointless enjoyment. I offer them because maybe it will be useful to "others" to see how truth unfolds and reveals itself through the messy life of one flawed human being in the middle of so-called ordinary reality. Otherwise, all this spiritual stuff can seem like a very abstract and distant ideal. People get discouraged by the apparent gap between what the books seem to describe and what they find going on in their own lives, and they keep trying to close the gap, to achieve that distant (imaginary) ideal.

The truth isn't an ideal, an abstraction, or a belief. It is utterly real, and it's right here, too close to ever be found. It has never for one single instant been absent or unrealized. You are it. Everything is it. There is nothing else. Wake up to the Holy Reality. Pull back the curtain and see your own face everywhere. Dance until you dissolve. This awakening is absolutely simple. There is literally nothing to it. It is what is, *just* as it is.

~❧

2011 Afterword

My mother Dorothy died at home at the age of 95 surrounded by friends and family. On the first anniversary of her death, the trees I loved so much outside my apartment windows were chopped down by the new owners of the building and a new view of the sky opened up. The lady who played her radio all night in the apartment next to mine died soon after my mother. New people moved into the building – families from Africa, Mexico, India and Pakistan, a woman who wore a full burqa, a Cuban woman who smoked cigars. It sometimes seemed as if the whole world were contained in that one apartment building, bumping up against each other in the laundry room. I stayed in Chicago for three more years after my mother died. Then in the spring of 2008, I moved to southern Oregon. I turned 60 that year. George Bush was replaced by Barack Obama. What ends and what doesn't? This is a wonderful question to explore, not philosophically or speculatively, but directly, in this moment.

I returned to Springwater for retreats and visits many times after this book was published. I scattered my mother's ashes in the woods there, and I remain in touch with Toni and others in the Springwater community. I saw Gangaji again long before I moved to Chicago, and over the years attended several more retreats with her. Once again, she and I have mysteriously ended up living in the same town – occasionally I run into her in the grocery store. I enjoyed being with several nondual teachers who visited Chicago while I was living there, especially Sailor Bob Adamson, and I even did a few Zen sesshins up in Minneapolis after my mother died because I wanted to meet and talk with Zen teacher Steve Hagen in person. Although I no longer feel any need for a teacher, I do on occasion still enjoy reading, hearing, talking or being with those with whom I resonate, and as always, I appreciate many different expressions of the One Reality.

For a long time, it seemed as if I had to choose between "be here now" (meditation and inquiry) and "all there is, is now" (radical nonduality), but this conflict slowly melted away, not because I finally found the correct answer or made the right choice, but simply because it became ever-more obvious that the conflict only existed conceptually. Reality itself is much simpler and can never be packaged up into any concept or formula, nor can it ever really be divided into separate and opposing camps.

I continue to enjoy sitting quietly – at home in my armchair, on a bench in the park, or wherever I happen to be – but I no longer think of it as meditation, and I'm not *doing* (or *not* doing) anything special. I still have an interest in exploring the nature of life, but I am no longer searching for some final enlightenment experience or any ultimate answer. Instead, there is an ever-deeper resting in the *answer-less-ness* of simple being. This bodymind can still be swept up at times in the story of separation, the rope can momentarily be mistaken for a snake, but in reality, this entrancement happens to no one. It is simply another fleeting appearance in the ever-changing weather of Here / Now.

I still write books and offer meetings. In my meetings, I invite people to investigate actual present moment experiencing, to see how it is, and perhaps to discover that this one eternal present moment is timeless, placeless, always Here, always Now, ever-present, ever-changing, seamless, boundless, uncontained, undivided and without self. *Painting the Sidewalk with Water,* a collection of talks and dialogs, most of them drawn from meetings held in Chicago while I was living there, has recently been published by Non-Duality Press, and another book focusing on death, aging and nonduality is in progress. My mother once told a nurse in the ER that my books were about "being who you are," a statement that can be heard on many levels.

I might say that my books and meetings are explorations, like a child exploring its toes or a lover exploring the beloved. There is no end to such explorations, all of which are forms of play.

As my very playful mother often said in her last year, "It's so freeing to realize that nothing really matters!" She said it joyously, as if a burden had fallen away. She became lighter and lighter, more and more transparent, until finally she disappeared completely. It all boils down in the end to love – this vast emptiness that includes absolutely everything and that holds on to nothing at all.

Joan Tollifson
Ashland, Oregon
April, 2011

Acknowledgements

Thank you to my mother Dorothy, exuberant and blithe spirit, for unwavering support, encouragement, and generosity. My life is infinitely enriched forever by your passionate delight in ordinary miracles, your sense of humor, your love, and your gift for seeing the divine in everyone. I love you with all my heart. Thank you also to my very wonderful father.

Thank you to Toni Packer for waking me up again and again to the simplicity of listening without knowing; to Gangaji for opening my heart and revealing the jewel that is everywhere present; to Tony Parsons for pointing so uncompromisingly to *what is,* for your irreverent and liberating sense of humor, and for including absolutely *everything* in the truth; to Sailor Bob Adamson for your clear expression and for encouraging me to trust what is expressing here; to Nathan Gill for pointing beyond all experiences and for encouragement on this book; to Steven Harrison for questioning all the answers; to Joko Beck for our talks. Thank you to Leo Hartong, Chuck Hillig, Wayne Liquorman, Francis Lucille, Adyashanti, Isaac Shapiro, Nirmala, Ngeton, Byron Katie and Nisargadatta Maharaj.

Thank you to the National Endowment for the Arts for the Creative Writing Fellowship grant that helped make this book possible. Thank you to Isabel Stukator for the beautiful job on layout and cover design. Thank you to Julian Noyce and Non-Duality Press for this beautiful new edition.

Special thanks to Fran Perry, D Allen, Pam Barry, Lola Moonfrog, Paula Kimbro, Mike Stiler, Tanis Walters, Dan Delorenzo, Randolph Pope, Rabbi Rami Shapiro, Waltraud Ireland, Betty Lacy, Charlie Ogle, Dennis Peak, Tom Fleming, Julie & Paul Rubin, and to everyone who has attended my meetings.

Finally, I bow to the mourning doves, the locust trees, the squirrels, the cicadas, the icecream vendors, the morning traffic, the garbage trucks, the snow storms, my wonderful neighbors, and the heartland that brought me home.

This book is dedicated to the One behind all the masks.

NON-DUALITY PRESS

If you enjoyed this book, you might be interested in these related titles published by Non-Duality Press.

Painting the Sidewalk with Water by Joan Tollifson

Dismantling the Fantasy and *Essence Revisited*, Darryl Bailey

Awakening to the Dream and *From Self to Self*, Leo Hartong

What's Wrong With Right Now Unless You Think About It? and *Presence-Awareness: Just This and Nothing Else*, Sailor Bob Adamson

Only That: the Life and Teaching of Sailor Bob Adamson, Kalyani Lawry

Already Awake and *Being*, Nathan Gill

The Transparency of Things, Rupert Spira

I Am and *Transmission of the Flame*, Jean Klein

The Almighty Mackerel and His Holy Bootstraps and *The Light That I Am*, J.C. Amberchele

The Wonder of Being and *An Extraordinary Absence*, Jeff Foster

Ordinary Freedom, Jon Bernie

Standing As Awareness, Greg Goode

This is Unimaginable and Unavoidable, Guy Smith

Eternity Now, Francis Lucille

I Hope You Die Soon and *The Book of No One*, Richard Sylvester

The Ultimate Twist, Suzanne Foxton